MARKETING IN THE SERVICE INDUSTRIES

MARKETING IN THE SERVICE INDUSTRIES

Edited by

GORDON FOXALL

LONDON AND NEW YORK

First published 1985 by
FRANK CASS AND COMPANY LIMITED

Published 2013 by Routledge
2 Park Square, Milton Park, Abingdon, Oxfordshire OX14 4RN
711 Third Avenue, New York, NY 10017

First issued in paperback 2014

Routledge is an imprint of the Taylor & Francis Group, an informa business

ISBN 13: 978-0-714-63270-4 (hbk)
ISBN 13: 978-0-415-76118-5 (pbk)

This group of studies first appeared in a Special Issue on 'Marketing in the Service Industries' of *Service Industries Journal*, Vol. 4, No. 3, published by Frank Cass & Co. Ltd.

Contents

Marketing *is* Service Marketing

by

Gordon Foxall

This editorial introduction expresses a personal view of the marketing of services and introduces the remaining papers in this special collection.

The classification of certain economic goods as 'services' and others as 'products' owes more to convention than to conception. The classification schemes which have been advanced to distinguish services from products rest all too often upon simplistic dichotomies into which our experience of the real world fits only with difficulty.

Thus it is frequently said that in contradistinction to 'products', 'services' are intangible. But, from the customer's viewpoint, the precise benefits gained from owning a lawnmower may be as elusive as those which a life assurance policy confers. This issue of intangibility has clearly caused some confusion and argument among marketing academics [cf., inter alia, Baker, 1981; Gronroos, 1978; Levitt, 1981; Lovelock, 1984; Middleton, 1983; Sasser *et al.*, 1978; Stanton, 1975]. No doubt, if he were aware of it, it would prove confusing to the individual about to enjoy a restaurant meal: clearly he is paying for and consuming tangibles as well as intangibles but the tendency, nevertheless, is to classify the industry which provides them as a 'service' industry. Even the end-product of life assurance can be tangible enough and the investor in an endowment policy may, like the diner-out, enjoy both tangible rewards such as cash and the things it buys and intangibles such as security and peace of mind.

Again, it is often asserted that services are distinguishable by their perishability. But the unsold dairy products which some supermarkets destroy at the end of the day's trading also suffer on this account; indeed, all agricultural and horticultural produce is ultimately perishable, although its life may be temporarily extended by means of the appropriate technologies. In connection with the desire to ascribe a unique quality of perishability to 'services', it is often stated that service marketing is characterised by problems of under- and over-capacity; but, once again, believers in a sharp dichotomy between products and services have, at best, established another dimension along which services and products differ in degree rather than kind. To state that 'Unused capacity in a service business is rather like having a running tap in a sink with no plug' [Lovelock, 1984: 5] may be to confuse stocks with flows. Since the dichotomisers are also keen to point out that the production or performance of a service coincides temporally with the consumption, there can be no flow in the absence of a buyer. In such absence of demand, nothing is draining away, although the potential provider of the service is certainly suffering from a lack of business – in precisely the same way as an ice-cream vendor may do on a cold day or a mackintosh manufacturer during a heatwave.

The other arguments adduced in the attempt to discriminate between 'services' and 'products' also fail to convince. Lack of homogeneity and consequent difficulties in controlling the quality of services are often used to distinguish them from 'products' but the distinction breaks down when one considers the off-the-shelf nature of most motor insurance policies and that no-one can dissect an apple with absolute certainty as to what he will find. Both 'products' and 'services' can be delivered by means of physical channels of distribution or equipment. Even the contention that services involve simultaneity of production and consumption does not provide an absolute distinction: the benefits which result from their repair to a motor car are not enjoyed while the repair takes place and may be consumed over several years.

Those who argue for clear-cut distinctions between services and products have actually demonstrated no more than that if *some* 'services' are located at or near one end of various continua, then *some* 'products' can be logically located at or near the opposing poles. Some authors, for example, Berry [1980] take care to stress the relative nature of the distinctions they draw but it should be constantly borne in mind that the bases of distinction are themselves weak and can break down completely when certain specific products and services are concerned. Given these considerations, it makes sense in a marketing context to conceptualise services and products in ways which emphasise their similarity in kind, while being open to the importance of differences of degree where they are locally relevant, just as the differences in degree between types of product and between types of service may assume importance in specific circumstances. Middleton [1983] has suggested that services constitute a subset of products and that the latter should be the generic term of description but he reverts, nevertheless, to a distinction between 'goods' and 'services' which appears to contain all the difficulties he attempts to overcome. Yet the suggestion that a single conceptual basis should be found for both 'products' and 'services' is sound in view of the fact that customers are interested in obtaining the same thing – benefits, satisfactions or services – whether or not they are supplied via a physical entity. The appropriate generic concept is, therefore, surely that of a *service*. Marketing analysts should recognise that that which is exchanged for customers' money in a market transaction is a *service* (or a bundle of services) which may or may not involve the transfer of a physical entity.

Recognising that customers inevitably purchase services has two further advantages. First, it overcomes the demonstrably false implication of the product/services dichotomy to the effect that all services have elements in common which they do not share with non-services. Often it is impossible to discern what two 'services' – say, telecommunications and fast food – have in common which neither shares with, say, electric clocks or alcoholic beverages. Recognition that buyers purchase and consume services, irrespective of the mechanism by which they are generated and supplied, allows the observed differences both within and between 'product' and 'service' categories to be noted where salient but does not force those observations to fit a spurious analytical dichotomy. Second, it overcomes neglect of the remainder of the marketing mix which comprises, essentially, *service* – most obviously in the case of marketing communications and distribution (which supplies time and place utilities) – but also in the case of price which serves to indicate quality, reputation, value and availability to customers. Also important is the recognition of customer service as an inevitable element in all transactions. None of this argues against the use of arbitrary categorisation in spheres beyond marketing. Macroeconomic analyses, for instance, may benefit from the classification of industrial sectors as primary, secondary, tertiary and quaternary and of economies as pre- or post-industrial; no doubt it is useful to make these distinctions in studies which deal, for example, with changes in employment levels and productivity. However, it must be stressed in the context of marketing that the prevailing convention rests upon arbitrary definitions which have little or no ultimate significance for the understanding of customer behaviour, competitive analysis or managerial action.

If these arbitrary definitions are tolerated it must be only for the time being and principally in order to overcome the imbalances in academia and industry which have led to an overemphasis: marketing has found overwhelming application in manufacturing industry but has been neglected elsewhere. There is no inherent reason why marketing study or marketing practice should be fragmented in the long term, and it is in the spirit of treating the marketing of services as a separate field of discourse, research, and practice with temporary advantages that should not ultimately obscure the unity of marketing that I have undertaken the editing of this collection of papers. The remainder of this introductory paper thus employs the term 'marketing of services' more as a limited convenience than to reify an essentially *ad hoc* classification.

THIS COLLECTION OF PAPERS

During the last several years, the marketing of services has shown signs of coming into its own in two ways. Managers in service industries have increasingly asked what marketing-orientated management has to offer them in an ever more competitive market-place. Marketing academics who, as noted above, appeared for so long to be exclusively concerned with manufacturing industry, have turned some of their attention to the service sector. This collection of original papers explores the marketing of services both as an area of managerial practice and in terms of an emerging academic contribution.

Much thought has been given to the intended audience and the final decision has been to the effect that the papers should be chosen so as to appeal as widely as possible. Certainly, there has been a great unwillingness to exclude either practitioners or academics. It is also obvious, however, that many practitioners and academics are primarily interested in *services*: hitherto their interest in *marketing* may have taken second place. Papers which discuss the nature and role of marketing itself and go on to apply its principles to service organisations have been, therefore, a high priority.

It has not been possible to cover every aspect of the marketing of services in this volume; already the publisher's initial guidelines on length have been severely breached. Individual specialists have been invited to write for practitioners and academics on the subject of their recent work, but no attempt has been made to form them into a particular mould, to encourage them to express a general view of what the terms 'marketing' or 'services' should embrace. Several authors have defined these terms in their own way and some have discussed the nature and scope of services marketing. The volume does not, therefore, attempt to be a textbook in the narrow sense but it should complement the serious and highly competent texts on the marketing of services which are now appearing (some of them by contributors to this issue). Some of the papers have clearly been written with practitioners in mind; others are aimed primarily at academics. Both practitioners and academics have much to gain from all of the papers; in particular academics who, to state the obvious, make up the bulk of the readership of academic journals, stand to profit from understanding the viewpoint of managers. This is especially so, given the present stage of development of services marketing. No attempt has been made, therefore, to try to impose a uniform style upon contributors who have chosen their own audiences, approaches and philosophies. Just as the academics' obvious need to delineate the scope of 'the marketing of services' suggests a discipline in transition, so the frequently-expressed view that many service organisations have far to go before their managements can claim to have implemented the marketing concept provides evidence of a field of application which is at an early state of development.

The first four articles are concerned with general issues which confront those involved in services marketing, whether as corporate managers or policy-makers. In the first article, John Lidstone who is a management consultant discusses the application of marketing principles to service organisations and draws specific attention to the use of marketing planning techniques. This article makes a valuable starting point for the collection by presenting a general account of what marketing is and the implications of ignoring it. Christopher Lovelock discusses the managerial problems of constrained demand, a situation that service organisations frequently face and one which some authorities on service marketing cite as distinguishing services clearly from products. Donald Cowell draws attention to the consequences of consumer protection regulations for the providers of services; and Keith Blois introduces a topical theme, marketing productivity, to the services sphere.

The following four articles are concerned with professional services including those of a financial nature. Barbara Lewis reviews recent advances in bank marketing while Simon Majaro reports on his researches into the adoption of the marketing concept by insurance companies and its implications for their financial performance. In another article, John Driver explores the application of marketing principles to estate agency, which for many firms represents a novel departure. Stanley Siebert argues in his article for the extension of competitive advertising to the activities of the legal and other professions.

The articles which complete this special volume demonstrate further the breadth of services marketing: transportation is represented by Norman Marr's exhortation to managers in that industry to become more customer-orientated, and by Peter White's analysis of the marketing of travelcards; local authorities' provision of leisure services is discussed by David Yorke. Tourism is the subject of two articles: Arthur Meidan's article is concerned with the extension of marketing generally to this areas of business while A.J. Burkart considers the package tours sector. The last two articles concern distribution. Nigel Piercy describes the accommodation of technological change in retailing and, in an article which resumes a general theme in the marketing of services, Martin Christopher discusses the importance of providing customer service whatever the 'product' or 'service' on offer.

The intention and, I hope, the outcome of this collection of essays has been to convey a practice and a discipline at a fascinating and important stage of development. More than one plausible view of what marketing is, and how it might be better applied in service organisations, has been expressed, and if practitioners and academics are a little confused as a result of the editorial policy which has fostered this result, then that is intentional, too. Dissatisfaction with the prevailing wisdom is a vital component of progress in commerce as well as academia. I am honoured to have been asked to make the selection of articles herein and I would like to thank the contributors for the interest, industry and consideration they have shown. I am also grateful to the regular editors for their guidance and advice.

REFERENCES

Baker, M.J., 1981, 'Services – Salvation or Servitude?', *Quarterly Review of Marketing*, Vol. 6, No. 3.

Berry, L.L., 1980, 'Services Marketing is Different', *Business*, May–June.

Gronroos, C., 1978, 'A Service-Orientated Approach to Marketing Services', *European Journal of Marketing*, Vol. 12, No. 8.

Levitt, T., 1981, 'Marketing Intangible Products and Product Intangibles', *Harvard Business Review*, Vol. 59, No. 3.

Lovelock, C.H., 1984, *Services Marketing*, Englewood Cliffs, NJ: Prentice-Hall.

Middleton, N.T.C., 1983, 'Product Marketing – Goods and Services Compared', *Quarterly Review of Marketing*, Vol. 8, No. 4.
Sasser, E., Olsen, R.P., and D.D. Wychoff, 1978, *Management of Service Operations*, Boston, MA: Allyn & Bacon.
Stanton, W.J., 1975, *Fundamentals of Marketing*, Englewood Cliffs, NJ: McGraw-Hill.

The Marketing of Professional Services

by

John Lidstone

The recognition by professional services firms of the need to become marketing-orientated and apply marketing techniques is of recent origin. Yet their need to identify, anticipate and satisfy client requirements profitably, rather than passively wait for clients to request their services, is overwhelming. The professional services provided by such specialists as accountants, advertising agents, banks, computer consultancies, consulting engineers, and management consultants are highly people-intensive. Consequently, there is more room for individual discretion, eccentricity, delay and error. This article argues that professional services companies can systematically plan the marketing of their services so that they can provide value satisfactions that will create and keep their clients and produce profits.

INTRODUCTION

Twenty years ago when I first became a marketing consultant in the United Kingdom, I was faced with the awesome challenge of helping to market a new company's services. Unlike products that can be seen and evaluated before purchase, professional services such as accountancy, advertising, architecture, banking, computers, consulting engineering, the law, public relations and indeed, management consultancy, too often have a mystique that makes evaluation difficult. Such services cannot be seen nor their potential benefits enjoyed at the time of purchase. Moreover, in 1964, the majority of those who managed professional services companies saw no necessity to market their services to their clients. In fact many of the professional bodies such as the Institute of Chartered Accountants, The Association of Consulting Engineers, The Law Society, The Management Consultants Association, The Royal Institute of British Architects expressly forbade their members actively to canvass for custom. The word 'marketing' was not used for the single reason that it did not exist in the vocabularies of those in professional services. Business came to them. Competition was non-existent because, like canvassing for clients, it too was forbidden.

Bank managers, for example, would never try to obtain new business by taking a customer away from another bank. This cosy atmosphere was not always so:

> In these days of keen competition between banks, one of the first special qualifications of a branch manager, and the one most likely – given certain attributes – to lead to promotion, is the ability to get new business of a satisfactory nature and to increase the magnitude and profitableness of the transactions of the branch.

That is the opening sentence of a chapter entitled, 'Getting New Business: Guidance for the more senior men', from the book – *How to Succeed in a Bank* by F.E. Steel – *published in 1926*. Without changing a single word, that sentence could be used with much greater force and relevance today and applied to all the professions [Lidstone, 1973].

Competition and greater freedom from financial controls has brought about changes in the traditional attitudes of the professional services. As a result 'marketing' has become an important factor in the thinking of those who manage such professional enterprises. First, however, there needs to be a clear understanding *of what marketing is* and how it applies to professional services.

WHAT IS MARKETING?

Perhaps it is time now to ask ourselves: what is marketing? There is a compelling case for it, despite its criticisms from academics, politicians and businessmen and women. In the UK many of the professional bodies and associations have eased their regulations governing advertising and promotional activities with the result that architects, accountants and, of course, management consultants are now planning how they can communicate to their clients in a persuasive way.

This is part of the problem of marketing. For many people it is just a fashionable word for advertising and promotion; for others, it means selling. Indeed, in some quarters marketing is seen as a Trojan Horse which releases hordes of salesmen upon the general public, persuading people to buy things they do not want. Marketing is not another name for selling, nor is it a department of a business. It is an all-pervading philosophy governing attitudes, objectives and direction of a business enterprise, and it is also a driving force for people in a business.

Marketing is the business of creating customers by looking at all your activities through the consumers' eyes and supplying value satisfactions at a profit. It sounds simple but implementation is difficult. Marketing ensures that a company first finds out the nature and scale of people's needs and then makes the products, services or ideas to satisfy them, rather than adhering to the traditional British approach of producing things and then trying to persuade individuals and companies to buy them. It sounds elementary, yet takeovers and mergers and, in the last few years, failures of famous names, the invasion of our markets by overseas competitors bear witness to the daily violation of this rule. In her book, *The Agents of Change*, Patricia Tisdall [1982] reminds us of the hands of British consultants thrown up in horror when the British Government called in McKinseys to carry out a major study at the Bank of England in preference to a British firm. Perhaps the British Empire must take some of the blame for the time it has taken for the marketing message and philosophy to take root in British boardrooms. For over a hundred years this country governed a quarter of the globe; it enjoyed the captive custom of millions of people wherever the Union Jack flew. Yet, when we gave away our empire, we overlooked the simple fact that with it we also gave to those same millions of people the freedom to satisfy their needs as they chose, not as we paternalistically conceived them to be.

Marketing is as much a developed social discipline as anything. It is always so much easier to think about ourselves and our needs than about the needs of our clients. Yet clients' needs must be thought about constantly. The one constant in this world of change is the need to give client satisfaction; it should be the inspiration and the principal objective of every business enterprise.

The Marketing-orientated Firm

Marketing arises as a natural response to the market conditions of the day, and so corporate philosophy seems to have passed through three stages:

> First, the 'product/service' orientation or fixation where the demand for a service is great enough to allow an expectation that business will follow as of right; the main concern under these conditions is primarily with the technical perfection of the services to be supplied.
>
> Second, as demand slackens or competition increases or, as our growth outstrips our client base, there arises a 'selling' orientation. It is concerned with communicating persuasively to potential clients what services we have to offer. Often the concentration is still on persuading clients to accept what the firm has to offer.
>
> Third, at times of major change, when business is still slow in emerging, the firm must consider a genuine 'marketing' orientation. The change is characterised by the identification of the range and mix of services that clients and the market at large will need, building up the facility to supply such services, and persuading clients that this is the service they require.

Does 'Marketing' Apply to Professional Services?

If a professional firm is to survive and prosper, then it must organise its activities in such a way that the fees and revenues it can earn from the supply of its services exceeds the costs of those services. Indeed, in many cases it must do more: it must produce sufficient growth both of profit and range of interesting work so that it can provide the satisfactions necessary to attract and keep the level of first-class staff to supply the partners of tomorrow; to provide a future for the firm as a whole. Therefore, the firm must be constantly aware of the need to offer services to clients which fulfil not only statutory but also commercial needs; and to fulfil these needs better than competition at cost-effective fee levels. If this is accepted, then the philosophy of marketing would seem to be inevitable [Levitt, 1981].

In order to fulfil such a philosophy, the needs of the client and the market must be defined, the appropriate services for today (and tomorrow) must be developed; the fees levels which are both competitive and profitable must be set; the services available must be communicated to existing and prospective clients so that they are persuaded to buy them. Thus the main marketing tactics, research, product/service development, pricing and promotion all have a part to play in the successful firm. Some marketing tools, appropriate to other industries, will be neither applicable nor effective. In-store merchandising or door-to-door selling are of little use to the industry. However, no commercial company can usefully employ all the marketing and promotional tactics. It is the company's or firm's decision as to which tactics are most appropriate or cost effective. However, it is hard to identify any examples of a company where marketing has no application at all.

Why Marketing is so Important Now

The current situation, both in the United Kingdom and internationally, makes the adoption of a marketing philosophy and the use of marketing tactics essential to survival. Professional services companies have begun to question previously held beliefs – 'selling is unprofessional and undignified' – and to debate the relevance of historically accepted ethical standards, for example, on advertising.

Change is always unsettling and much of the opposition to debate is little more than a distaste for change. The phenomena we have noted, however, will not go away if they are ignored. Any firm which wishes to maintain its position, and grow to ensure its future must pay particular attention to its marketing.

CONCLUSION

The responsibilities of everyone in a professional services enterprise concerned with directing or managing one or more of its services is twofold: the first concerns today's business and is met by the daily functional decisions that the manager makes; the second involves tomorrow's business and this requires *planning*.

Looking ahead at the pressures from technological advances, increasing competition and more demanding clients, the professional services offered must inevitably change; so, too, with the businesses that provide them. Marketing planning will help make the transition from today to tomorrow. Planning for changed circumstances provides the single opportunity to gain significant growth and advantage over competition. Individual professional regulatory requirements, services innovation, new technology and other realities of life all combine to even out companies. Yet these same factors which account for market changes also provide opportunities.

Finally, it should be realised that marketing planning is not something set apart from the rest of the business. For a professional services company to be successful, this planning determines the objectives, direction and activities, and provides the driving force for everyone. This needs to be recognised by the whole company and an example set by the directors, partners and managers.[1]

NOTE

1. A complete guide to marketing planning and its application to service organisations can be found in Forsyth and Senton [1983].

REFERENCES

Forsyth, P., and D. Senton, 1983, 'The Marketing and Selling of Accountants' Services', *Accountants' Digest*, No. 140.

Lidstone, J., 1973, *How to Sell Banking Services*, London: Marketing Improvements Ltd.

Levitt, T., 1981, 'Marketing Intangible Products and Product Intangibles', *Harvard Business Review*, Vol. 59, No. 3.

Steel, F.E., 1926, *How to Succeed in a Bank*, London: Pitman.

Tisdall, P., 1982, *Agents of Change: The Development and Practice of Management Consultancy*, London: Heinemann.

Strategies for Managing Demand in Capacity-Constrained Service Organisations

by

Christopher H. Lovelock

A major problem facing managers of capacity-constrained service organisations is how to balance demand against available capacity. Unlike their counterparts in manufacturing firms, service marketers cannot rely on inventories of finished products to act as a buffer between a tightly constrained level of supply and a widely fluctuating level of demand. This article argues that managers of capacity-constrained services who seek to smooth demand to match available capacity must address themselves to two key issues: (1) What type of customers they wish to have using the service at particular points in time; and (2) how to achieve high – and profitable – levels of utilisation over time. Developing appropriate strategies should begin with an understanding of the patterns and determinants of demand: are fluctuations in demand random or do they follow a predictable cycle over time? What causes these fluctuations and how do they vary between different market segments?

This article discusses five approaches to managing demand and relates each to three alternative capacity situations: insufficient capacity (relative to demand), sufficient capacity, and excess capacity. A review of marketing tools shows that each of the elements of the marketing mix – product elements, distribution, pricing, and communication – has a role to play in managing demand, sometimes alone but often in concert with the others. Finally, there is discussion of the need for marketing information systems that will provide managers with specific data to formulate and evaluate appropriate demand management strategies.

INTRODUCTION

Recent years have seen a continuing debate on whether or not service organisations require a distinctive approach to marketing management. Several authors have argued that while the products of service firms are undoubtedly different from those of manufacturing firms, the goal of marketing should be to focus on the universal task of determining and satisfying customers' needs [Blois, 1983; Enis and Roering, 1981].

Many needs, in fact, can be met either by purchasing a good or by renting it. However, just because a good and a service may satisfy the same central customer need does not mean that the marketing management tasks are the same [Lovelock, 1981]. Thus, marketing cars is different from marketing car rentals; packaged foods require a different marketing approach to that entailed in marketing a fast-food restaurant; and a marketing executive for a manufacturer of heavy industrial equipment will need to develop a new managerial style – as well as new strategies – if transferred to the same company's equipment servicing division.

Problems Facing Capacity-Constrained Services

One important characteristic that distinguishes service organisations from manufacturing firms is the former's inability to inventory finished products. In the manufacturing sector, imbalances between supply and demand are usually irregular and temporary phenomena, since inventories can generally be employed as a buffer between the two. It is only during periods of resource shortages that marketers of physical goods need to develop strategies for dealing with scarcity [Kotler and Balachandran, 1975; Monroe and Zoltners, 1979].

The lack of inventories of finished services is not a problem for all service businesses. However, it raises significant issues for management in capacity-constrained service organisations that regularly face significant variations in demand levels. This happens in such important industries as transportation, lodging, food service, repair and maintenance, entertainment, and health care, and in many professional and commercial services. Financial success in these industries is, in large measure, a function of management's ability to use productive capacity – staff, labour, equipment, and facilities – as efficiently and as profitably as possible. When demand is low, productive capacity is wasted, since a service business cannot normally store its product as inventory, and when demand is so high that it exceeds the organisation's ability to meet it, potential business is likely to be lost.

One solution to the demand problem, which falls within the province of operations, is to tailor *capacity* to meet variations in demand [Sasser, 1976]. For example, during peak periods management can add part-time staff and rent extra facilities. During periods of low demand capacity can be reduced by laying off staff and scheduling employee vacations, and also by renting out surplus equipment and facilities or taking these out of service for maintenance and renovation.

Another solution which should logically be entrusted to marketing is modifying *demand* to match available capacity. (Many service organisations, of course, seek to manage both demand and capacity.) Such an approach requires a good understanding of the underlying determinants of demand and how these may be influenced.

Economists have long recognised the role of the price mechanism in bringing supply and demand into balance. However, pricing is only one of several tools available to marketing managers who can also look to modifications in product features and distribution elements, as well as communication efforts, to help smooth the peaks and valleys of demand – a marketing task that Kotler [1973] has called 'synchromarketing'.

Despite the importance of effective demand management strategies for the success of so many service businesses, there has not been significant coverage of this topic in the marketing literature. Some writers have cited the need to manage demand in services and have thrown out a few brief ideas as to how to achieve this through marketing [Berry, 1980; Kotler and Levy, 1976]. However, there has been no systematic attempt to develop a conceptual framework that would help managers to identify and evaluate the alternative strategies available.

Scope of the Article

This article argues that managers of capacity-constrained service organisations must address two key issues: what types of customers they wish to have using the service at particular points in time and how to maintain high utilisation levels. To develop appropriate strategies, managers must understand the patterns and determinants of demand, breaking these down by segment. This article discusses five approaches to managing demand and relates each to three alternative capacity situations: insufficient capacity (relative to demand), sufficient capacity, and excess capacity. A review of specific marketing tools shows that each of the elements of the marketing mix – can be used to help manage demand, sometimes alone but often in concert with the others. Finally, there is a discussion of the need for marketing information systems that will provide managers with specific data to formulate and evaluate appropriate demand management strategies.

UNDERSTANDING THE PATTERNS AND DETERMINANTS OF DEMAND

The search for demand management strategies should start with an understanding of what factors govern demand for a specific service at a given point in time. Managers should address the following questions:

I. Does the level of demand for the service follow a regular *predictable* cycle?
   A. If so, is the duration of that cycle:
      1. One day (varies by hour)
      2. One week (varies by day)
      3. One month (varies by day or by week)
      4. One year (varies by month or by season; or reflects annually occurring public holidays)
      5. Some other period.

B. What are the underlying causes of these demand variations?
   1. Employment schedules
   2. Billing and tax payment/refund cycles
   3. Wage and salary payment dates
   4. School hours and vacations
   5. Seasonal changes in climate
   6. Occurrence of public holidays and so forth.

II. Are changes in the level of demand largely random in nature? If so, what are the underlying causes?
   1. Day-to-day changes in the weather affecting relative use of indoor and outdoor recreational or entertainment services.
   2. Health events whose occurrence cannot be pinpointed exactly (for example, heart attacks and births affecting the demand for hospital services).
   3. Calls for assistance resulting from accidents, acts of nature, and certain criminal activities requiring fast response by emergency services.

III. Can demand for a particular service over time be disaggregated by market segment to reflect such components as:
   A. Use patterns by a particular type of customer or for a particular purpose;
   B. Variations in the net profitability of each completed transaction?

Disaggregating Demand by Market Segment

Generally, marketing efforts can do little to smooth out *random* fluctuations in demand over time, since these are usually caused by factors beyond the service organisation's control. However, detailed market analysis may sometimes reveal that a predictable demand cycle for one segment is concealed within a broader, seemingly random pattern, and can thus be addressed by marketing strategies. For instance, a repair and maintenance shop may know that a certain proportion of its work consists of regularly scheduled contractual business, representing routine preventive maintenance. The balance may come from 'walk-in' business and emergency repairs, and it may be hard to predict or control the timing and volume of such work.

The ease with which total demand can be disaggregated depends on the nature of the records kept by the service organisation. If each customer transaction is recorded separately, and backed up by detailed notes (as in a hospital visit or accountant's audit) then the task of understanding demand is greatly simplified. For subscription services, where each customer receives itemised monthly bills, managers can gain some immediate insights into usage patterns. If the identity of the subscriber is known, consumption of the service can be related to type of user (household versus commercial or industrial), geographic location, and total usage volume. Some services – such as telephone – even have the ability to track subscriber consumption patterns by time of day. Although these data may not always yield specific information on the purpose for which the service is being used, it is often possible to make informed judgements about the volume of sales generated by different user groups. Similarly, if there are variations in the prices charged to different customers (and/or the costs incurred in serving them), then managers can assess the relative profitability of serving various customer segments.

Analysis may also show that part of the demand for a particular service is undesirable, for instance, calls to emergency services to rescue cats from trees. Demand that represents a poor fit with institutional goals may constitute a special problem for public and non-profit organisations which define their missions in non-financial terms. Although discouraging undesirable demand through marketing campaigns or screening procedures will not eliminate random fluctuations in the remaining demand, it may bring the peaks of that demand within the service capacity of the organisation.

When demand for a service fluctuates widely but follows a predictable pattern over a known cycle, it may be economically worthwhile to develop marketing strategies designed to smooth out major fluctuations over time. However, no strategy is likely to succeed unless it is based on an understanding of *why* customers from a specific market segment choose to use the service when they do. For example, most hotels find it difficult to convince business travellers to remain on Saturday nights since few executives do business over the weekend. Instead, hotel managers should consider promoting use of their facilities for other purposes at weekends, such as conferences or pleasure travel. Similarly, attempts to get commuters on public transport to shift their travel to off-peak periods will probably fail, since the timing of most commuter travel is determined by people's employment hours. Instead, marketing efforts should be directed at employers to persuade them to adopt flexitime or staggered working hours [Lovelock and Young, 1979].

STRATEGIES FOR MANAGING DEMAND

At any given point in time, a fixed-capacity service organisation may be faced with one of four conditions:

1. Demand exceeds maximum available capacity with the result that potential business may be lost.
2. Demand exceeds the optimum capacity level; no one is turned away, but all customers are likely to perceive a deterioration in the quality of service delivered.
3. Demand and supply are well balanced at the level of optimum capacity.

4. Demand is below optimum capacity and productive resources are under-utilised; this poses the risk (in some instances) that customers may find the experience disappointing or have doubts about the viability of the service.

Note the distinction between *maximum available* capacity and *optimum* capacity. When demand exceeds maximum capacity, some potential customers may be disappointed because they are turned away – and their business may be lost forever. However, when demand is operating between optimum and maximum capacity, there is a risk that all customers being served at that time may receive inferior service and thus become dissatisfied.

The optimum level of capacity is likely to vary from one service business to another and even from one market segment to another. Sometimes optimum and maximum capacities are the same. For instance, at a live performance in a theatre or sports arena, a full house is generally regarded as very desirable, since it stimulates the players and creates a sense of excitement and audience participation, thereby enhancing the service experience. In other cases, however, customers may feel that they get better service if the facility is not operating at full capacity. The quality of restaurant service, for instance, often deteriorates when every table is occupied. Passengers travelling alone in aircraft with high density seating usually feel more comfortable if the seat adjacent to them is empty. When repair and maintenance shops are fully scheduled, delays may result if there is no slack in the system to allow for coping with unexpected difficulties in completing particular jobs. Hence, smoothing demand to the optimal level may be a desirable goal even for service organisations that rarely encounter demand in excess of maximum available capacity.

Optimising the use of capacity requires looking at the *mix* of business obtained as well as at the total volume. Some market segments may be more desirable than others because the customers fit particularly well with the organisation's mission, reinforce the ambiance that the service organisation is trying to create, have needs that match the professional skills and interests of staff members, or pay higher rates and are more profitable. Marketing managers should examine the components of overall demand and seek to stimulate or discourage demand from particular segments on a selective basis.

Five common approaches to managing demand can be identified. The first, which usually reflects the absence of any strategy, involves taking no action and *leaving demand to find its own levels*. This approach does have the virtue of simplicity; eventually customers may learn from experience or word-of-mouth when they can expect to stand in line to use the service and when it will be available without delay. The second and third strategies involve *managing demand*: taking active steps to reduce demand in peak periods and to increase it when demand is low, respectively. The fourth and fifth approaches involve *inventorying demand*. This objective can be accomplished either by introducing a reservations system or by adopting a formalised queuing system (or by a combination of the two).

Table 1 links these five approaches to three alternative demand/capacity situations and offers a strategic commentary on each of the 15 resulting cells. To achieve the best results over the duration of the demand cycle, service organisations should consider using a combination of two or more of the options described.

Managing Demand

The *product demand cycle* is the periodic cycle influencing demand for a particular service; it may vary in length from one day to 12 months. In many instances, multiple cycles may operate simultaneously. For example, demand levels for public transport may vary by time of day, day of week, and season of year. The demand for service during the peak period on a Monday in summer may be different from the level during the peak period on a Saturday in winter, reflecting day-of-week and seasonal variations jointly.

Many permutations may exist. For instance, two time-of-day periods (peak and off-peak), two day-of-week periods (weekday and weekend), and three seasonal periods (peak, shoulder, and off-peak) can be combined to create 12 different demand periods. In theory, each of these periods might have its own distinct demand level (at a particular price) and customer profiles. By careful analysis of both the demand level and the mix of business in each demand period, a manager can determine whether there are close similarities between any of the demand periods. This would make it possible to collapse the framework into clusters of cells, with each cluster receiving a distinct marketing treatment in order to optimise use of available capacity and achieve the most desirable customer mix. During the 1960s, the Canadian National Railway developed such an approach for pricing its passenger services. The entire year was divided into 162 'red' (or bargain) days, 143 'white' (or economy) days, and 60 'blue' (or standard) days – essentially representing dates on which rail travel was in low, average, or high demand – with prices being set accordingly and communication efforts publicising the dates through the use of an eye-catching red, white, and blue calendar [Harvard Business School, 1966].

Inventorying Demand for a Service

Service businesses, for the most part, can rarely inventory supply, but they can often inventory demand.[1] This can be done by asking customers to wait in line on a first-come, first-served basis (queuing), or by offering them the opportunity of reserving space in advance.

A marketing approach to queuing involves determining the maximum amount of time that people will wait for service and then finding ways to make this time pass quickly and pleasantly. Strategies for accomplishing this include agreeable surroundings (for example, a comfortable

TABLE 1
CAPACITY SITUATION RELATIVE TO DEMAND

Strategy	*Insufficient Capacity (Excess Demand)*	*Sufficient Capacity* (Satisfactory Demand)*	*Excess Capacity (Insufficient Demand)*
Take no action	Unorganised queuing results. (May irritate customers and discourage future use.)	Capacity is fully utilised. (But is this the most profitable mix of business?)	Capacity is wasted. (Customers may have a disappointing experience for services like theater.)
Reduce demand	Pricing higher will increase profits. Communication can be employed to encourage usage in other time slots. (Can this effort be focused on less profitable/ desirable segments)?	Take no action, (but see above).	Take no action, (but see above).
Increase demand	Take no action (unless opportunities exist to stimulate and and give priority to more profitable segments).	Take no action (unless opportunities exist to stimulate and give priority to more profitable segments).	Price lower selectively (try to avoid cannibalising existing business; ensure all relevant costs are covered. Use communications and variation in products/ distribution (but recognise extra costs, if any, and make sure appropriate trade-offs are made between profitabiliy and usage levels).
Inventory demand (1) Reservation System	Consider priority system for most desirable segments. Make other customers shift (a) outside peak period or (b) to future peak.	Try to ensure most profitable mix of business.	Clarify that space is available and that no reservations are needed.
(2) Formalised Queuing	Consider over-ride for most desirable segments. Seek to keep waiting customers occupied and comfortable. Try to predict wait period accurately.	Try to avoid bottleneck delays.	Not applicable.

* *Note*: 'Sufficient capacity' may be defined as *maximum available capacity* or *optimum capacity* depending on the situation.

temperature, a seat, and restful music), taking preliminary information from the customer, disseminating advance information on the service, promoting other products offered by the organisation, or offering supplementary services (for example, entertainment, reading materials, or food and drink).

Market segmentation may sometimes be used in designing queuing strategies so that certain users of the service obtain a higher priority than others. This may be based on the importance of the customer (or the job), how long it will take to provide service (with 'express lanes' for shorter jobs), or faster service in return for a premium price.

Usually goods that require servicing can be kept in a waiting line longer than people can. But sometimes their owners do not wish to be parted from them for long. Households with only one car, for example, or factories with a vital piece of equipment often cannot afford to be without such items for more than a day or two. So a reservations system may be necessary for service businesses in fields such as repair and maintenance. By requiring reservations for routine maintenance, management can keep time free for handling emergency jobs at premium prices which yield a much higher contribution margin.

Taking reservations serves to pre-sell the service. In theory, it benefits customers by avoiding the need for queuing and, to help the service firm balance capacity, guaranteeing service availability at a specific time. Demand can be deflected from a first-choice time to earlier or later times, and even from first-choice locations to alternative locations. However, problems arise when customers fail to show up or when service firms over-book. Marketing strategies for dealing with these operational problems include requiring an advance fee for all reservations (not always feasible), cancelling non-paid reservations after a certain time, and providing compensation to victims of overbooking.

ASSET REVENUE GENERATING EFFICIENCY

Ideally, capacity-constrained service firms would like to be operating at a high level of capacity (which, as discussed earlier, may or may not be 100 per cent of available capacity) at all times outside scheduled downtime periods. Many capacity-constrained service organisations use percentage of capacity sold as a measure of operational efficiency. For instance, transport services talk of the 'load factor' achieved, hotels of their 'occupancy rate', and hospitals of their 'census'. Similarly, professional firms can calculate the proportion of a partner's or an employee's time classified as billable hours, and repair shops can look at utilisation of both equipment and labour. However, by themselves, these percentage figures tell us little of the relative profitability of the business attracted, since high utilisation rates may be obtained at the expense of heavy discounting.

What is needed, then, is a measure of the extent to which the organisation's assets are achieving their full revenue–generating potential. This must take into account the relationship between the average price actually obtained per unit of service and the maximum price that might potentially have been charged – what might be termed the unit price efficiency rate. By multiplying the capacity utilisation rate by the unit price efficiency rate, we can derive an index of *asset revenue generating efficiency* (ARGE). Consider, for example, a 200-room hotel where all rooms carry a maximum posted price of £50. If only 60 per cent of rooms is occupied one night, with 60 rooms being sold at £50 and another 60 at £30, then the average unit price efficiency rate is 80 per cent and the ARGE is $(0.6 \times 0.8) = 48$ per cent. Another way to arrive at the ARGE is to divide total revenues received (£4,800) by the theoretical maximum revenues that could have been obtained by selling all rooms at the highest unit price (£10,000).

Improving Advance Sales Decisions

The value of the ARGE approach to performance measurement is that it forces explicit recognition of the opportunity cost of accepting business from one segment when another might subsequently yield a higher rate. Consider the following problems facing sales managers for different types of capacity-constrained service organisations:

(1) Should a hotel accept an advance booking from a tour group of 200 room-nights at £30 each when these same room-nights might possibly be sold later at short notice to business travellers at the full rack rate of £50?
(2) Should a railway with 30 empty freight wagons at its disposal accept an immediate request for a shipment worth £100 per wagon or hold the wagons idle for a few more days in the hope of getting a priority shipment that would be twice as valuable?
(3) How many seats on a particular flight should an airline sell in advance to tour groups and passengers travelling at special excursion rates?
(4) Should an industrial repair and maintenance shop reserve a certain proportion of productive capacity each day for emergency repair jobs that offer a high contribution margin and the potential to build long-term customer loyalty, or should it simply follow a strategy of making sure that there are sufficient jobs, mostly involving routine maintenance, to keep its employees fully occupied?
(5) Should a computer service bureau process all jobs on a first-come first-served basis, with a guaranteed delivery time for each job or should it charge a premium rate for ‘rush’ work, and tell customers with ‘standard’ jobs to expect some variability in completion dates?

Good market information supported by good marketing sense is the key to making appropriate decisions in such instances. The decision to accept or reject business should represent a realistic estimate of the probabilities of obtaining the higher rated business, together with a recognition of any incremental costs involved.

Based upon past experience and an understanding of current market conditions, prices can be set that reflect the demand curves of different market segments. At the same time, 'selective sell' targets can be assigned to advertising and sales personnel, reflecting how management expects to allocate available capacity among different market segments *at a specific point in time*. These allocation decisions by segment also constitute vital information for reservations personnel, indicating when to stop accepting reservations from certain segments. To simplify the task, customers from different segments can be assigned different telephone numbers or mailing addresses for making reservations.

Allocating Capacity Over Time by Service Class

Service organisations often offer different classes of a particular service, with the premium version containing added value elements such as more comfort, more speed, and extra amenities. Marketers of multi-class services often develop a framework for establishing pricing policy and capacity allocation decisions by both service class and time period. Figure 1 shows a hypothetical example in which three service classes – top-of-the-line, standard, and budget – have been combined with four time periods – peak, first shoulder, off-peak, and second shoulder – to form 12 cells, each of which may require a distinctive marketing approach. The size of each cell reflects the percentage of total capacity allocated to it over the duration of the product demand cycle (in this case, one year). For instance, top-of-the-line/peak has been assigned nine per cent (30 per cent x 30 per cent) of total annual capacity. Clearly, accurate demand forecasting and understanding of customer behaviour are important to this assignment process. Fine tuning can be achieved by monitoring results and changing capacity allocations, prices, and other marketing actions for future demand cycles.

This type of exercise may need to be performed separately for each operating unit (for example, each service facility in a chain of repair shops or each corridor in a transportation system). Relevant criteria include strength of market demand, competitive price levels, quality of product relative to the competition, and variations in cost structure. Alternatively, individual units can be clustered into similar groups (for example, hotel units located at airports versus hotels located in central business districts) for the purpose of establishing appropriate marketing programmes. The challenge is to be responsive to individual market situations but to avoid creating a pricing scheme so complex that it confuses customers, intermediaries, and service personnel alike (as many airline pricing schemes are alleged to do).

In order to ensure that profitability goals are met, the marketer must not only set an appropriate price but also understand the variable cost per

FIGURE 1
DEVELOPING A PRICING MATRIX:
ALLOCATING CAPACITY OVER TIME BY SERVICE CLASS
(HYPOTHETICAL EXAMPLE)

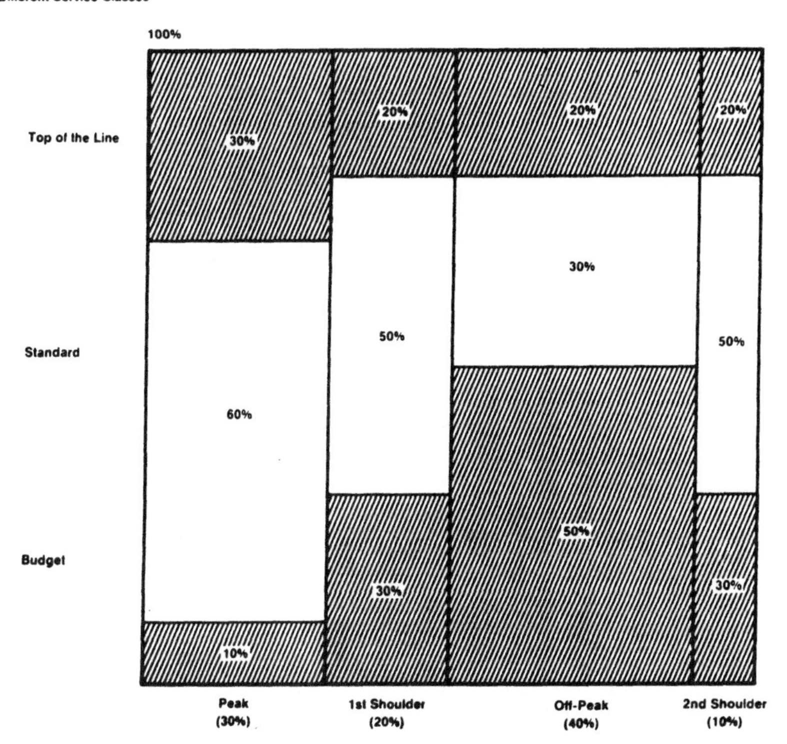

sales unit, such as a seat, a room, or a specific repair task. This cost is likely to vary by service class when extra value is added by providing extra service, such as more floor space, more personal attention, or use of superior equipment. In some instances, however, as in theatres with identical seat sizes, the extra value to customers is created by better locations, and no extra costs are incurred by the marketer. Additionally, a decision must be made on how to allocate fixed costs among the different cells. When the marketer would like to price close to variable cost in order to stimulate off-peak demand for budget-class service, it may be appropriate to allocate no fixed costs to that cell at all. (However, all fixed costs must be allocated and recovered *somewhere* within the matrix!) The final issue is to recognise that 100 per cent utilisation of the assigned capacity within each cell may not be achieved. Hence, cost allocations per sales unit must reflect the anticipated utilisation rate in each cell. Again, this places a premium on accurate forecasting.

MODIFYING MARKETING MIX ELEMENTS TO MANAGE DEMAND

All the elements of the marketing mix have a role to play in stimulating demand during periods of excess capacity and in decreasing it (demarketing) during periods of insufficient capacity.

Price is often the first variable to be proposed for bringing demand and supply into balance, but product and distribution modifications and communication efforts can also play an important role. The relative effectiveness of each depends both on the underlying causes of demand variations and on the nature of the demand cycle. Although each element is discussed separately below, effective demand management efforts often require changes in two or more elements jointly.

Product Variations

Although pricing is the most commonly advocated method of balancing supply and demand, it is not quite as universally feasible for services as for goods. A rather obvious example is provided by the respective problems of a ski manufacturer and a ski slope operator during the summer. The former can either produce for inventory or try to sell skis in the summer at a discount. If the skis are sufficiently discounted, some customers will buy before the ski season in order to save money. However, no skiers would buy ski lift tickets for use on a midsummer day at *any* price. To encourage summer use of the lifts, the operator has to change the product by installing an alpine slide or by promoting the view at the summit. Solutions of a similar nature have been adopted by tax preparation firms that now offer bookkeeping and consulting services to small businesses in slack months, and by landscaping firms in many parts of the US and Canada that seek snow removal contracts in the winter. These firms recognise that no amount of price discounting is likely to develop business out of season.

Although many service offerings remain unchanged throughout the year, others undergo significant modifications according to the season. Hospitals, for example, tend to offer the same array of services throughout the year. By contrast, resort hotels sharply alter the mix and focus of their peripheral services such as dining, entertainment, and sports to reflect customer preferences in different seasons.

There can be variations in the product offering even during the course of a 24-hour period. Restaurants provide a good example, marking the passage of the hours with changing menus and levels of service, variations in lighting and decor, opening and closing of the bar, and presence or absence of entertainment. The objective may be to appeal to different needs within the same group of customers, to reach out to different customer segments, or to do both, according to the time of day.

Different versions of the same service can also be offered simultaneously in response to variations in customer preferences and ability to pay. For example, airlines offer first-class, business-class, and tourist-class service; hotels have different room and service categories; and theatres and concert halls offer different seating categories. To reflect variations in demand among different customer groups over the course of the product demand cycle, some service marketers vary the mix of capacity allocated to the different product categories (for example, by adding or removing first-class seats from an airliner). But when the capacity mix is fixed – as it is in hotels and concert halls – changes in category allocations are tantamount to price increases or decreases (for example, when hotels charge only the price of a regular room for a suite).

Another form of product variation reflects the customer's need for speedy service. Examples include different priority classes for surgery, airfreight service, printing, and computer processing. Higher priority classes have first claim to the limited productive capacity available.

Variations in Distribution

Rather than seeking to modify demand for a service that continues to be offered at the same time in the same place, it may be worthwhile to respond to market needs by modifying the time and place of delivery.

Four basic options are available. The first option represents a strategy of no change: regardless of the level of demand, the service continues to be offered in the same location at the same times. By contrast, the second strategy involves varying the times when the service is available to reflect changes in customer preference by day of week, by season, and so forth. For instance, theatres often offer matinees over the weekend when people are free during the day as well as in the evening; during the summer in hot climates, banks may close for two hours at midday while people take a siesta, but remain open later in the evening when other commercial establishments are still active.

The third strategy involves offering the service to customers at a new location. One approach is to establish mobile units that will take the service to customers, rather than requiring them to visit fixed-site service locations, as an inducement to use. Mobile libraries and vans equipped with primary care medical facilities are two examples that might be emulated by other service businesses. A cleaning and repair firm that wishes to generate business during low demand periods could offer free pickup and delivery of movable items that require servicing.

Alternatively, a viable strategy for a service whose productive assets are mobile may be to follow the market when that, too, is mobile. For instance, some car rental services establish seasonal branch offices in resort communities. In these new locations, it may be necessary to change the schedule of service hours (as well as certain product features) to conform with local needs and preferences. This results in a fourth strategy that involves simultaneous variations in both scheduling availability and location. One New England airline, for instance, operates between Boston and Cape Cod in the summer; in the winter, the aircraft and crews move to Florida and operate a different route network and schedule down there.

Pricing

For price to be effective as a demand management tool, the marketing manager must have some sense of the shape and slope of a product's demand curve (that is, how the quantity of service demand responds to increases or decreases in the price per unit) *at a particular point in time*. It is important to determine whether the aggregate demand curve for a specific service varies sharply from one time period to another. If so, significantly different pricing schemes may be needed to fill capacity in each time period.

To complicate matters further, there may be separate demand curves for different segments *within* each time period, reflecting variations in the need for the service or ability to pay between various customer groupings.

One of the most difficult tasks facing service marketers is to determine the nature of all these different demand curves. Research, trial and error, and analysis of parallel situations in other locations or in comparable services are all ways of obtaining an understanding of the situation. This information is needed not only for demand management purposes, but also to maximise profits in service businesses (or to optimise the social value of a public or non-profit service).

Many service businesses explicitly recognise the existence of different demand curves for different segments during the same period by establishing distinct classes of service, each priced at levels appropriate to the demand curve of a particular segment. In essence, each segment receives a variation of the basic product, with value being added to the core service in order to appeal to the higher paying segments. For instance, top-of-the-line service in airlines offers travellers larger seats, free drinks, and better food; in computer service bureaus, product enhancement takes the form of faster turnaround and more specialised analytical procedures and reports.

In each case, the objective is to maximise the revenues received from each segment. However, when capacity is constrained, the goal in a profit-seeking business should be to ensure that as much capacity as possible is utilised by the most profitable segments. For this reason, various usage conditions may have to be set to discourage customers willing to pay top-of-the-line prices for trading down to less expensive versions of the product. Airlines, for instance, may insist that excursion tickets be purchased 21 days in advance and that the passenger remain at the destination for at least one week before returning – conditions that are too constraining for most business travellers.

Communication Efforts

Even if the other variables of the marketing mix remain unchanged, communication efforts alone may be able to help smooth demand. Signing, advertising, and sales messages can remind prospective customers of the peak periods and encourage them to avoid these in favour of the uncrowded, off-peak times when service is, perhaps, faster or more comfortable. Examples include postal service requests to 'Mail Early for Christmas', public transport messages urging non-commuters – such as shoppers or tourists – to avoid the crush conditions of the commuter hours, and communications from sales reps for industrial maintenance firms advising customers of periods when preventive work can be done quickly. In addition, management can ask service personnel – or intermediaries such as travel agents – to encourage customers with discretionary schedules to favour off-peak periods.

If there are changes in pricing, product characteristics, and distribution, it is vital to communicate these clearly to the target markets. Obtaining the desired response to variations in marketing mix elements depends, of course, on fully informing customers about their options.

INFORMATION NEEDS

It is clear that marketing managers in service organisations require substantial information if they are to develop effective demand management strategies and to monitor subsequent marketplace performance.

The information required includes:

(1) Historical data on the level and composition of demand over time, including responses to changes in price or other marketing variables.
(2) Forecasts of the level of demand by segments under specified conditions.
(3) Ability to distinguish between periodic cycles and random fluctuations in demand on a segment-by-segment basis.
(4) Good cost data to enable the organisation to distinguish between fixed and variable costs and to determine the relative profitability of incremental unit sales to different segments and at different prices.
(5) In multisite organisations, identification of meaningful variations in the levels and composition of demand on a site-by-site basis.
(6) Customer attitudes towards queuing under varying conditions.
(7) Customer opinions on whether the quality of service delivered varies with different levels of capacity utilisation.

Where might all this information come from? Although some new studies may be required, much of the needed data is probably already being collected within the organisation – although not necessarily by marketers. As Little [1979] has noted:

> A stream of information comes into the organization from the world at large in many ways ... especially from distilling the multitude of individual transactions of the business .... The amount of data handled by a large company is staggering. Business runs on numbers. Sales alone have vast detail.

Most service businesses collect detailed information for operational and accounting purposes. Although some do not record details of individual transactions (examples include urban public transportation, cinemas, and sports arenas), a majority can identify specific customers with specific transactions. Unfortunately, the marketing value of these data tends to be overlooked and they are not always stored in ways that permit retrieval and analysis for marketing purposes. Nevertheless, the potential exists to reformat collection and storage of customer transaction data in ways that would provide marketers with some of the information they require, including how existing segments have responded to past changes in marketing variables.

Other information may have to be collected through special studies, such as customer surveys, or reviews of analogous situations. On the other hand, information on competitive performance must be gathered on an ongoing basis, since changes in the capacity or strategy of competitors may require corrective action.

The ultimate goal is to develop a marketing decision support system that organises the different data bases within a service organisation and then combines them with models and analytical techniques that can be directed at forecasting demand by segment under alternative assumptions. These projections can then serve as the basis for developing the most appropriate demand management strategy at specific points in time. Ongoing data collection should quickly reveal whether actual performance met the projections. By monitoring performance in this way, and by evaluating the reasons for significant deviations, management should be able to improve its strategies in the future.

CONCLUSION

Managers of capacity-constrained service organisations often face the problem of balancing demand against available capacity, especially when the level of demand varies sharply over a reasonably predictable time cycle. However, it is not enough just to maintain high levels of utilisation. If the organisation is to meet its goals, action must be taken to attract the most appropriate type of business at specific times. Such efforts require breaking down existing and potential demand over time and by segment. This analysis will make it possible for management to establish time-based priorities, stating how much demand is sought from various segments at particular points in time. Establishing such objectives allows management to create a precisely scheduled marketing programme to attract the most desirable segments at the busiest time, to encourage lower priority segments to use the service when capacity is more freely available, and to actively discourage use (or misuse) of the service by unwanted segments.

Marketing strategies for managing demand to match capacity include taking steps to increase or decrease demand, as appropriate, or introducing such procedures as reservations and customer-orientated queuing. Each element of the marketing mix has a role to play in helping the service organisation make optimum use of its capacity, and often the best results are achieved when several elements are used in conjunction with each other.

The availability of good data for planning and evaluation purposes is central to creation of effective demand management strategies. Many service organisations already collect much of the needed data, but store it in formats that meet the needs of the operations and billing departments, rather than of marketing. An integral part of the shift to a greater marketing orientation in service businesses is re-evaluation of current data collection and storage procedures.

Because capacity-constrained service organisations tend to have heavy investments in fixed facilities and equipment, and incur substantial fixed labour costs, even modest improvements in capacity utilisation can have a significant effect on the bottom line. Similarly, changes in the mix of business to emphasise the most profitable segments during periods of excess demand can also have an important impact on profits. The service organisation that can combine a strong marketing management orientation with the marketing decision support systems needed to develop effective demand management strategies will thus be well placed to achieve – or improve upon – success.

NOTE

1. Inventorying the supply of a service is usually only possible for repair and maintenance services involving homogeneous, interchangeable goods. For instance, an industrial service shop may handle large numbers of identical electric motors. Regular customers who bring in such a motor for repair can be given a substitute motor, already serviced and sitting on the shelf, then billed subsequently for the work on their own motor, which will be offered later to another customer bringing in a similar piece of equipment at some future point in time.

REFERENCES

Berry, Leonard L., 1980, 'Services Marketing is Different', *Business* (May–June) 1983.

Blois, K.J., 1983, 'Service Marketing: Assertion or Asset?' *The Service Industries Journal* (July).

Enis, Ben M., and Kenneth J. Roering, 1981, 'Services Marketing: Different Products,

Similar Strategy', in J.H. Donnelly and W.R. George, *Marketing of Services*, Chicago: American Marketing Association.

Harvard Business School, 1966, 'Canadian National Railways', 9–513–038, Boston: Harvard University, HBS Case Services.

Kotler, Philip, 1973, 'The Major Tasks of Marketing Management', *Journal of Marketing*, Vol. 37, October.

Kotler, Philip and V. Balachandran, 1975, 'Strategic Remarketing: The Preferred Response to Shortages and Inflation', *Sloan Management Review* (Fall).

Kotler, Philip and Sidney J. Levy, 1976, 'Demarketing, Yes, Demarketing', *Harvard Business Review*, (November–December).

Little, John D.C., 1979, 'Decision Support Systems for Marketing Managers', *Journal of Marketing* (Summer).

Lovelock, Christopher H., 1981, 'Why Marketing Management Needs to be Different for Services', in J.H. Donnelly and W.R. George, *Marketing of Services*, Chicago: American Marketing Association.

Lovelock, Christopher H., and Robert F. Young, 1979, 'Look to Consumers to Increase Productivity', *Harvard Business Review*, May–June.

Monroe, Kent B., and Andris A. Zoltners, 1979, 'Pricing the Product Line During Periods of Scarcity', *Journal of Marketing*, 43 (Summer).

Sasser, W. Earl, Jr., 1976, 'Match Supply and Demand in Service Industries', *Harvard Business Review*, November–December.

Service Markets: The Effects of Competition Policy and Consumer Protection

by

Donald Cowell*

This article outlines the current status of Competition Policy (Monopolies and Mergers; Anti-Competitive Practices; Restrictive Trade Practices) and Consumer Protection (Legislation; Consumer Protection Agencies; Voluntary Codes of Practice) in services markets. The relative neglect of services markets until recently is reflected in the fragmented and patchwork systems, mechanisms and agencies available in this important sector of the economy and further developments are likely.

INTRODUCTION

Two features of government policy which affect services marketing are the measures taken to encourage competition and the measures taken to control practices which are considered to be restrictive or anti-competitive. Coupled with these are the policies employed to encourage fair trading and protect consumers. Competition policy and consumer protection are issues of great importance in the service sector of the economy. This paper gives an outline of how competition policy and consumer protection apply to services. Many government departments exercise some functions with regard to competition policy and consumer protection. However, the main department concerned with such matters is the Department of Trade and Industry. The Minister of State for Consumer Affairs, who is answerable to the Secretary of State for Trade and Industry, has special responsibilities for competition policy and on consumer matters. These include trading standards, fair trading, weights and measures, consumer credit and consumer safety. Significant agencies of government for whose work the Secretary of State is ultimately responsible include the Monopolies and Mergers Commission and the Office of Fair Trading. The latter is headed by the Director General of Fair Trading.

* This article is based on a chapter in the author's book, *The Marketing of Services*, London: William Heinemann, 1984.

COMPETITION POLICY

Over the years the competition policies of different governments in Britain have led to the development of procedures and methods for examining and controlling monopolies and mergers, anti-competitive practices and restrictive trade practices. The current situation (1984) is that the Director General of Fair Trading administers the Fair Trading Act 1973 which regulates anti-competitive practices; and the Restrictive Trade Practices Acts 1976 and 1977 which regulate restrictive trading agreements. These three areas of competition policy – monopolies and mergers, Anti-Competitive Practices and Restrictive Trade Practices – are examined in turn with specific reference to services.

Monopolies and Mergers

The Secretary of State for Trade and Industry and the Director General of Fair Trading can refer monopolies for investigation to the Monopolies and Mergers Commission. A monopoly is defined in law as a situation where at least a quarter of a particular kind of goods or service is supplied by or to a single person or two or more people acting in a common manner. Local monopolies which prevent, restrict or distort competition as well as public monopolies can be referred to the Commission. Where a monopoly is found to operate against the public interest the Secretary of State for Trade has powers to make orders and to remedy and prevent the harm which may exist. Alternatively, the Director General of Fair Trading may be asked to negotiate undertakings to remedy the effects identified by the Commission. The Commission does not distinguish between goods and services and therefore service industries are not treated in any 'special' way.

During 1981, for example, the Monopolies and Mergers Commission reported on a number of services. These included Roadside Advertising Services where a monopoly was found to exist and remedial measures were adopted. The Commission also found that the monopoly position enjoyed by British Posters Ltd. and its ten-member companies operated against the public interest. The Commission recommended that the company should be broken up and not reformed. This occurred during 1982. Proposals for a merger may be referred to the Commission by the Secretary of State for Trade and Industry if it would result in a monopoly (25 per cent market share) or if gross assets taken over exceed £15 million (formerly £5 million until April 1980). If the Commission finds the merger to be against the public interest the Secretary of State can prevent it from taking place or reverse it if it has already taken place. Two recently approved mergers in the service sector have been that between British Rail Hovercraft and Hoverlloyd and that between Godfrey Davis Car Rentals with Europcar (both approved during 1981).

One effect of the increased assets criterion necessary for consideration by the Commission has been to reduce the number of mergers examined by the Office of Fair Trading. In 1980, for example, 182 mergers were examined by the office. Of these the largest number were in the Distributive Trades and the Insurance, Banking and Finance sectors. The service sector as a whole (roughly comparable to Standard Industrial Classification (SIC) orders 21 to 26) accounted for 88 out of the 182 examined or about 48 per cent of the total. In 1981, 164 mergers were considered. The financial and distribution sectors continued to be major areas for merger and the Director General reported that an increasing number had taken place in the leisure and entertainment fields.

Official figures are of course not an accurate reflection of all merger activity in Britain as there are special provisions relating to newspapers (like the Lonrho takeover of *The Observer*) and certain other mergers. The Director General of Fair Trading usually refers in his annual report to the work of the Monopolies and Mergers Commission. The 1980 Report, for example, referred to the investigation on UK credit card franchise services. In this case the Commission recommended that the 'no discrimination' policy between cash and credit being pursued was against the public interest. This was reflected in garages making an additional charge on petrol sales when a credit card was used to make a purchase. The Director also reported that previous reports from the Commission relating to services still to be considered by ministers included:

(a) whether individual solicitors should have greater freedom to advertise their services as he had recommended. (Certainly in the US where advertising restrictions have been lifted, the American Bar Association has reported that the profession's new-found freedom has resulted in new clients and lower fees);
(b) that discussions were continuing on the removal of restrictions on advertising of veterinary surgeons' services and accountants' services. (In the 1981 report the Director General reported the progress made; the four main professional accountancy bodies had agreed to amend their rules to permit members to advertise their professional services in local newspapers and other local publications);
(c) in respect of other services the Director General reported that as far as architects' services were concerned the Office of Fair Trading was having difficulty during 1980 in obtaining an undertaking from the professions for a more competitive fee system. (Interestingly, an internal poll during 1980 showed 28 per cent of the profession to be against advertising by architects);
(d) the Institute of Quantity Surveyors was reported to be moving towards a more competitive fee policy. (The conservatism of the profession at this time was reflected however in the opposition to the move by the Abbey National Building Society when it began to reveal the contents of surveyors' valuations to prospective housebuyers. This practice has since been followed by other building societies.)

By the time of the 1981 report, the Director General was able to report that his discussions with the professional bodies representing veterinary surgeons, architects and surveyors were concluded and advice had been submitted to the Secretary of State.

Anti-Competitive Practices

The Competition Act has been on the statute book since 1980. This abolished the Price Commission, transferring some of its powers to the Director General of Fair Trading and the Monopolies and Mergers Commission. Subject to certain exemptions the Director General is now empowered to investigate anti-competitive practices in the public or in the private sector. Such practices should have, or are intended or likely, to have, the effect of restricting, distorting or preventing competition in the production, supply or acquisition of goods or services in Britain. The Director may also investigate particular prices and charges on reference by the Secretary of State. If, as a result of enquiries, an anti-competitive practice is found, then the Director General can either refer the matter to the Monopolies and Mergers Commission or accept an undertaking to remove the practice by the business under investigation. If the Monopolies and Mergers Commission finds the practice against the public interest it can recommend remedial action to the Secretary of State, who is ultimately empowered to make an order prohibiting the practice.

One novelty of the Act is that the Secretary of State may also refer to the Commission any question relating to the costs and efficiency of the services provided or the possible abuse of monopoly power by named bodies in the public sector (that is, nationalised industries). The Commission, however, cannot take account of the financial obligations and objectives imposed upon such a public body by statute or ministerial direction. Nor may it consider conduct permitted by the Restrictive Trade Practices Act. A recent illustration of the work of the Commission in its investigation of public bodies was the controversy raised over the hold British Gas had over the supply of gas appliances through over 200 gas showrooms in the United Kingdom. The Commission recommended that British Gas should discontinue its retailing function but implementation was fiercely opposed.

On the working of the Competition Act 1980, the Director General of Fair Trading concluded in his report for 1980 that, at that time, it was too early to assess its effects. However, he did report that the number of complaints received which had justified preliminary enquiries was smaller than might have been expected. He did, however, differentiate between those concerning goods and those concerning services.

Restrictive Trade Practices and Services

Restrictive Trade Practices have to be registered with the Director General of Fair Trading under the Restrictive Trade Practices Act 1976. Basically an agreement has to be registered if two or more parties to the agreement who are engaged in business in Britain accept some limitation on their actions in matters connected with such things as:

(a) charges to be made for services;
(b) the terms or conditions of supply of such services;
(c) the extent to which such services are made available;
(d) the form or manner in which such services are to be made available;
(e) the persons or classes of person for whom services are to be made available.

If an agreement is not registered any restrictions are void and the parties involved are liable to legal action. Equally, registered agreements may be referred to the Restrictive Practices Court by the Director General of Fair Trading to decide, according to criteria laid down in the Act, whether the agreement is against the public interest. The Act chiefly attempts to prevent 'market sharing'.

In practice, however, many services are excluded from the provisions of the Act. These include:

(a) Professional services such as: legal services of barristers, advocates and solicitors; medical, dental and opthalmic services; veterinary services; nursing and midwifery services; architects services; accounting and auditing services; patent agents services; surveyors services; the services of ministers of religion; the services of professional engineers and technologists; financing terms (for example, making a loan);
(b) Services relating to: international sea transport; carriage by air; road passenger transport; building societies; financial control by the Treasury of the Bank of England; banking services (in Northern Ireland); insurance services; unit trust schemes; implementation of decisions of the city panel on takeovers and mergers.

In addition to the above, other exclusions to the Act may apply. These include agreements authorised by Statute; certain agricultural and marketing agreements; know-how agreements; and agreements affecting exports. The Secretary of State is also empowered to exclude agreements of 'importance to the national economy'.

These exclusions obviously cover many services within the service sector of the economy. While it can be argued in respect of certain professional services that restrictive practices can be justified because they protect the consumer (for example, from those unqualified to practice by training and licence) the nature of many other exemptions remains controversial. This is in spite of the fact that the professions ultimately may be scrutinised by the Monopolies and Mergers Commission (for example, the recent Royal Commission on Legal Services). In addition to exclusions from the Act there is the possibility that many restrictive agreements for services are not registered. Both the Office of

Fair Trading and the National Consumer Council have produced evidence of undisclosed agreements for goods and services. Non-disclosure may be due to ignorance on the part of the parties concerned. It may also be due to blatant evasion. This is particularly where the consequences of ignoring the law and subsequent prosecution under the Act are outweighed by the commercial benefits of not registering an agreement.

The Director General of Fair Trading in his annual report for 1981 indicated that 191 new agreements for services were entered on the register in 1981. This took the total entered since 1976 to 686. Of these 686 he reported that: 94 had been ended; 35 had all restrictions removed; 86 were the subject of representations to the Secretary of State (on 82 of which directions have been given); five were (now) before the courts (Aerodromes Owners Association; Society of West End Theatres (two); Association of British Travel Agents; Stock Exchange). In addition he reported that discussions were continuing on agreements affecting a range of services. These included mortgage lending, advertising, actuarial services, commodity markets, bookmaking, freight transport and storage.

The number of agreements registered for goods during 1980 (63) and agreements terminated during 1980 (18) were similar to those for services; however, the number of agreements entered in total on the register for goods (3,873) and terminated for goods (3,211) were larger. This is because Restrictive Trade Practices for goods have been in force (and, therefore, enumerated) since 1956. For services the starting date for enumeration was 1976. Examples of services on which some of the most onerous restrictions have been removed in recent years are:

Bailiffs
Banks
Commodity dealers
Football pools promoters
Goldsmiths
Investigators
Local coach operators groups
Local hotel associations
Motoring schools
Shipbrokers and shipowners
News agencies
Recording and film studios
Wharfingers

Price restrictions have been given up but there was still work to do on the services of:

Cold storage
Commercial/home removals
Electrical testing
Freight forwarding
Road haulage

Also at the end of the year discussion on some 250 services agreements were under way. At that time the Director General was able to report that particular progress had been made in the banking sector.

In addition to these main exclusions the Director General of Fair Trading has discretion in adjudicating whether certain trade practices are of 'significance' enough to call for investigation by the Restrictive Trade Practices Court. Broadly each case is considered on its merits but the discretionary element does mean that the Director General can reach agreement with the parties concerned without resort to a court hearing. The Director General's 1980 report contained a number of illustrations relating to acceptable restrictions on trade. These were in respect of such things as standard terms and conditions, joint ventures and codes of practice with a variety of service organisations.

CONSUMER PROTECTION

In the United Kingdom the Fair Trading Act 1973 now provides machinery for the review of consumer affairs, for action to deal with trading practices and offenders under the law and for the development of codes of practice to raise trading standards. In respect of services the most visible consequences of consumer protection attempts are: Legislation; Consumer Protection Agencies; Voluntary Codes of Practice.

Legislation

There are still a number of differences in England between the law as it applies to 'goods' and as it applies to 'services'. A major problem as far as the law as it applies to services is concerned is that it is still being developed and there are disagreements about interpretation. The law about services is not yet as well codified as the law about goods. It is likely that in the 1980s further laws will be introduced to regulate practices in respect of the marketing of services. Such laws will be in response to changes occurring both in Britain and in the EEC.

Some of the main pieces of legislation related to services marketing are outlined below:

(a) *Sale of Goods Act 1893 as amended by the Supply of Goods (Implied Terms) Act 1973*: Services are not covered by the Sale of Goods Act. But anyone offering a service – things like hairdressing, holidays, car parks – must carry it out in a careful and workmanlike way. If a job is not done properly, or loss or damage is suffered, then it may be possible to claim compensation. However, there is no legislation covering services which is equivalent to the Sale of Goods Act.

(b) *Unfair Contract Terms Act 1977*: Some service firms try to escape responsibility by using 'exclusion clauses'. Until recently exclusion clauses were valid for services as long as the exclusion clause(s) were brought to the attention of consumers when a contract was entered into. Under the Unfair Contract Terms Act 1977 liability is put on a proper footing. A trader is not allowed to restrict or limit liability, or contract out of liability, for death or personal injury which result from negligence or breach of duty.

For claims which do not involve death or personal injury, exclusion clauses are only valid if they are fair and reasonable in the circumstances. The guidelines in the Act used for the reasonableness test include: the strength of the bargaining positions of the various parties to the contract; whether the customer received an inducement to agree to the exclusion clause; whether the customer knew or ought reasonably to have known of the existence of the exclusion clause; in the case of an exclusion clause which applies when some condition is not complied with, whether it was practicable for the condition to be fulfilled.

In addition some businesses cannot exclude liability for their own breaches of contract; cannot use small print to allow them to provide a substantially different kind of service from that reasonably expected of them; nor are exclusion clauses in guarantees valid. In hiring agreements, for example, TV or car rental, the company renting the goods cannot use exclusion clauses to take away its responsibility for seeing that the goods are fit for their purpose. The act applies to a wide range of services including government departments, local authorities and nationalised industries. It does not apply, however, to insurance, the sale of houses, copyright, trade marks or shares in a company.

(c) *Trade Descriptions Act 1968*: The Act makes it a criminal offence for a trader to describe inaccurately the goods he is selling or the services he is offering and he can be fined or imprisoned. A spoken false description is just as much an offence as a written one. A wide range of information is covered such as size, quantity or strength; how, where and by whom something was made or what it is made of; what it is for and how well it will work; any standards to which it conforms; its previous history. Under this Act some kinds of false price reductions or 'markdowns' are also an offence.

In theory this Act should mean that consumers can rely upon descriptions given of services they buy. Thus if a holiday tour operator describes a hotel as 'secluded and peaceful' or as 'one kilometre from the beach' then these statements must be true. If a theatre is displaying a notice which is clearly false it can be prosecuted under this Act. However, if you book in advance to see a play with a famous actor taking the lead you cannot claim your money back if he is unwell and not performing on the night, although the theatre should protect itself against misrepresentation on the night by announcing any change.

In practice the rules for goods and services are different. A service business is liable only if a wrong description can be proved to have been made 'knowingly or recklessly'. In addition certain kinds of service producers are excluded. Estate agents are immune from responsibility under the Act because houses are not legally either goods or services. According to the Annual Report of the Director General of Fair Trading 1980, there were 125 convictions under the

Act for false statements about services compared with over 1,000 convictions for false descriptions about goods – about the same order of magnitude as the previous year.

(d) *Unsolicited Goods and Services Act 1971*: The main way this Act effects the general public is to make it an offence for traders to demand payment for goods or services which people have not ordered. If you receive goods which you did not ask for and you do not agree to keep them, the sender can take them back during the six months after you have received them. If you have not agreed either to keep or send back the goods they become your property after six months. You can then use them, sell them or otherwise dispose of them as if they had been a gift. You can, if you like, cut short the six months' period by writing to the sender giving your name and address and stating that the goods were unsolicited. If the sender then fails to collect them within 30 days they become your property. But in either case you must give the sender reasonable access to collect them. Anyone who demands payment for unsolicited goods can be fined. Corresponding legislation in Northern Ireland is the Unsolicited Goods and Services Act (Northern Ireland) 1976.

In addition it is a criminal offence for the sender of unsolicited goods or services to make any demand for payment from the recipient, unless he has reasonable cause to believe there is a right to payment. The consumers position has been further improved by the Unsolicited Goods and Services (Invoices etc) Regulations 1975 which require the notification of price to be clearly shown as not one obliging payment. Further there are penalties if senders threaten to bring legal proceedings, places or threatens to place the consumers name on a black list of defaulters or invokes any other collection procedure.

(e) *Negligence*: In recent years the Law of Negligence has been widened and applied increasingly in services situations. That is, where there is reliance by an inexpert individual on the care, skill and advice of an expert; and where it can be proved that there was negligence – the failure to employ skill and reasonable care – liability will arise. What was originally thought to apply only to manufacturers has now been extended to many others including banks, accountants, solicitors, surveyors, local authorities and government departments, although the application of the law remains a grey area. Thus a bank manager who gives investment advice could be liable; an estate agent or insurance broker could be liable; and the Unfair Contract Terms Act 1977 nullifies any disclaimer which may have been used in the past unless it can be proved fair and reasonable.

Solicitors have long accepted that the negligent handling of a client's affairs can oblige them to compensate the client. Every practicing solicitor has to be insured against liability of this kind. Barristers, however, are immune from liability for errors in their handling of court cases. In a recent case in which a firm of investment brokers was taken to court (Stafford v. Conti Commodity Services) [*Money Management*, 1981: 177], the judge expressed the view that a broker cannot be right all the time about the advice he gives. Incorrect advice, it was ruled, is not necessarily proof of negligence.

(*f*) *Other legislative and quasi legislative controls*: There are of course other forms of control to try to ensure that people who provide services are qualified and honest. These include giving a public body like the Office of Fair Trading the power to issue or withhold a licence for certain occupations as under the Consumer Credit Act 1974; or by establishing some body to control membership as with the Solicitors Act 1974, and the Insurance Brokers (Registration) Act 1977.

In his 1981 report, for example, reviewing licensing under the 1974 Consumer Credit Act the Director General identified a number of sectoral practices found to be unfair or illegal. These included services like double glazing, debt collection and money lending. The Director General's actions varied in each case but included receiving an undertaking to improve trading conduct, issuing a public warning about unfair methods and strong arm tactics, to withdrawing a traders' licence.

Consumer Protection Agencies

In addition to the framework of legislation relating to services there are a large number of consumer protection agencies which have been established. These agencies collect and distribute information and advice, negotiate on behalf of consumers and exert pressure to reform and improve trading standards and other standards of practice. A major difficulty faced by consumers is the sheer number of agencies with interests in consumer protection and the difficulty of finding out who does what.

It is inappropriate here to describe in detail the activities of the various consumer protection agencies that exist to work at a general level to improve consumer protection or at the specific level to obtain redress for particular grievances. The institutional framework reflects the state of development in Britain and like any institutional arrangement is subject to change and adaptation over time. An excellent guide to the agencies involved is produced by the Office of Fair Trading ['Fair Deal'] and detailed descriptions are available in books and articles specifically devoted to the topic. A number of general observations are however appropriate about the institutional framework:

(a) There is no separate system of institutions to deal with services. Certain institutions may restrict their work to goods (for example, British Standards Institute) but this is due to their range of concern rather than the deliberate separation of goods and services by the system.
(b) There are a great number of public, semi-public, independent and

voluntary organisations involved in consumer protection whether directly or indirectly. They are funded in different ways. The Consumers Association, for example, is funded by subscription while the Citizens Advice Bureaux receive a government grant and rely on voluntary help and subscriptions. Their range of interests can be wide, as with the Office of Fair Trading, or narrow, as with a local consumer group concerned with specifically local issues. Many government departments have interests in the general field of consumer protection (for example, the Ministry of Agriculture, Fisheries and Food, the Department of Health and Social Security, the Home Office) but the Office of Fair Trading, ultimately responsible to the Secretary of State for Trade and Industry, is the main official body in this field.

(c) A broad distinction can be made between institutions concerned with making policy and those concerned with implementation. Usually policy is formed at central government level through the influence of pressure groups, government-sponsored bodies like the Consumers Association. Generally policy is implemented at the local level through Local Authority Trading Standards or Consumer Protection departments. In addition, advice is available locally through Consumer Advice Centres, Mobile Advice Centres, Citizens Advice Bureaux, Local Consumers Groups and Law Centres.

(d) Inevitably there is overlap between many of the agencies involved in the institutional systems of consumer protection. Also, the range of possible sources of advice, information and help is complicated by the separate consumer councils that exist for the nationalised industries to say nothing of the international dimensions such as the effect of EEC membership. The range is often too complex for the consumer to comprehend.

(e) Consumer protection is very much a political arena with arguments about who should be involved; whether it is necessary for the state to be involved; who should pay for services and how; whether there is an unnecessarily large number of agencies and parties involved, and so forth. Such issues are likely to be fiercely debated in the 1980s with the increasing polarisation of views between politicians of left and right of the role that the state should play in economic and social life.

(f) Institutions for consumer protection are, in the main, characteristic of economies in an advanced stage of economic development. Economies in an advanced stage of economic development tend to be service economies. The services of consumer protection are spawned by the service economies of which they are a part.

Voluntary Codes of Practice

Certain professional and trade associations have codes of practice relating to the services they provide. For example, professional bodies concerned with accounting, architecture, management consulting and market research have established codes of practice, and trade associations representing such fields as package holidays, shoe repairs, car repairs, laundering and dry cleaning have also laid down codes for their members. Under the Fair Trading Act 1973 the Director General of Fair Trading has a duty: 'to encourage relevant associations to prepare ... codes of practice for guidance in safeguarding and promoting the interests of consumers'. These codes are designed to improve traders' standards of service and to ensure the consumer gets a fair deal. The first Director General, John Methven, placed great emphasis on the need for voluntary codes as a means of improving standards, arguing that the more effective voluntary controls there were the less would be the need for statutory control.

The advantages of codes of practice are that they do help to establish minimum acceptable standards for services; they deal with a specific trade or profession; and they are probably cheaper to establish and operate than using statutory measures. On the other hand, they are voluntary; they do not give an immediate solution to all consumer problems; and they only apply to members of the association. Furthermore, they do not give extra rights in law, although they do usually supplement legal remedies. An additional weakness of codes of practice is that they are often drawn up by members of the profession or trade without outside help or advice. However, the Office of Fair Trading is taking an increasing role in assisting associations to draw up codes of practice and has been actively involved in helping to draw up some of the recent codes issued. The office also encourages the strengthening of existing provisions within codes of practice, for example, improving conciliation and arbitration of disputes under codes. Thus the revised code of practice for the Glass and Glazing Federation incorporated suggestions made by the Office of Fair Trading.

Certain conditions must apply if the code of practice operated by an association is to be effective. The association must have a respected and representative central body; it must be efficient in operating the code; and it must have the will and enthusiasm to be more than a self-protecting organisation. In particular, membership of the association must be valued by those who belong to it or who aspire to belong to it, if the code of practice is to have any impact. Codes of practice are specific to a particular profession or trade and therefore vary considerably in content. The Office of Fair Trading issues explanatory leaflets dealing with codes of particular interest to consumers. The example below is for services dealing with dry cleaning and laundries.

Dry Cleaning and Laundries

Cleaning, laundering, dyeing and garment repairing are covered by a code of practice produced by the Association of British Launderers and Cleaners (the ABLC) whose membership encompasses over 75 per cent of launderers and dry cleaners in England, Scotland and Wales. The code deals in particular with the following:

(i) *Disclaimer*: The members of the ABLC agreed not to use disclaimers (now illegal anyway!) limiting their liability for negligence if an article is damaged. A cleaner cannot therefore rely on any condition to the effect that the article is left at the owner's risk or that the cleaner 'cannot be responsible for any damage'. If a cleaner or launderer negligently loses, destroys or damages one of your articles, you are entitled to receive fair compensation (the value of the article). If the article can be repaired the launderer or cleaner will pay the cost of repair, up to the value of the item at the time.
(ii) *Fire or burglary*: ABLC members will pay compensation if your article is lost or damaged as the result of a fire or burglary while in their care.
(iii) *Faulty processing*: If an article of yours is unsatisfactorily processed the launderer or dry cleaner will process it again free of charge if you ask for this to be done.
(iv) *Prices*: A price list for standard items should be displayed in the shop or should be available from a van driver in the event of a collection or delivery service. Carpet cleaning prices will normally be expressed as a cost per square metre or square foot.
(v) *Delicate or valuable items*: Should you point out that an item is delicate or valuable the shop may decide to send it away to their main office for examination, in which case they must give you, if you so require, a quotation for the processing before the work is commenced.
(vi) *Delays*: ABLC members will try to ensure that they keep to their indicated delivery times. If an item has been mislaid or its treatment delayed you should be able to get a reduction in the charges.

If you have cause for complaint, you should take the matter up first with the particular shop. If the problem is not satisfactorily resolved (and provided that the launderer or dry cleaner is a member), you can take the matter up with the ABLC and make use of their Customer Advisory Service at Lancaster Gate House, 318 Pinner Road, Harrow, Middlesex, HA1 4HX. The Advisory Service will ask you to submit details of your complaint in writing, and they will try to bring about a satisfactory conclusion by conciliation. They may arrange for a laboratory test to be carried out – which will be free of charge. You will, however, be expected to accept the test findings.

The Director General of Fair Trading reported in his 1980 Annual Report that his office had so far been involved in helping to draw up codes of practice for 19 different types of goods and services. Preliminary discussions were taking place on site and letting arrangements for holiday caravans; he foresaw the likely completion of a code of practice for mechanical breakdown insurance for motor vehicles although the discussions on launderettes had ended without a code being accepted. He also indicated that the Office of Fair Trading is encouraging a move towards flexible but standard procedures and systems of arbitration in the light of its experience so far. A year later in the 1981 Annual Report the Director General indicated that he was not willing to continue negotiations for a code for site and letting arrangements in view of the conditions usually applied to purchase and resale of holiday caravans and to security of tenure. He put pressure on the trade associations involved to make further proposals.

Thus the Office now takes an active role in encouraging the formation of trade associations and codes of practice. According to one press report marriage bureaux and dating agencies have been urged to form a trade association and improve their business methods [*Daily Telegraph*, 1981]. Failing voluntary action, the report suggests, the Office of Fair Trading would press for legislation for some form of licensing system.

THE NATIONALISED INDUSTRIES

The nationalised industries are 'public corporations' with a separate legal personality conferred by statute or charter. They fulfil a range of functions which often gives them a monopoly of the supply of goods or services. In Britain services like Water, Gas, Electricity, Postal and Telecommunications services are all provided chiefly by the nationalised industries. Their very existence apparently contradicts the measures taken by various governments to encourage competition, to restrict competitive practices and thereby encourage fair trade and protect consumers. The political, economic and social arguments for and against nationalisation need not be rehearsed here. However, it is worth noting that the role of the state does vary in different industries and in different countries.

The activities of the nationalised industries can be controlled to some extent through Parliament. As far as the interests of the consumer are concerned, however, the main representative mechanism is the appropriate consultative council or committee. These vary considerably in their structure, powers and influence. For example, there is no consumers council dealing with the water industry. In contrast the Electricity Consultative Council is an active body which helped to sponsor a code of conduct for the industry and which included provision for using an independent arbitration scheme. Further, the Post Office Users National Council was influential in securing reductions in tariff increases proposed by the Post Office during 1981.

Consumers Councils, where they exist in the nationalised industries, seem to have three main problems. First, they are only consultative bodies. Neither the boards of the nationalised industries nor the government has to take note of or act on their views. Second, they need to develop their independence and expertise if they are to be effective representatives of consumers. The annual government grant of around £2 million goes only some way towards helping them assert their independence. Third, there seems to be ignorance still at local level of the existence of such councils. This ignorance acts as an obstacle to their more effective operation.

THE EUROPEAN ECONOMIC COMMUNITY

As a member of the European Economic Community, Britain is affected by its competition rules which are set out in the Treaty of Rome. Article 85 of the Treaty of Rome deals with practices likely to affect trade and prevent, restrict or distort competition. Article 86 is concerned with the abuse of a dominant market position. Policy on mergers is less clear. In all cases only a limited amount of case law is available and some of the provisions of the articles have yet to be tested. However, they do only apply where trade between member states is concerned. The articles of the treaty are implemented by the Directorate General IV and fall within the scope of the European Court of Justice which acts as a court of appeal if firms are dissatisfied with the Commission's findings. In some cases the Commission will exempt certain agreements which, although they may restrict competition, are of ultimate benefit to the European Economic Community. The Office of Fair Trading has a number of liaison functions with the European Economic Community Commission and represents the United Kingdom on the Advisory Committee on Restrictive Practices and Dominant Positions. This committee is consulted on matters connected with the infringement, enforcement, exemption procedures and so forth which relate to the Community's competition rules.

Consumer protection has become an important part of the European Economic Community's work. In 1975 the Council of the Commission adopted a Consumer Protection and Information Programme covering a number of important topics such as health, safety, protection of the consumers' economic interests when purchasing goods and services, consumer education and stronger representation of consumer interests. In addition, the Environment and Consumer Protection service within the Commission received help and advice on consumer affairs from the Consumers Consultative Committee and the European Bureau of Consumers Unions. The views of British organisations interested in consumer affairs are represented by the European Community Group (UK). Some of the products, services and practices which have come under the scrutiny of the Commission in recent years include public transport, doorstep sales, correspondence courses, consumer credit, advertising and after sales services and repairs.

COMPLAINTS ABOUT SERVICES

Each year there are over half a million formally recorded complaints about goods and services in Britain. An analysis of consumer complaints by type of goods or service shown in Table 1 reveals that under 25 per cent of these complaints were to do with services (123,759 in total). Of course figures of this kind are only the tip of the iceberg as many complaints do not find their way into official figures as reproduced here from the Annual Reports of the Director General of Fair Trading. Two general features of the recorded data are revealing:

(a) complaints about goods substantially exceed complaints about services;
(b) the number of complaints decreased in 1979–80 compared with 1978–79, the previous year for which comparable data were available

TABLE 1
CONSUMER COMPLAINTS ANALYSED BY TYPE OF GOODS OR SERVICE

	No. of complaints 1979–80	*Complaints per £m spent 1979–80*
Goods		
Food and drink	39,672*	1.22
Footware	26,225	14.02
Clothing and textiles	54,633	5.92
Furniture and floor coverings	55,794	18.06
Household appliances	61,158	25.88
Toilet requisites, soaps, detergents, etc.	2,498	1.86
Toys, games, sports goods, etc.	8,928	12.11
Solid and liquid fuels	6,439	1.19
Motor vehicles and accessories	65,009	11.61
Other consumer goods	83,199	–
Non-consumer goods	2,665	–
Land, including houses	1,491	–
Services		
Home repairs and improvements	15,315	3.93
Repairs and servicing to domestic electrical appliances (excluding radio and TV)	4,390	23.93
Repairs and servicing to motor vehicles	12,752	10.44
Other repairs and servicing	13,031	39.25
Cleaning	8,093	36.54
Public utilities and transport	13,006	0.84
Consumer credit	5,693	–
Entertainment and accommodation	12,715*	1.65
Holidays	8,060	2.90
Professional services	10,650	2.05
General services, etc.	20,054	–

* Consumer complaints reported by Environmental Health Officers are included in these sectors. They are:

Food and drink	18,111
Entertainment and accommodation	7,482

Source: Annual Report of the Director General of Fair Trading, London: HMSO, 1981.

(123,759 against 150,460). Also, the number of complaints for each individual service category shown decreased except for consumer credit which increased from 5,121 to 5,693. This may be partly attributed to the implementation of the Consumer Credit Act. Equally the substantial decrease in the number of complaints about 'Repairs and Servicing to Motor Vehicles', 'Other Repairs and Servicing' and 'General Services', may be partly attributed to measures introduced in recent years to protect the consumer. These include the provision of mechanisms for complaint and redress, as set out, in Codes of Conduct.

The National Consumer Council's own Consumer Concerns Survey reveals discontent with services [Service Please 1981]. Their survey conducted by Research Services Ltd between November 1979 and November 1980 contained a sample size of nearly 2,000 people. It identified three main problems in connection with consumer services:

poor quality workmanship (for example, with car repairs; domestic appliance servicing; plumbers; hairdressers; professional services);
delays in carrying out work (for example, legal profession; building trade);
prices charged (for example, TV set repairs; car crash repairs).

The Consumer Concerns Survey suggests that in some cases up to one-fifth of respondents were dissatisfied with some aspects of the service they received. The survey also showed that in spite of problems with services, consumers often do not take the trouble to make a formal complaint to a trading standards department, advice agency or solicitor. It suggests that consumers may not necessarily be able to avoid problems by careful 'shopping around'. This is because either they may be limited in their choice anyway or it is often difficult to assess a contractor's reliability in advance. The National Consumers Council therefore recommend that where it is difficult for consumers to protect themselves before they make a contract they should be given the best avenues for redress after the contract is made. Their belief is that law reform is the best method of obtaining minimum standards with which all traders must comply. In their report they make detailed legislative proposals for ensuring that at the very least services are performed with reasonable care and skill, within a reasonable time and at a reasonable price.

CONCLUSION

Overall then the situation in the service sector of the economy in respect of consumer protection is complex and inadequate. The imperfection of much machinery in existence to protect the consumers' interest (whether legislative, institutional or in the form of codes of conduct) in the service sector, was amply illustrated during 1981 by various 'incidents' in the City of London. These exposed many weaknesses. The failure of investment advisers Norton Warburg led to calls for controls of financial advisers by the Government. The City 'watchdog' – the Council of the Securities Industry – suspended stockbrokers Halliday Simpson, an unprecedented act although they were not insolvent. There was an investigation into the activities of executives in the firm of Arbuthnot Latham. There were a series of 'dawn raids' on the shares of companies like Consolidated Gold Fields. There were 'hammerings' of firms like Norman Collins and Hedderwick Sterling. Equally, the reactive measures of the Council of the Securities Industry in drawing up a much criticised set of draft rules for the management of clients investment funds, and the belated appointment by the Government of Professor J. Gower to review existing legislation covering investment management to prevent fraud and control dealers in securities were all signs that all was not well. They revealed that the mechanisms currently available to protect customer interests – clients, investors, institutions – were far from adequate. All this in a relatively sophisticated services marketing setting.

Unfortunately, as this brief review has suggested, imperfections and anomalies in respect of competition policy and consumer protection remain, as applied to services markets. The correction of these weaknesses is likely to become a significant issue for the service sector of the economy plays such an important role in economic and social life. Further, as the consumer movement extends its influence, service markets represent a new frontier for its activities.

REFERENCES

Annual Report of the Director General of Fair Trading, 1980, London: HMSO, 1981.

Annual Report of the Director General of Fair Trading, 1981, London: HMSO, 1981.

Daily Telegraph, 24 July 1981.

'Fair Deal – A Shopping Guide', prepared by the Office of Fair Trading and the Central Office of Information, Various dates.

Money Management, 'Legal Light on Duties of Investment Brokers', August 1981, p. 777.

'Service Please', Services and the Law: A Consumer View, National Consumer Council, October 1981.

Productivity and Effectiveness in Service Firms

by

Keith J. Blois

Service firms are facing pressures which are leading them to seek increases in productivity. While attempts to increase productivity in goods-producing organisations seldom affect customers, such attempts in service firms are very likely to impinge upon customers' perceptions of the service. The need for service firms' marketing personnel to be involved in the assessment of the impact of attempts to raise productivity is thus clear. Furthermore, the need to assess the impact of increases in productivity on the firm's effectiveness rather than in traditional efficiency terms is emphasised.

INTRODUCTION

'Anonymous and characterless' is the phrase that has been suggested might soon be applied to British Clearing Banks as they continue to introduce more 'mechanisation' of the provision of their services [Bevan, 1983: 3–19]. The introduction of these new methods of providing services is the result of a complex set of changes in the banks' environment, but similar changes are also affecting other service industries. This paper describes some of the pressures for change which are forcing service industries to re-examine their methods of 'producing' services and some possible responses. It points out the dangers which can arise from changing the method of production and suggests some of the information which management requires if it is to make an appropriate response to these pressures.

PRESSURES FOR INCREASED PRODUCTIVITY

The search for increased productivity can be observed in most organisations. In the case of firms in the service sector of the economy the reasons for it seem to have been:

(*i*) *Price inflation*: A faster rate of price increase for services than for the rest of the economy [Whiteman, 1981: 6]. This has occurred because of the high proportion of most service firms' costs accounted for by salaries, national insurance, etc., such costs having risen more rapidly than inflation. In those service industries with a high proportion of female employees this has been accentuated by legislation concerned with equal pay for women and maternity leave.

(ii) *Increasing demand*: A steadily increasing demand for many services; attempts by firms to increase their supply of services, even at higher prices (see *i* above), have not always been successful because of bottlenecks within their organisations. In some firms these bottlenecks are created by a shortage of appropriately trained and experienced personnel and attempts to 'buy' new supplies of such resources are often unsuccessful and may lead to further wage inflation.

(iii) *Increased competition*: This may arise from a number of sources. First, there is the entry of new firms into an existing industry as, for example, has occurred in packaged tours. Even when demand is rising such new entrants put pressure on existing firms. Second, changes in legislation and professional regulations affect the degree of competition as the opticians and solicitors are about to find. Third, competition may arise from unexpected sources due to technological developments as the Post Office and British Telecom have discovered.

(iv) *Company objectives*: Some service firms are recognising that their profitability must be raised if they are to be able to create sufficient reserves to finance future developments.

(v) *Management attitudes*: Greater use of managerial skills in industries which have traditionally adopted a 'professional' as distinct from 'managerial' ethos.

Overall productivity in the service sector of the UK economy has been rising even more slowly than in the manufacturing sector, although the service sector has apparently been more competitive than manufacturing in overseas markets [Whiteman, 1981: 14]. The pressures for increased productivity are thus very apparent and consequently many service firms are investigating methods of increasing their productivity.

METHODS OF RAISING PRODUCTIVITY

There are broadly two approaches to raising productivity: first, the more effective use of inputs and second, changing the nature of the demand for the service.

Amongst those methods which come into the first category is the possibility of changing the range of services being offered. For example, it may be possible to identify additional services which could be offered without increasing the firm's staff or facilities. Alternatively, products may be deleted from the range for it may be possible that some services, currently offered, are creating neither much direct revenue or much custom for other services in the firm's range, and yet do make demands in terms of resources and thereby increase costs. Another method of raising productivity is to ensure that scarce resources, such as highly skilled personnel, are not used on work which could be performed by less fully trained staff. Such an approach is followed in hospitals where nurses and then junior doctors will often collect data and carry out tests on a patient prior to them being seen by a consultant. However, in some service firms, even where the level of demand would justify assistants, scarce and expensive personnel may be observed carrying out mundane functions. Finally, the use of technology can displace relatively expensive labour and also free labour to undertake work which makes fuller use of their skills. For example, a word-processor can reduce the number of typists required and also free a secretary from repetitive re-typing of documents requiring minor alteration.

The second approach, namely changing the nature of demand, can involve attempts to match demand with capacity more effectively and also encouraging customers to undertake some of the work themselves. In both approaches price is often used as the mechanism which affects the change. For example, price discounts can be used to encourage customers to accept a service at a time of low demand. Such an approach increases capacity utilisation – a critical point in service firms because of their inability to store their product. Finally, customers can be encouraged to undertake some work themselves. For example, a petrol station may offer petrol at a lower price to those customers who are prepared to serve themselves. By encouraging customers to act in this way fewer staff will be required thus reducing costs.

There are, of course, problems in raising productivity in any organisation, but service firms are distinctive in that it is an issue with which marketing personnel must concern themselves, the reason being that raising productivity nearly always leads to changes in the way the service is provided and such changes may affect actual and potential customers' perceptions of the service being offered. It is therefore necessary to consider some of the problems of measuring productivity which are met in all organisations, and then to specifically discuss the problems faced by service firms.

MEASURING PRODUCTIVITY

The difficulties in measuring productivity are three fold. First what are the appropriate measures of inputs to a system? Second what are the appropriate measures of output? Third, what are the appropriate ways of measuring the relationship between inputs and outputs?

(i) *Inputs*: It is difficult to imagine a productive organisation which does not use more than one type of input. However, most measures of

productivity use a single input – labour being the most common. This is obviously unsatisfactory but considerable difficulties arise once attempts are made to simultaneously take account of more than one category of input. These difficulties exist even with regard to measuring the input of labour, for just as when seeking to combine several categories of input, a common measure has to be used and this may be unsatisfactory. Thus labour input may be measured by numbers of employees but this equates the highly skilled with the less skilled. On the other hand, if cost of employees is used as a measure of input then it is being assumed that relative wages actually relate to relative productive value! Comparable problems exist with other measures of labour input.

(ii) *Outputs*: A similar set of problems arises with regard to measuring ouput as to those of measuring inputs – that is, the problem of finding a measure which is applicable to more than one category of output. For example, should output be measured in terms of units or value of output?

(iii) *Inputs relationship with outputs:* There are a variety of measures of this relationship each of which is appropriate to some, but not all, circumstances. As a starting point to determining the relevant measure, it has been suggested that it should be decided whether the intent is to measure input creativity or conversion efficiency [Gold, 1976: 17]; measures like output per employee falling in the former category and value added per man-hour being in the second category.

In the case of a service firm additional difficulties arise when measuring productivity. These are:

(i) *Inputs:* The intangible nature of service products and the interaction of customers and employees creates a problem with the measurement of inputs. For two employees similar in training and experience and receiving the same salary may differ greatly in their effectiveness in dealing with customers – thus in service firms labour inputs are probably more variable within any given category of employee than in manufacturing firms. As manufacturing industry becomes more capital-intensive, the ability of individual production workers to affect the rate of production is lessened, and so contrasts strongly with the variability of employee effectiveness observed in service organisations, especially those which provide little electronic/mechanised support for their employees.

(ii) *Outputs:* The most obvious difficulty in measuring the output of service firms is that those attributes of the product which are measurable may relate only very indirectly to the value of the product to customer or to producer. For example, in the case of estate agents their product has a measurable attribute, namely number of houses sold. However, clearly sales of ten small houses are not

equivalent in terms of value to sales of 10 larger houses, although the amount of the estate agent's time involved may vary little between these sales. In some situations the problem is to determine which of the available measures is the most appropriate (or least inappropriate) to use. In the case of a conference centre, is room occupancy rate a better measure than drinks sold in the bar (which is where the profits may arise)?

However, the critical problem of seeking to measure the output of many service firms arises from their intangible nature. As Inman says 'how do you value the reassurance that a Doctor offers a patient?' [Inman, 1983] Again, although in a less emotive context, how can the value of an evening at the theatre be valued? For some people the artistic performance is the essence of the experience. Others will evaluate the evening in terms of a broader experience – the comfort of the seating; the ease of obtaining refreshments; the behaviour of the audience; etc. In such circumstances the intangibility of the product, together with the heterogeneity of the demand which is supplied by a single product, creates the difficulty of measuring ouput. This is particularly the case if it is assumed that the degree of customer satisfaction affects the probability of repeat purchases.

(iii) *Inputs relationship with outputs*. The variability in the forms of customer satisfaction all combine to create difficulties in establishing appropriate measures in service firms. However, one aspect of services which here creates particular difficulties is their lack of storability. For example, a bank clerk sits doing nothing productive for part of a day simply because there are no more customers to serve and the fact that he expects to be very busy the next day in no way enables him to store up unused capacity. In other words, many service employees' productivity is determined to a considerable degree by the variability of demand during the period of time rather than total demand in that period.

In addition to these problems the effect of variable levels of customer interaction and the intangibility of the product can make valid comparisons between the productivity of branches of a service organisation difficult. Thus the amount of time which bank clerks in small towns spend on friendly, neighbourly chat with customers exceeds that observed in London. In that customers' satisfaction with a bank is linked with their perception of the 'quality' of the exchange experience, attempts to increase cashiers' productivity may be counter-productive in some areas but produce little negative customer reaction in other areas.

CUSTOMERS' PERCEPTIONS OF SERVICES

It is possible to raise productivity in manufacturing organisations without the customer being aware of what has happened. A car manufacturer can automate parts of its assembly line without there being any change in the physical specification of the car. By comparison in the case of service industries, it is seldom that productivity can be increased without some impact upon the offering made to the customer and therefore, possibly, upon the customers' perception of the service [Blois, 1983: 258].

For example, the introduction of a computer support system may enable insurance clerks to answer customer enquiries more speedily which may raise the customers' view of the quality of service offered. However, the introduction of computers to banks has made it impossible for customers to know what their balance is 'at this moment' and some customers do regard only knowing yesterday's balance as unsatisfactory.

It should be stressed that the reason why customers' perception of a service may be affected by attempts to increase productivity is not, as is so often claimed, that the production and consumption of services are simultaneous. In fact, there are many services where production and consumption are not simultaneous. However, this is not to deny that the process of production may be a significant element in the consumers' perception of the product. Levitt considers this by discussing the way the good or service is 'delivered' stating that 'manufacturing an intangible product is generally indistinguishable from its actual delivery' [Levitt, 1981: 98]. The term 'delivery' is not defined and the examples he provides are open to a wide range of the possible interpretations.

However, for services, it does seem that 'delivery' is an activity where production and consumption at least overlap. Thus delivery for a haircut would include the physical process of cutting the hair and also the environment within which the process is carried out. Both these factors will influence a customer's feelings of satisfaction with the product even though the consumption of the product goes on after its production. Similarly, for an insurance policy, delivery includes the process of issuing the policy to the customer and the way any queries or claims are treated – both these being production activities and both affecting consumers' satisfaction but only representing a part of the consumption.

There is, however, an additional aspect of the marketing of services which, although a part of the production of the service, is not always part of the process of consumption. This is the 'signal' which the consumer accepts as an indication that the service will be performed satisfactorily. Such a 'signal' may be a document, a verbal statement, that part of the service organisation which is visible to the customer or any number of things and will not necessarily involve personal contact. To use insurance as an example again, for the average individual, the acceptable signal is physical possession of a policy issued by a recognised insurance company accepting the risk to be covered. For a businessman a verbal commitment from an authorised representative of an insurance company may be the acceptable signal. In the latter case personal contact has occurred; in the former the policy may be obtained from a slot machine! Such signals may arise from various stages of the production process and the nature of the acceptable signal will vary with the needs and experience of the potential customer. Thus, the decor of a restaurant may be the signal which determines if a potential new customer enters the restaurant. In the case of an established customer the signal may be the contents of the day's menu.

It follows that, whether or not the production and consumption of a service are simultaneous, changes in the method of providing a service will affect either 'the delivery' and/or 'the signal', the concept of 'delivery' and 'signal' drawing attention to the need to examine the impact on consumers' perception of the service of any change in the method of providing the service. Pressures to raise productivity may therefore lead to changes in the nature of the service itself. It is, however, the customers' *perception* of the service which is critical. This is well illustrated by the dilemma facing organisations concerned with the possibility of introducing electronic fund transfers at the point of sale. Although it would appear that this scheme offers advantages to customers (for example, the need to carry less cash and not to carry a cheque book), early indications are that customers do not perceive it as an attractive method of payment. Obviously the concern of those who will need to make the massive investment necessary to create the scheme – which could increase the productivity of the banking system – is to avoid a repetition of their experience of introducing automatic teller machines (ATM). Here, customer resistance originally existed (and still does exist to a lesser extent) towards the use of ATMs.

THE EFFECTIVENESS OF A SERVICE FIRM

As indicated most discussions of how to measure productivity relate to the process of manufacturing physical goods. Marketing's distinctive contribution to a firm should be its customer-orientation and therefore, marketing management should seek to ensure that the measure of productivity used does not permit a mechanistic analysis of the relationship of inputs to outputs to become dominant. What is important is 'the effectiveness' of the organisation by which is meant the ability of the organisation to attain its specified objectives. In contrast productivity, whether high or low, is a worthless measure unless it is related to an objective. Indeed the danger is that productivity can be increased at the cost of an organisation's effectiveness – especially when inter-firm comparisons often regard a firm as necessarily more efficient than a competitor, if its productivity is higher. Yet the less efficient firm may be the more effective in meeting its goals.

The difficulties of evaluating an organisation's effectiveness are considerable; in particular, in spite of the acceptance of the fact that it is important to make a distinction between productivity and effectiveness, some definitions of effectiveness come markedly close to the concept of productivity. For example, Mott defines effective organisations as 'those that produce more and higher quality ouput and adapt more effectively to environmental and internal problems than do similar organisations'

[Mott, 1972]. It is, recognised however, that some 'disagreements over the definition of effectiveness arise from the fact that organisations and the people who run them often have *multiple* and *conflicting* goals' [Jackson and Morgan, 1978: 320]. It follows that some method has to be found of evaluating effectiveness with regard to the various constituencies of the organisation. Amongst these constituencies would be 'customers'.

Obviously, marketing with its central concern with the firm's customers will have its own criteria for evaluating the firm's effectiveness. In the case of service firms, as the earlier discussion of productivity indicated, the need to take account of the customers' views is greater than in manufacturing organisations. It follows, therefore, that in service firms marketing's appraisal of effectiveness merits greater emphasis. The need, therefore, is to develop measures of productivity in terms of effectiveness in relation to marketing objectives. Such an approach can produce a radically different view of the appropriateness of certain policies. For example, an organisation can become less effective as a result of raising its productivity as is illustrated by comparing large British post offices with those in some European countries. In British post offices counter-clerks will deal with any type of business and therefore customers only queue once. In other countries, the clerks are specialised – one clerk for stamps, another for the giro, etc., – in consequence not only can less highly trained staff be used, but the clerks can use their time more efficiently, but at the cost of the customers' use of time in waiting in several queues! Which system is the more effective in achieving its marketing objectives (which must surely include some measure of customer satisfaction) and which is the more productive in conventional terms?

A MEASURE OF MARKETING PRODUCTIVITY IN SERVICE FIRMS

The need, therefore, is for marketing managers to develop measures of productivity which are appropriate to their needs. Such measures should be concerned primarily with effectiveness within a given budget rather than productivity in its traditional meaning. The measure derived by Heaton illustrates this approach.

Heaton suggests that the productivity of a service organisation should be measured as the product of four operating functions: input; processing; output or follow-up; and timing and co-ordination. Applying this concept to a mental hospital he suggests [Heaton, 1977: 145–7] that: (i) input should be measured as a percentage of those admitted to the hospital who actually required hospitalisation; (ii) processing should be a measure of the percentage of patients helped by the treatment received; (iii) output or follow-up should be a measure of the percentage of patients receiving appropriate treatment after 'processing', that is, after discharge; and (iv) timing and co-ordination should be a measure of the percentage of patients receiving treatment at the appropriate time.

Heaton calculates gross productivity by taking the product of these four measures. Further, he considers net productivity – which is similar to the concept of 'effectiveness' – when he allows for the damage done to some patients.

This might appear to be a rather unusual example. However, what is so striking about Heaton's approach is that its measures are all related to customers and as such could be claimed to have a marketing orientation. Furthermore, it suggests approaches to measuring productivity and effectiveness of service organisations in a variety of markets. Consider how Heaton's terms could be applied to the examples of hotels and of estate agents:

	Hotel	*Estate Agent*
Inputs	% of quotations resulting in business	% of enquiries (sales and purchases) appropriate to agent's market (geographical or social class segment)
Process	% of clients using facilities in addition to bedrooms (e.g. resident guests using squash court)	% of purchase enquiries resulting in sales
Output	% of clients which is repeat business	% of house sales on behalf of previous purchasers
Timing and co-ordination	% of enquiries rejected because of capacity limitations	% of houses sold within client's specified time limit

These measures of effectiveness, of course, do suffer from limitations. The most obvious is that both can indicate a high level of effectiveness even if only one enquiry was received! It is therefore necessary to incorporate an additional function, namely, 'prerequisite' which could be measured by 'number of enquiries received as a percentage of a target figure'.

The case for claiming that this is, with the addition of the 'prerequisite' element, a good measure, is based on the view that: a) each of the components is affected by marketing activity; b) the data required, while relating to customer activity, are available within the firm; and c) the components all relate to objectives which a firm should incorporate in its marketing plan. Thus, to consider the Estate Agent example:

Prerequisite: If the number of enquiries being made is lower than a target figure (this figure being high enough to be expected to generate sufficient business for the firm to be profitable), then this points to a failure to communicate effectively.

Input If only a small proportion of all enquiries are from market segments with which the firm plans to do business, then this points to a failure by the firm to communicate effectively. Enquiries from other market segments may actually have a negative effect upon the business.

Process If the number of enquiries about properties for sale which result in actual sales is lower than planned for, then this points to inefficiency in the basic function of the Estate Agent – namely, matching vendors with potential purchasers.

Output If purchasers of a house are satisfied with the Estate Agent's service (something only assessable after completion of the purchase), it would seem likely that on selling their houses at a later date they would place their property in that Estate Agent's hands.

Timing and Co-ordination House sales and purchases are often completed at times which do not satisfy the client. Obviously delays in completing a transaction can be caused by events outside the Estate Agent's influence. However, an increase in the proportion of transactions failing to be completed 'on time' might indicate some lack of efficiency on the Estate Agent's part. Indeed, an efficient Estate Agent will have a norm against which to judge this issue.

What is so important about this approach is that, as stated, it is customer-orientated whereas most productivity measures are not. For example, Sevin (still one of their most quoted references on Marketing Productivity) takes a mechanistic view and relates inputs to outputs in terms of their value [Sevin, 1965]. In comparison, Heaton points to the danger that 'Where output is difficult to measure, attention shifts to the process of assigning work to people' [Heaton, 1977: 39]. Furthermore, he suggests that 'Where processes are difficult to standardise, organisational resources are measured' [Heaton, 1977: 39]. Yet neither measurement of resources or their allocation can really control the quality of service offered by an organisation, but concentration on either measure can easily lead to a lowering of the service offered.

For example, emphasis on the process of assigning work can lead to a lowering of the service offered by reducing the flexibility of the organisation's staff. Again, measurement of organisational resources may say nothing about the quality of the service and selection of particular measures may, through subsequent re-allocation of resources, lower service. Thus a hotel classification based on physical resources may lead to a hotel increasing the number of bathrooms at the expense of staff training.

The obvious weaknesses of Heaton's approach are that it contains no input data nor does it provide any financial evaluation of the firm's output. Nevertheless, where an organisation is working with a fixed budget, Heaton's measure would be a valid way of comparing the effectiveness of different combinations of inputs within the budget. Furthermore, the measure could incorporate some element of the financial implications of the firm's activity. For example, in the case of the Estate Agent it might be possible to make this measure for a number of price categories of dwellings and then combine the results by means of a simple weighting procedure. The problem of inputs can probably only be handled by the relatively crude mechanism of relating the measure of effectiveness to levels of expenditure. This would do little more than show a positive or negative relation between, say, increased expenditure and the effectiveness measure. [Hall, Knapp and Winston, 1961: 37] However, it would probably be no less accurate than many measures currently used.

CONCLUSIONS

There is evidence from many sources that cost pressures are forcing those responsible for managing the provision of services to seek ways of increasing their organisation's productivity. This paper points out that the traditional measures used to assess it may be inappropriate for use by marketing managers. Furthermore, it suggests that the use of such measures may lead an organisation to institute changes in the way a service is supplied which radically and possibly adversely affects the consumers' perceptions of the service itself.

REFERENCES

Bevan, T.H., 1983, 'Personal Customers – A Changing Approach', in Institute of Bankers, *The Banks and Personal Customers*.

Blois, K.J., 1983, 'The Structure of Service Firms and their Marketing Policies', *Strategic Management Journal*, Vol. 4.

Brisley, C.L., and W.F. Fielder, 1983, 'Unmeasurable' Output of Knowledge/Office Workers Can and Must Be Measured', *Industrial Engineer*.

Gold, B., 1976, 'A Framework for Productivity Analysis', 16–39 in S. Eilon, B. Gold, and J. Soesan, (1976), *Applied Productivity Analysis*, Oxford: Pergamon Press.

Hall, M., J. Knapp, and C. Winston, 1961, *Distribution in Great Britain and North America*, Oxford: Oxford University Press.

Heaton, H., 1977, *Productivity in Service Organisations*, New York: McGraw-Hill Inc.

Inman, R., 1983, 'The Future of the Service Economy', ARA/Wharton Conference unpublished paper.

Jackson, J.H., and C.P. Morgan, 1978, *Organisational Theory*, Englewood Cliffs, NJ: Prentice Hall Inc.

Levitt, Theodore, 1981, 'Marketing Intangible Products and Product Intangibles', *Harvard Business Review*, Vol. 59 (May–June).

Mott, P.E., 1972, *The Characteristics of Effective Organisations*, New York: Harper & Row.

Sevin, C.H., 1965, *Marketing Productivity Analysis*, New York: McGraw-Hill Inc.
Whiteman, J., 1981, *The Services Sector – A Poor Relation*?, National Economic Development Office, London (Discussion Paper 8).

Marketing Bank Services

by

Barbara R. Lewis

This paper considers recent research and practice in the marketing of bank services, and reviews literature which pertains to the adoption and implementation of marketing in the banks' personal, corporate and international market sectors.

INTRODUCTION

Throughout the 1970s and 1980s, the nature of banking has altered and progressed as a result of a combination of changes in the market-place, relating to the legislative, economic and business, technological and social environments, which affect both personal and corporate customers. As a result, the marketing concept has become increasingly relevant and important for the banking industry. In this article, environmental trends will be summarised, and recent research and practice pertaining to the adoption and implementation of marketing will be reviewed. Attention will be focused on the acceptance of marketing within the banks; bank priorities and strategic issues; the development of the sales function; together with examples of marketing research and segmentation in the personal account sector; and issues in the corporate/ international arena – such as the US banks' expansion into the UK and the purchasing of financial services.

CHANGES IN THE MARKET-PLACE

Legislation

Legislative developments in industrialised countries have had a major impact on banking activities. For example, in the UK, a number of government reports and Acts of Parliament in the 1970s had the objective of encouraging competition in the financial sector, and led to the abandonment of bank cartels and controls over lending, and increasing competition between banks. Also, 'de-regulation' in the US has led to a less regulated environment (for example, with regard to the amount of interest holders of US dollars can receive, and interstate banking operations), and the banks are re-evaluating their geographic limitations, interest rate ceilings and product limitations.

Competition is intensifying and the US banks are pursuing new opportunities with regard to market segmentation and effective positioning in the market, product testing and development, and flexible pricing.

Economic and Business Environment

An important consideration for banks around the world at present is the increasing competition they face from non-banks – some of which are new institutions – who, as a result of reduced barriers to entry, are expanding into the financial services field. The traditional boundaries between financial institutions are becoming blurred as non-banks develop and extend their product ranges and encroach on the banks' territory.

However, to their advantage, the banks must increasingly be aware of, and respond to, the changing and expanding needs of their customers, both personal and corporate. The corporate business environment is increasingly complex, and organisational expansion is prevalent – both at home and in international markets – due to expansion of the world economy, growth in exports and international trade, and improvements in communications. This implies expanded financial needs: for example, multinational corporations require trade finance, transnational investment, project finance, etc. But, at the same time, economic factors such as rising funds costs, high inflation rates, volatile interest rates, and rising operating costs, dictate cost pressures on those responsible for buying financial services. Thus, many major corporations have a pattern of financial needs which necessitate sophisticated, yet cost-effective, advice and solution. For example, they require high productivity from idle funds, on-line cash management systems, more flexible funding, and are increasingly engaging in split-banking to satisfy their diverse demands.

Socio-Economic Trends

The changing needs of customers in the personal sector are a function of socio-economic trends, resulting from such factors as educational opportunities and technological advance. One can focus on the re-distribution of individual disposable income, with a narrowing of the gap between skilled and unskilled workers and the increasing prosperity of manual workers; the growing proportion of women in employment; and rising living standards – which, in general, have brought more people into the groups of interest to the banks (in particular, in the UK). Additionally, consumer changes in attitudes towards saving, spending and borrowing are leading to financial horizons becoming broader and longer, especially for those of low socio-economic status, to include saving and budgeting. Further, traditions and values are being modified so that credit and borrowing are more acceptable. In all, those in consumer markets are becoming more sophisticated and discriminating.

Technological

Developments in technology and operations have been spurred by market needs to be product, price and service conscious, and recent years have witnessed the arrival of high technology products *and* service delivery mechanisms. These include computerisation and the growth of cheque cards and bank-based credit cards; automatic teller machines providing a variety of services including extended hours via 'lobby-banking' in consumer markets and electronic funds transfer; in-home terminals; and cash management services. Most computerised facilities represent, to the banks, the opportunity to provide new/more efficient services and/or a saving in human and physical resources.

The Marketing Concept

As a consequence of the aforementioned changes, banks' customers in all segments have developed expanded and increasing needs and more sophisticated purchasing behaviour, in an increasingly competitive environment. Thus, the banks have been forced to become more marketing-orientated and to some extent the acceptance of the marketing concept and a marketing philosophy has been forced on them, as discussed in the early literature on bank marketing [e.g. Hodges and Tillman, 1968; Berry and Capaldini, 1974; Reekie, 1972; Ornstein, 1972; Berry and Donnelly, 1975; Baker, 1977a and 1977b; and Wilson, 1980].

The remainder of this paper focuses on the acceptance of marketing within the banking community, and provides illustrations of some of the ways in which banks are adopting marketing principles with regard to identifying markets for their products and services, and providing services to meet customer needs, whilst fulfilling their own organisational goals.

THE ACCEPTANCE OF MARKETING WITHIN THE BANKS

The acceptance of the marketing concept within banks has been considered and researched at two levels: branch management and senior executive level. At branch level, the increased pressures on managers to widen their role and perform marketing tasks has been highlighted by early writers such as Ornstein [1972]; Reekie [1972]; Waterworth [1973]; Dibbs [1974]; Berry and Capaldini [1974]; and Berry and Donnelly [1975]; and more recently by McIver and Naylor [1980]. In particular, they stressed the need for branch managers to recognise and accept the importance of personal communication between themselves and customers.

However, Watson [1974] found evidence of rejection of marketing by branch management, and Brack [1977] concluded that bank managers dislike the marketing approach being forced on them, and research by Turnbull and Wootton [1981], designed to discover the existing role of a manager and how he perceives his role and his customers' needs, found similar attitudes. The managers that Turnbull and Wootton interviewed, in a UK clearing bank, demonstrated a lack of understanding of the marketing concept. Most equated marketing with selling and few recognised the need for understanding customer needs, researching the market, or product planning; but most recognised the importance of good personal relationships with customers, although such contact was limited. The authors concluded that managers lack knowledge of the principles of marketing and commitment to implementing them due to lack of motivation, ability and time available.

Recent research in this area is reported by Watson [1982 and 1984], who surveyed both senior executives and branch managers in UK clearing banks, and compared their perceptions of the impact of marketing in four areas. First, organisational issues: both groups perceived some change in organisational structure following the introduction of marketing and recognised and emphasised that new skills are required and, therefore, extensive training in marketing. Second, satisfaction with results: with regard to achievement of financial targets, ability to respond to competitive pressure, corporate image, and personal job satisfaction and professional image – branch managers being less positive in their responses than senior management. Third, specific areas of application: the usefulness of marketing was cited with regard to new business ventures, harnessing new technology, and for long-term planning. Fourth, continuing difficulties: there remained reluctance of some to accept marketing.

Overall, Watson concluded that, at branch level, marketing is being accepted but is not yet the integrating dimension of branch activity that it might be. He pointed out the danger if marketing initiatives are largely head-office prerogatives with nationwide programmes; they might stifle the development of branch marketing initiatives based on local conditions and knowledge. Further, at executive level, it seemed that marketing is better accepted and was judged to be delivering satisfactory results, implying that education programmes are being successful; but judgements are subjective and were probably measured against initial expectations which were not very high. In conclusion, Watson emphasises the need for bank executives to look to longer-term issues of marketing and the strategic aspects, and not just the short-term action implications which focus on selling and communications. Indeed, the future priorities for bank marketing and strategic issues have recently been the focus of attention for several academics and practitioners.

PRIORITIES AND STRATEGIC ISSUES

All banks naturally set objectives which indicate what they hope to achieve in relation to profit, growth, size, etc., from which strategies follow which attempt to suggest how they can best reach their goals within their available resources. Varadarajan and Berry [1983] present a framework, based on Ansoff's work in corporate strategy [1957 and 1965], for thinking strategically about avenues for growth. They discuss market penetration, that is, increasing sales of present services in present markets (for example, increasing the average account size by reducing loan rates or service fees for customers with balances over a certain level); market development, that is, creating new markets for present services; product development, that is, developing new services for present markets (for example, paying interest on credit balances on charge cards); and diversification, that is, developing new services for new markets. They provide numerous examples and also look at the evaluation of such growth strategies.

An alternative framework is presented by Meidan [1983] who focuses on growth and competitive strategies. Growth strategies embrace geographical expansion, including the establishment of new branches; market penetration; new market strategy; and cost cutting strategy, for example, substituting capital for labour. Competitive marketing strategies aim to be a market leader, employed by large dominant banks; market challenger, employed by 'trailing' banks who are trying to grow and typically have aggressive marketing tactics; market follower, trying to keep a market share; and market nicher, aiming to specialise in particular niches.

A third approach is that of Thompson [1983] who considers the positioning choices confronting US financial industry managers and marketers, in response to the realities of de-regulation. He suggests seven types of positioning, namely: institutional, that is, whether to operate on a national, regional or community basis, and within the retail or wholesale arenas; product line; delivery system, that is, determining the most efficient mix of people and machines; price; people, that is, matching customer wants with staff expertise, training and motivation; customer; and profitability.

Also, in a strategic planning vein, Landon and Donnelly [1973] identify five changes they believe will occur in bank marketing. They suggest that marketing will become a line function as well as a staff function; organisation structures will change from functional to product lines/markets; pricing analysis will increase in importance; channels of distribution will change, that is, there will be fewer bank buildings but more alternative delivery systems; and selling skills will be emphasised including 'relationship' banking, that is, viewing customers as clients, acquiring and retaining them, creating loyal clients. Indeed, the emphasis on relationship banking is one of four priorities considered by Berry [1982], who also discusses the development of multi-tier delivery systems, that is, moving from high cost, labour intensive, distribution, to a mix of full service branches, mini-branches (for example, in retail stores), automatic teller machines, and electronic in-home banking facilities); marketing to investors via 'investment portfolios' tailored to customer needs; and building a personal selling organisation, that is, encouraging the acceptability of selling in banks.

SELLING/DEVELOPMENT OF THE SALES FUNCTION

The acceptability and development of the sales function in banking is generally treated separately in the literature from considerations relating to the adoption of the marketing concept, although in the work already reported (for example, by Turnbull and Wootton [1981]), marketing was equated with selling by many bank managers/personnel – managers did not like the idea of being salesmen.

The need for personal selling and its changing role is highlighted by Berry [1980] and Edwards [1981], in particular, the need to focus on customers and tailor packages to satisfy their individual financial needs. Subsequently, Futrell, Berry and Bowers [1984] have surveyed 714 senior marketing executives in US banks to appraise the state of personal selling in their banks, and assess the managerial interest in, and commitment to, improving bank sellig performance. They found that the implementation of bank selling programmes, and sales training, lags behind the recognition that bank employees do need to sell, that is, that management interest in improving bank selling performance and management commitment to making it happen are not the same thing. They concluded that personal selling is far from a mature function in US banks in the mid-1980s, and identified a problem of lack of control systems for measuring success of sales goals, and priorities for increasing selling performance, that is, a need for better sales planning, management, training and measurement/rewards/incentives.

Futrell's findings mirror those of Cheese [1983] who concludes that senior management in UK banks have accepted that the branch system, that is, the manager and his staff, is the field sales force and that they need appropriate sales training. Cheese also discusses approaches for the organisation/management of the sales function, the identification of sales training needs, and sales training programmes. Johnson [1983] goes one stage further and reports on the actual planning and organisation of a bank sales management system in a US regional bank. In his case study he describes a management-by-objectives planning procedure which is used to set sales goals, together with the identification of the tasks of the line sales organisation, the branch banking system and the staff sales department. Thus, this bank now has a framework for its selling efforts and Johnson suggests that this is an example of *internal marketing* (as presented by George [1977]; and Gronroos [1980 and 1981]), whereby it is necessary to 'sell' bank employees on their responsibilities to serve their customers and prepare them to do this, that is, as Coates [1983] concludes 'to develop genuine staff involvement – to get them to want to sell the bank's products and services in the market place'.

A second application, on a much larger scale, is that reported by Wills and Day [1984] who describe a unique marketing and selling training programme for one UK bank, designed to revitalise the marketing function among 70,000 staff in 3,200 locations. Rather than continuing to rely on their own training department and programmes, the bank used an outside force or '*change agent*' (a major business school) to help 'change its culture', in particular to try to adopt a selling stance. The programme comprised training courses for senior managers and specially developed distance teaching resources for them to use at lower levels, that is, it was a cascade approach to training, for managers in both the domestic and international divisions. The activity has resulted in a change in both attitude and practice among bankers, marketing managers, and staff working throughout the bank, towards a greater acceptance of marketing and selling.

In light of the findings and discussion of authors referred to so far it would appear that marketing and selling is becoming widely accepted in banks, in the US and UK, and that attention is being given to various strategic issues and priorities. Thus, it would seem to be appropriate to consider now some of the more 'tactical' marketing activities of banks, especially those relating to market and marketing research, and market segmentation.

MARKET RESEARCH AND SEGMENTATION

Market research and segmentation are integral and increasingly important elements of the banks' marketing orientation. Market research helps banks to identify their target market segments, their size, and the services they need; and research information aids them in tailoring and adjusting their marketing mix to satisfy the demands of particular segments. Thus, effective market research and segmentation become vital to the banks' long-range profitability and ultimate survival.

Yorke [1982] discusses the basic task of linking the concept of 'what business are we in?' to the structure of the total market in order that banks can develop a suitable range of products/services to meet specific market needs (for example, in the personal account market – cash accessibility, asset security, money transfer, deferred payment, and financial advice). He also reviews bases for segmentation in the personal market (for example, age, sex, socio-economic class, stage in the life cycle, psychographic, benefits sought, etc.) and in the corporate sector (for example, type of industry, management structure, size, location, etc.), and stresses that segments should be identifiable with regard to possessing specific common needs, measurable, accessible, and (potentially) profitable.

Early American examples of market segmentation are reported by Robertson and Bellenger [1977] who considered high income consumers and found that they placed special importance in their choice of bank on integrity, ego enhancement and expertise; and by Stanley *et al.* [1980] who focused on high income consumers' perceptions of personal service and convenience – and found that a high quality personalised service, rather than convenience, would seem to be crucial in attracting and keeping such consumers.

In the UK personal sector the major clearing banks have, during the last decade, identified a number of segments from which they try to attract new account holders, and it may well be of interest to the reader to review some of the marketing activities and evaluative research which have been completed in respect of such segments.

Students/School-Leavers

In the early 1970s the UK clearing banks identified school-leavers progressing to college as a segment of interest. They believed that it might be in their interest to attract students to open accounts in the anticipation that they would remain, after graduation, with the bank and be profitable in the long term. Consequently, campaigns were developed to educate students with regard to bank services, promote a student-orientated image, and to obtain and keep as many student accounts as possible.

The success of such campaigns has been evaluated by Gray [1977] and Brockman-Smith [1979] – who assessed factors such as the opening of bank accounts and choice of bank, awareness and use of bank services, and reaction to bank advertising and promotion. Findings showed that students are not influenced in their initial choice of bank by the services offered or bank promotions and gifts, but by locational convenience and parental influence – with substantial family loyalty to banks, and the opening of accounts before going to college.

The attraction of college students was based on the assumption that the majority do not switch banks on graduation and their accounts will be profitable in the long run, but Clarke [1975] found evidence of graduate mobility in early careers with many switching jobs and banks within a couple of years. Therefore, the banks cannot anticipate keeping their accounts, and so have more recently turned their attention to school-leavers in general, that is, those going into immediate employment who are also less likely to be mobile and switch banks (with many being of lower socio-economic status – with unbanked parents). Campos [1980] argues that this group is more adaptable to change and innovation than their parents and, therefore, more likely to alter their attitudes with regard to the management of personal finances, including acceptance of payment by cheque and opening of bank accounts. Nevertheless, his survey work among a sample of school-leavers showed that they rated the saving, advice and borrowing functions of banks more important than the money transmission function, that is, that they seemed to lack an awareness of the services and functions of a bank. Consequently, it would appear that the banks have a way to go in attempts to build and maintain a good corporate image and reputation among school-leavers.

Women Customers

A second demographic based segment which has been the focus of marketing activities is women, and Yorke and Hayes [1982] engaged in research dealing with working women specifically. They considered the increasing number of women in the labour force, due to economic necessity, a desire to increase standards of living, or for personal achievement; recent legislation designed to protect working women; and the improvement in the position of their earnings relative to men. They identified a trend towards working women as a market segment, and set out to discover what sort of financial services they require.

They built on previous studies by MAS [1975] and NOP [1976] and investigated, by group discussion, five segments based on marital status and position in life cycle. The women were questioned about banking behaviour and attitudes towards banks; awareness and independent use of financial services; and attitudes towards saving, borrowing and spending. The segments were found to have different needs (for example, unmarried women, over 25 years, show the greatest need for a variety of services and would appear to be targets for loans, mortgages, credit cards, financial advice, and perhaps a need for female advisers), which the banks should recognise and design appropriate marketing strategies to meet.

In addition, it must be realised that as a result of societal changes, women – whether they are working or not – have a growing influence on, and involvement in, the level and direction of family expenditure and financial management. Further, many have a desire for their own financial holdings, and so are increasingly potential bank customers.

Weekly, Cash-Paid Workers

The third example of a consumer market segment comprises those of lower socio-economic status, the majority of whom in the UK do not have a current bank account, but many of whom are unlikely to perceive a need for one whilst they continue to be paid weekly and in cash (40 per cent of the UK workforce). Buswell [1977] found such people to be reluctant to be paid other than by cash (and weekly), and had a cash orientation and short-term financial horizons – although with rising income levels and living standards, attitudes towards saving/spending and borrowing are changing and financial horizons are perhaps becoming less limited. Their attitudes towards banks were not favourable, with evidence of fear and ignorance, for example, fears that cash will become inaccessible, that they may lose control over spending, of a loss of privacy, of the unknown with regard to bank behaviour, and of intimidation by bank surroundings and staff. These fears, also found by Smith [1980] and King [1981], represent a hurdle for the banks to overcome when attracting accounts from this segment.

Regarding the possibilities for revising payment methods in the UK, Lewis [1982] concludes that weekly, cash-paid, workers have unfavourable attitudes towards monthly payment and/or bank credit transfer, and this has been a restraining influence on employers – although some have taken initiatives with regard to change. Further, as the banks resent weekly cash pay, due to the costs of holding and moving cash and the associated security risks, it is in their interests to encourage weekly, cash-paid, workers to cross the psychological and attitudinal barrier between 'cash' and 'non-cash' and move towards changing payment methods and having bank accounts.

MARKETING RESEARCH IN CONSUMER MARKETS

In addition to the banks' activities which pertain to specific market segments, as just described, they may also participate in marketing research as it is relevant for elements of their marketing mix, for example, product, price, promotion and customer service. Once again, examples of such work, completed by both academics and practitioners, are available. A product-related example is reported by Bellur [1984] who considers the recent introduction of NOW accounts in the US. All federally regulated finance institutions can offer such interest-bearing checking accounts, which gives them the opportunity to generate new business, and has led the commercial banks to follow suit. Bellur investigated the awareness of NOW accounts, and the knowledge and use of such accounts among a sample of households.

Advertising as a marketing tool has been researched by Stafford and King [1983], who explore the significance of media selection in approaches adopted by UK banks for market segmentation. The pricing of these banks' services was the concern of Lawson and Watt [1983], who used consumer group interviews to investigate attitudes and perceptions of banks and their services; understanding of, and reaction to, pricing policies and their importance in decision-making; and reaction to price increases and possible alternative methods of pricing accounts. Lawson and Watt conclude that price is not a major factor in bank choice; that consumers would pay more for some services, for example, standing orders, as a function of utility and the opportunity cost and inconvenience of other methods of payment of recurrent debts; and that there is some scope for competition on a price basis, among those who derive less utility from accounts. Thus, a market-orientated pricing policy would suggest charging a high rate for exclusive services and a lower rate where competition exists.

Concerning customer service, two researches are relevant. Watkins [1984] considers till service provision, for example, queuing problems and the potential negative effect of queuing time on consumers which might cause them to transfer accounts. He postulates that computer simulation techniques may be used to minimise the total cost of till provision – that is, in optimisation terms, to balance till costs, including personnel, against the potential loss of profit opportunity to a bank from transfer of accounts by dissatisfied customers – to provide pointers to actionable decision rules for service management, for example, with regard to the number of service provisions. The second example of customer service research is reported by a market research manager [Buswell, 1983], and took place in one UK bank (with 202 branches), to quantify customers' assessments of quality of service received. The bank was aiming to develop a system which would be able to reveal changes in service at the same branch over time and distinguish between branches at the same point in time. 131 components of service were used in pilot interviews among customers of all the major banks, to cover knowledge of products, banking practice and branch methods; communications; expertise; willingness to lend; and branch design. Some of these incur one-off costs (for example, new branches, refurbishment), others continuous costs (for example, provision of statements, staff training), and some no direct cost (for example, politeness, helpfulness). These components were finally reduced to 24 for use in a postal questionnaire to samples of customers of the various branches of the research bank.

Consequently, a bench-mark for the quality of in-branch customer service was established against which branches and time can be tested. This has led to regular surveys of the bank's branches, and results have been used to guide decisions with regard to branch design and refurbishment; as a basis for 'customer service' discussion on training courses; for feedback to branch managers, for corrective action; and for focusing on the quality of service they provide.

CORPORATE/INTERNATIONAL MARKETS

The examples of marketing and market research presented so far have been focused on the personal account sector. Indeed, most of the early writings concentrated on the adoption of the marketing concept in consumer markets. However, bank marketers and researchers have for some time been giving attention to the corporate/international activities of the banks – which may now be reviewed.

International banking embraces two main areas or markets, as discussed by Turnbull [1982b], the international money markets and overseas markets for the domestic banks of various countries – where the marketing strategies adopted in each market will be dependent on the banking regulations and operating conditions in that market. In a further research paper Turnbull [1982c] goes on to highlight some of the current product developments in international capital markets which are of most significance to the international marketing strategies of UK banks, namely, syndicated loans run by consortium banks; project finance which has emerged from the increasing size, complexity and cost of projects; and the growth of the foreign exchange market.

US Expansion in the UK

Regarding overseas markets for domestic banks, the marketing activities of the US banks in the UK have been of particular interest. Carter [1980] and Turnbull [1982e] consider the reasons behind the US banks' need to move overseas, together with the attraction of the British market. Emerson [1983] also discusses the attractive features of the retail and corporate sectors of the British market such as: size to accommodate depth of competition, a well-educated population, an advanced industrial economy, political stability, London as a financial centre, and relative freedom from regulations such as credit ceilings or exchange controls. These advantages have to be balanced against the possible disadvantages of a static population, a tendency to conservatism in financial dealings (for example, reluctance to change banks and experiment), and uncertainty with regard to future changes as governments fine-tune the economy.

Carter [1980] and Turnbull [1982f] go on to survey the expansion and success of US banks in the UK and comment on how they have tended, until relatively recently, to concentrate in the wholesale (corporate) sector. They have tried not to replace the UK clearing banks over the whole range of services, and so avoided the need to establish a costly retail branch network, but concentrated on profitable foreign exchange and merchant banking transactions.

Purchasing of Financial Services

Further research in corporate/international banking has been the province of Turnbull [1982d, 1982f and 1983] who has worked with Carter [1980] and Vaughan [1980] in close liaison with a major UK clearing bank. In one project [Turnbull, 1983], the relationship between medium-sized corporate customers and their sources of financial services were examined, through interviews with financial decision-makers. It was found that all respondents had used a foreign bank at least once – such banks (in particular the US ones) seeming to be pursuing a strategy of incremental commitment, by selling one service to a company in the hope of getting more business in the future. Another major finding was that the companies viewed UK clearers as being too conservative in attitude with regard to providing business finance, an area where the foreign banks have been successful. In addition, they were critical of the quality of financial information and advice provided by their main bank, and believed that bank staff lacked expertise in this service. The implication for the UK clearers was that they may be creating awareness of their products/services, but need to develop expertise to provide them as expertly as foreign banks or more specialised organisations.

In a related project [see Turnbull, 1982f; and Carter, 1980], the use of foreign banks by large British companies was investigated via interviews with corporate treasurers. It was found that a great deal of 'split-banking' prevailed together with extensive use of foreign US banks. The success of the US banks seemed to be built on the inadequacy of the UK clearers in respect of their general marketing ability; ability to put together flexible tailor-made product packages; ability to provide large sums of finance rapidly; and their organisational structure for corporate business. However, the present signs are that the UK clearers are reacting to the success of the US banks by emulating their marketing approach; recognising that a prerequisite to establishing relationships with new clients is the use of calling officers and account relationship managers; using corporate finance divisions for large companies, and introducing international finance executives.

A third piece of work [Turnbull, 1982d; and Vaughan, 1980] focused on UK-owned companies with overseas subsidiaries in Europe, and investigated the use of international financial services by the subsidiary companies, and the factors which influenced their choice of supplier. They found evidence of highly centralised purchasing authority controlling group finance, with an increasing expertise of corporate treasurers; complex relationships between the UK parent, the subsidiary and their banks; extensive split-banking arrangements; and critical attitudes towards the quality of financial advisory services, reflecting a lack of knowledge about customer industries. Resulting implications for the banks were that financial services are perhaps best marketed to the corporate centre and not to individual subsidiaries, and that split-banking provides for aggressive marketing, but more effort is needed to understand customer needs and bank–customer relationships.

Product Development

The final topic of marketing concern which is available to report in this paper is specific to product development, namely, cash management services – which are fee earning and in addition to the traditional main bank products of money transmission, lending, etc. White [1984] investigated cash management concepts through research in banks and with 435 companies in Canada and the US. The companies ranked 19 services which they might require, the most important being automatic funds transfer, foreign exchange, balance reporting, computerised payroll and cash concentration. White also measured the companies' interest in, and usage of (presently low), these services and his conclusions dealt with methods for market segmentation (by industry segment, type of service, etc.) for cash management services.

Cash management services were developed in the US, so that one bank could report on a company's overall cash position across the country and then develop a service incorporating electronic funds transfer. Then it became clear that US banks could use cash management as an entrée to the UK corporate market. However, at least one UK clearing bank has retaliated by developing its own (international) cash management system, as reported by Haaroff [1983] – which comprises a set of modules including balance reporting, to provide information to different branches, banks, currencies and countries; transaction reporting; netting of intra-company debits and credits; minimum balance reporting; electronic funds transfer; cash flow projection to aid management control; and information and advisory services. Haaroff reviews the steps taken to introduce this service and the indications of its acceptance by the market. The advantages to customers which together would contribute to improved management/business information and, therefore, increased profitability were seen to be: minimising the volume of unproductive cash and maximising the proportion of cash earning a return; reduction in exchange risk and administrative expense; speedier transmission of funds; and savings in managerial time and taking of better informed financial decisions.

CONCLUSION

In this paper, various factors have been reviewed which have contributed to an awareness of the need for adopting the marketing concept in the provision of financial services – in particular, those of traditional banking institutions. Additionally, a number of the more recently published articles in which the focus has been marketing/marketing research and/or implementation in the market-place, have been introduced. The authors' concerns range from the acceptance of marketing and selling by bank personnel and subsequent training for bank marketing, to specific issues relevant to personal, corporate and international markets. Market research and segmentation have been the focus of some researches and elements of the marketing mix for others. Corporate/international aspects have tended to be concerned with attitudes towards banks and the use of financial services – with emphasis on the expansion of banks and companies abroad.

It was not intended to provide a comprehensive statement on the current practice of bank marketing, but rather to provide a 'state-of-the-art' commentary in respect of recent/current published papers available to the author. Hopefully, these will provide 'food for thought' with regard to the various aspects of bank marketing and future developments as banks face their continuing challenges in the market-place.

REFERENCES

Ansoff, I.H., 1957, 'Strategies for Diversification', *Harvard Business Review*, September–October.

Ansoff, I.H., 1965, *Corporate Strategy*, New York: McGraw Hill.

Baker, M.J., 1977a, 'The Marketing of Services', *The Scottish Bankers' Magazine*, May.

Baker, M.J., 1977b, 'Bank Marketing' *The Scottish Bankers' Magazine*, August.

Bellur, V.V., 1984, 'NOW Accounts: Awareness and Impact', *International Journal of Bank Marketing*, Vol. 2, No. 1.

Berry, L.L., and L.A. Capaldini, 1974, *Marketing for the Bank Executive*, Maison and Lipscombe Inc.

Berry, L.L., and J.H. Donnelly, 1975, *Marketing for Bankers*, Washington, DC: American Institute of Banking.

Berry L.L., 1980, 'Bank Marketing will Come of Age in the 1980s', *American Banker*, March 19.

Berry, L.L., 1982, 'Bank Marketing Priorities in the United States', *European Journal of Marketing*, Vol. 16, No. 3.

Brack, R.D., 1977, 'The Bank Manager as an Adviser to Small Firms', *Journal of the Institute of Bankers*, December.

Brockmann-Smith, M.B., 1979, 'Bank Marketing to Students', unpublished dissertation, Department of Management Sciences, UMIST.

Buswell, D., 1977, 'An Exploration of the Attitudes and Behaviour of Weekly, Cash-paid Workers to Banks and Other Financial Institutions', unpublished M.Sc. thesis, Department of Management Sciences, UMIST.
Buswell, D., 1983, 'Measuring the Quality of In-Branch Customer Service', *International Journal of Bank Marketing*, Vol. 1, No. 1.
Campos, J., 1980, 'An Investigation into the Awareness and Attitudes of School-Leavers towards Banks and Other Financial Institutions', unpublished M.Sc. thesis, Department of Management Sciences, UMIST.
Carter, M.I., 1980, 'The Penetration of the UK Corporate Market by US Banks – A Marketing Analysis', unpublished M.Sc. thesis, Department of Management Sciences, UMIST.
Cheese, J., 1983, 'Development of the Sales Function in Banking', *International Journal of Bank Marketing*, Vol. 1, No. 2.
Clarke, M.J., 1975, 'Graduates' Attitudes to Banking Services', unpublished dissertation, Department of Management Sciences, UMIST.
Coates, J., 1983, 'Getting Bank Marketing to the Staff', *International Journal of Bank Marketing*, Vol. 1, No. 3.
Dibbs, A., 1974, 'What a General Manager Expects from his Branch Manager', *Bankers Magazine*, May.
Edwards, R.D., 1981, 'Special Report – Relationship Banking', *United States Banker*, September.
Emerson, R., 1983, 'Banking Strategies in the UK: A US Perspective', *International Journal of Bank Marketing*, Vol. 1, No. 1.
Futrell, C.M., Berry, L.L., and M.R. Bowers, 1984, 'The Personal Selling Orientation of Banks in the United States', *International Journal of Bank Marketing*, Vol. 2, No. 1.
George, W.R., 1977, 'The Retailing of Services – A Challenging Future', *Journal of Retailing*, Fall.
Gray, A.D., 1977, 'Student Attitudes Towards Banking', unpublished dissertation, University of Strathclyde.
Gronroos, C., 1980, 'Designing a Long Range Marketing Strategy for Services', *Long Range Planning*, April.
Gronroos, C., 1981, 'Internal Marketing – An Integral Part of Marketing Theory', in J.H. Donnelly and W.R. George (eds.), *Marketing of Services: 1981 Special Educators Conference Proceedings*, Chicago: American Marketing Association.
Haaroff, K., 1983, 'An Exercise in Product Development for the 1980s: International Cash Management Service', *International Journal of Bank Marketing*, Vol. 1, No. 3.
Hodges, L.M., and R. Tillman, 1968, *Bank Marketing: Text and Cases*, Reading, MA: Addison-Wesley.
Johnson, E.M., 1983, 'Planning and Organising a Bank Sales Management System: A Case Study', *International Journal of Bank Marketing*, Vol. 1, No. 2.
King, S., 1981, 'How Non-Customers see Banks', *Journal of the Institute of Bankers*, December.
Landon, E.L., Jr., and J.H. Donnelly, Jr., 1983, 'Marketing's Emergence in the New Banking Environment', *International Journal of Bank Marketing*, Vol. 1, No. 1.
Lawson, R. and A. Watt, 1983, 'Market Orientated Pricing for U.K. Banks', *International Journal of Bank Marketing*, Vol. 1, No. 2.
Lewis, B.R., 1982, 'The Personal Account Sector', *European Journal of Marketing*, Vol. 16, No. 3.
MAS, 1975, *Bank Account Monitor: Account Ownership Report*, MAS Survey Research Ltd. October.
McIver, C. and G. Naylor, 1980, *Marketing Financial Services*, London: Institute of Bankers.
Meidan, A., 1983, 'Bank Marketing Strategies', *International Journal of Bank Marketing*, Vol. 1, No. 2.
National Opinion Polls, 1976, *Radio Commercials*, National Opinion Polls Market Research Ltd. October.
Ornstein, E.J., 1972, *The Marketing of Money*, Aldershot, Hants.: Gower Press.

Reekie, W.D., 1972, 'Marketing in Banking', *Bankers' Magazine*, Vol. 214, August, pp. 56–60, and September.

Robertson, D.H., and D.N. Bellenger, 1977, 'Identifying Bank Market Segments', *Journal of Bank Research*, Vol. 7.

Smith, H.M., 1980, *Credit Unions: Past, Present and Future*, unpublished M.Sc. thesis, Department of Management Sciences, UMIST.

Stafford, D., and S. King, 1983, 'Banking on the Unbanked', *International Journal of Bank Marketing*, Vol. 1, No. 2.

Stanley, T.T., Berry, L.L., and W.D. Danko, 1980, 'Personal Service versus Convenience: Perceptions of the High Income Consumer', *Journal of Retail Banking*.

Thompson, T.W., 1983, 'Marketplace Positioning in a De-regulated Environment', *International Journal of Bank Marketing*, Vol. 1, No. 3.

Turnbull, P.W., and W.A. Wootton, 1981, 'The Bank Manager: Marketer, Salesman or Administrator?', *European Journal of Marketing*, Vol. 14, No. 8.

Turnbull, P.W., 1982a, 'The Role of the Branch Bank Manager in the Marketing of Bank Services', *European Journal of Marketing*, Vol. 16, No. 3.

Turnbull, P.W., 1982b, 'International Aspects of Bank Marketing', *European Journal of Marketing*, Vol. 16, No. 3.

Turnbull, P.W., 1982c, 'The Development of U.K. Banks into International Markets', *European Journal of Marketing*, Vol. 16, No. 3.

Turnbull, P.W., 1982d, 'The Purchasing of International Financial Services by Medium and Large Sized U.K. Companies with European Subsidiaries', *European Journal of Marketing*, Vol. 16, No. 3.

Turnbull, P.W., 1982e, 'The Penetration of the U.K. Corporate Market by U.S. Banks', *European Journal of Marketing*, Vol. 16, No. 3.

Turnbull, P.W., 1982f, 'The Use of Foreign Banks by British Companies', *European Journal of Marketing*, Vol. 16, No. 3.

Turnbull, P.W., 1983, 'Corporate Attitudes towards Bank Services', *International Journal of Marketing*, Vol. 1, No. 1.

Varadarajan, P. and L.L. Berry, 1983, 'Strategies for Growth in Banking: An Exposition' *International Journal of Bank Marketing*, Vol. 1, No. 1.

Vaughan, C.P., 1980, 'An Examination of International Banking Markets with Particular Reference to the Purchasing of International Financial Services by the Subsidiaries of UK Companies', unpublished M.Sc. thesis, Department of Management Sciences, UMIST.

Waterworth, D., 1973, 'Banking Behind Bars', *Marketing*, November.

Watkins, T., 1984, 'Optimising Bank Service Provision: A Simulation Approach', *International Journal of Bank Marketing*, Vol. 2, No. 1.

Watson, T., 1974, 'What Future for the Branch Manager?', *The Bankers' Magazine*, April.

Watson, I.J., 1975, 'The Implementation of the Marketing Concept in U.K. Banking Branches', University of Warwick, School of Industrial and Business Studies, Working Paper No. 23.

Watson, I., 1982, 'The Adoption of Marketing by the English Clearing Banks', *European Journal of Marketing*, Vol. 16, No. 3.

Watson, I., 1984, 'Some Current Issues in U.K. Bank Marketing', *International Journal of Bank Marketing*, Vol. 2, No. 1.

White J., 1984, 'Cash Management Services: Researching Segmentation Strategies', *International Journal of Bank Marketing*, Vol. 2, No. 2.

Wills, G., and A. Day, 1984, 'Marketing and Selling at Work: The IMCB/National Westminster Development Programme', *International Journal of Bank Marketing*, Vol. 2, No. 1.

Wilson, R., 1980, *The Marketing of Financial Services*, Bradford: MCB University Press Ltd.

Yorke, D.A., 1982, 'The Definition of Market Segments for Banking Services', *European Journal of Marketing*, Vol. 16, No. 3.

Yorke, D.A., and A. Hayes, 1982, 'Working Females as a Market Segment for Bank Services', *European Journal of Marketing*, Vol. 16, No. 3.

Marketing Insurance Services: The Main Challenges

by

Simon Majaro

On the basis of the author's recent researches among US insurance companies, this article demonstrates that the more marketing-orientated companies have fared better then those which have relegated marketing to a relatively less important role in their managerial priorities. The article lists a number of issues that the top managements of insurance firms should consider in some depth if they intend to espouse the marketing concept fully.

INTRODUCTION

In common with most 'service' industries the world of insurance has been slow in absorbing the marketing concept and all its panoply of tools and disciplines into its midst. The industry has been intrigued by the notion of 'marketing' and indeed many organisations in the insurance world have introduced some kind of marketing presence. Yet is it true to say at the very outset that very few companies in the field fully understand the role that an effective marketing function can contribute to the success of their respective organisations. A brief exploration of the industry will show that at best one can find companies that have a marketing department that deals with a number of peripheral, albeit important, activities which do not amount to a fully-fledged marketing function. At worst one encounters insurance companies that do not see the point of applying new-fangled ideas which are more appropriate to manufacturers of biscuits and cereals. This latter remark is that of a senior general manager of one of the most prestigious insurance companies in the City of London.

We have recently seen the trauma that was created for the life assurance industry through the abolition of the tax relief on life policies' premiums. It is difficult to comprehend why the industry got itself into such a state. After all, the idea that tax relief might be abolished was discussed for a number of years and any competent planner should have had a contingency plan available for such an emergency. Regrettably only a small number of firms in the insurance industry were proactive enough to prepare the ground for such an important change in the marketing environment. Albany Life Assurance deserves a compliment in this regard. It was one of the few companies that emerged with a campaign, a few days after the Budget, communicating the fact that 'We've always given people better reasons for life assurance than 15% tax relief'. Indeed the post-Budget campaign reiterated the various messages that had been communicated to the market-place during the previous few years. Tax relief was either not mentioned or referred to as a minor benefit only.

During recent work in the United States I discovered that even in a country which we tend to consider very marketing-orientated, the insurance industry is finding the full integration of the marketing concept a daunting task. Yet it was interesting to note that companies that have made some strides towards assimilating marketing principles are the ones that are able to demonstrate better overall performance. I have examined the annual reports of around 50 companies in the insurance field. My sample was selected carefully in accordance with strict criteria of size, 'product' mix and geographical coverage in order to maintain comparability of analysis. US insurance organisations provide a plethora of information about their activities, performance and costs. It was possible to gauge the level of marketing-orientation that these companies achieved through the analysis of the following items:

(1) The level of expenditure declared in the published reports regarding what one would classify as marketing activities.

Clearly one can assume that companies that allocate funds to such items as promotion, product development and innovation, consumer research, etc. are more aware of the role of marketing than those that spend very little on such items.

(2) The number of new products that the companies announced and referred to in their annual report.

Once again and in a fairly pragmatic way one can deduce that firms that spend time and creativity in developing new products are more responsive to a dynamic market-place than those who do not.

(3) The prominence that companies give to 'marketing' in their structure.

This is simply manifested in the way marketing and its concomitant activities are incorporated in the firm's managerial and functional hierarchy.

An insurance company that has a Marketing Director or a Vice President of Marketing on its Board seems to suggest that it has recognised the importance of marketing principles. Having a Marketing Director is no proof that the company is attaining excellence in this area. None the less, it is not illogical to believe that the company has taken an important step towards accepting the value of marketing principles as a factor in a successful operation.

(4) The emphasis that the annual reports and supportive publications place on the firms' response to identified marketing challenges.

Thus if a company highlights the fact that it has introduced special contracts in response to the needs of working women or single-parent families one can deduce that that particular organisation has identified significant demographic changes and responded thereto.

(5) The suggestion that the company has discovered specific segments upon which to target its marketing effort.

Surely the realisation that target marketing is more efficient than undifferentiated marketing must be one of the indicators that would give an organisation an extra accolade in the test of its orientation.

(6) The general appearance of the annual report itself.

This in itself is a 'plus point' in support of the firm's marketing orientation. Obviously the firm's management has recognised the value of an attractive, comprehensive and readable report as an instrument of communication with the company's stakeholders including customers.

I developed a screening matrix incorporating marketing criteria based on the above perception and listed all the organisations in the sample in a descending scale that emanated from this kind of analsysis. The gratifying outcome was that with very few exceptions the companies that received a high score on the 'marketing checklist' analysis were among the high-fliers in the batch. Crude a method as it was it proved to me that marketing has a powerful role to play in the insurance industry and that some 'cause and effect' between effective marketing and performance does exist.

Since then this approach has been used as a training device for students, who 1) undertake a traditional ratio analysis in order to establish the financial health of the organisation; 2) prepare a list of 'indicators' against which the 'marketing orientation' of the firm can be gauged.

The lessons that can be learnt from this kind of exercise are valuable and the impact on budding managers remarkable. I must admit that in no industrial sector did I find the consistency more instructive than in the insurance industry. In fact when asked to comment upon the suitability of a company for acquisition in the field of insurance I immediately direct my attention to its marketing health and quality as described above. A company that fails this primitive acid test is probably not worth buying and is sure to give headaches to its acquirer!

MARKETING IN INSURANCE COMPANIES

Before discussing the marketing issues that face insurance firms it is appropriate to review a fundamental point which would help to set the scene for this paper.

'Marketing' in any industry and in any environment can have two distinct, albeit interrelated, aspects:

(1) 'Marketing' is a corporate culture or attitude whereby everyone in the organisation, and at all times, understands that the customer's needs must be fully identified, anticipated and met;

(2) 'Marketing' is a function consisting of a cluster of disciplines,

activities and methodologies which must be carried out in seeking to attain the firm's commercial objectives.

It is not always appreciated that a firm can excel in the former but be extremely poor in the latter and vice versa. Ideally a company must develop both aspects in parallel. However, if forced to make a choice between the two it is probably more valuable to stimulate the first, namely, the customer-orientated creed and philosophy. The latter without the former may well mean having an effective marketing organisation operating in an isolated and somewhat sterile climate.

When one is talking about a corporate culture which is customer- or consumer-orientated one assumes that such an attitude pervades every level and every function of the organisation. In firms in which such a philosophy exists it is not seen purely as the duty of a small number of people carrying titles with marketing/selling connotations. This means that everyone in the firm has been brainwashed to recognise that the 'customer is king' and what is good for him or her is good for the firm's business. Such an attitude one would expect to find not only among the firm's personnel who have contact with the customer, but also among those who work behind the scenes such as the R & D people, finance department and manufacturing personnel. In fact it is often not realised that in some organisations it is the switchboard operator who is the first contact point with the customer. If this contact is unsatisfactory the firm's marketing task has become that much more difficult.

Most people could recount sad stories as to how they have changed patronage as a result of unfortunate encounters with clumsy and unsympathetic employees of a company. Indeed quite often the culprits were no more than relatively junior members of the organisations. Yet the consumer reacts to the people he has to deal with. We all judge the quality of an airline by the way we are being treated by the steward or stewardess. Very few passengers have an opportunity to meet the airline's Chief Executive or Marketing Director. The fact that they are both charming, persuasive and effective is totally irrelevant. The same airline may have a powerful marketing department that carries out the various marketing activities that effective organisations have to undertake. None the less if the corporate culture is apathetic to the customer, his needs and motivational stimuli, the chance of the company attaining marketing excellence is doubtful.

In this connection one may mention Marks and Spencer. This is an organisation which is universally acclaimed as a most effective and responsive one to customers' needs and expectations. It is rare to meet people who are less than complimentary of this company's products, quality, standard of service and courtesy, etc. This customer-orientation pervades every part of the company. There is a general recognition throughout the firm that what is 'good for the customer is good for the company's business'. None the less 'marketing' as a cluster of activities structured under that heading does not appear to exist there. In their eyes everyone working for them is involved in marketing activities in the broadest sense of the word. A firm may be able to achieve the development of a culture in which everyone is sensitive to clients' needs and responds thereto at all times and in a wholehearted way without the word 'markting' crossing anybody's lips. Such a firm is truly marketing-orientated, although in methodological and functional terms it might have failed to harness the armoury of tools that modern marketing theory offers. To me this is a greater achievement than the firm that has managed to encompass every technique, tool and discipline that have emerged during the last few years but has failed to come close to their customers and establish permanent and interactive communication bridges with them.

At the risk of emphasising a platitude this is a point which deserves careful ventilation especially when one addresses people from service industries. Banks, transport companies, and insurance organisations must remember that the cultural/attitudinal aspects of 'marketing' are of paramount importance to their success. The customer judges these organisations by the quality of contact that he or she has with the immediate interlocuter with whom business is transacted. Such a person may even be the telephone operator. To that extent the operator is part of the firm's 'product' and a poor or unhappy contact derogates from the quality of the product and the image of the organisation as a whole. In how many insurance companies is the responsibility for the switchboard training and control vested in the hands of a marketing department? Many similar examples can be highlighted in order to illustrate that 'marketing' in service industries in general and in insurance companies in particular entails a lot more than just running a marketing department on the fringe of the main business of the firm.

MARKETING CHALLENGES FACING THE INSURANCE INDUSTRY

One of the major problems that afflicts the insurance industry is the fact that the nature of the business calls for a sophisticated understanding of 'risk management' and the laws of probability. Insurance companies must be able to calculate estimated future losses on the basis of past experience. The business depends on people in the industry being able to quantify the probability of a risk taking place and the severity of such losses if they occur. The whole industry is based on the idea of transferring to an insurer the financial loss which may arise if a specified event occurs. The industry and the legal system of most countries have assembled over a long period a code of practice and rules which control the subtleties of what is insurable and who could insure against any risk. Thus the Life Assurance Act 1774 prescribes that any policy on the life of any person or other event in which the person for whose benefit or on whose account the policy is made has no insurable interest at the time of the policy is illegal. This 1774 Act is still one of the cornerstones of the insurance industry!

Another important feature of the industry is the 'Duty of Disclosure'. The proposer is under a legal obligation to disclose all material facts that he knows or would know if he made reasonable enquiries. Failure to disclose material facts can cause the insurer to regard the policy as null and void and refuse to honour claims when they occur. Clearly this rule can be the antithesis of good marketing in the hands of an unscrupulous or highly pedantic company.

These points and many others pertaining to legal, quasi-legal and institutional rules and procedures have meant that the industry has tended to be managed by people with specialised training steeped in mathematical, legalistic and procedural jargon and theories. Their role is to ensure that premiums received are judiciously balanced against the incidence of losses resulting in profits at the end of a given period. 'Marketing' as a subject seldom appears in the curricula of those seeking to join the industry either as actuaries or budding managers. There are notable exceptions to this remark but on the whole the industry could derive considerable benefits from the development of a systematised training module in the marketing theory and practice geared for the specific needs of the insurance world.

Stemming from this educational gap a number of marketing challenges face the industry and the companies that manage to deal with them should be among the high-fliers of the next decade:

(1) Developing a 'customer-orientated' culture: This is probably the most important challenge that top management of an insurance organisation must attempt to grapple with. As explained earlier it means a relentless effort at brainwashing every member of the organisation towards the acceptance of the notion that what is good for the customer is likely to be good for the firm.

To a company operating in consumer goods this statement is almost trite inasmuch as such companies have come to accept such a fundamental tenet a good few years ago. None the less, for insurance companies this basic concept is a difficult one to absorb in the firm's operational environment. It implies a total change in managerial and clerical attitudes towards customers and their needs and expectations. Whilst intellectually most senior people can understand the need for such an orientation, very few managers are prepared to change their demeanour and style in order to accommodate what appears to them a pious goal.

Thus, for example, it means designing policies which are more readable and more understandable and without hidden escape clauses. Unfortunately, the rigours of the legal system have provided a plausible alibi for non-action.

It should also mean responding to claims in an empathetic manner. How many insurers volunteer to do so without persistent pressure from clients or their brokers?

It should also mean trying to understand more closely the changing needs of a dynamic society in relation to product design, pricing policy, distribution strategies and communication. Unfortunately, all this is as yet the practice among the more effective few.

(2) Corporate image: This is an important part of an insurance company's marketing effort. In common with all service organisations the insurance industry is marketing intangible products. In fact an insurance policy is even more intangible than transport and banking. An insurance policy is a promise to pay some money if a certain contingency takes place. Until such a contingency occurs the 'product' is purely a piece of paper. None the less some people would consider a piece of paper issued by Company 'A' a better 'product' than the one issued by Company 'B'. It is a question of perception based on the quality of the 'image' that the firm has managed to develop for itself and its employees. What matters to customers is not 'objective quality' but 'perceived quality'.

Top management must be deeply involved in the task of developing the most suitable face for the company to project. It calls for a lot of care and thorough appreciation of the firm's aims and capabilities.

A number of points should be added in this connection:

(a) A corporate image strategy must be fully congruent with the firm's objectives, target markets and its identified 'strengths and weaknesses'.

It is pointless to develop an image which aims to convey the impression that the company is seeking to deal with large insurers only when in fact the marketing objectives are the complete opposite.

(b) Image building can be an expensive strategy. It is therefore important that the needs of the next decade are considered before undertaking such a project. It would be highly extravagant for a company to undertake a major corporate image programme without taking full cognisance of the future direction and aims of the firm.

(3) Reactive or Proactive Marketing: This challenge is being addressed to top management of insurance companies and not only to managers responsible for evolving marketing strategies. The industry tends to be reactive to events. The more enlightened organisations react quickly; the more dormant ones react slowly. This of course applies to most industries. However, my observation of the industry at close quarters has convinced me that very few firms in the business take steps to forecast changes in the market-place and plan a strategic programme capable of catering for such proactive assessments.

In those companies where a senior person looks after strategic planning one normally finds that very little marketing 'input' is incorporated into the preparation of such plans. The manager who is prepared to respond to this challenge, should consider the following:

(a) Changes are taking place in the demographic structure of the UK.
The pensionable proportion of the UK population has increased from 14.5 per cent in 1959 to 18 per cent in 1981.
The over 65 old increased from 5.9 million in 1959 to 8.3 million in 1981. It is easy to forecast the figures for year 2000.
Size of average household has decreased from 3.08 to 2.73 during the same period.
(b) Significant changes have taken place in the occupational status of households.
In 1959 the percentage of owner-occupiers was 38. In 1982 the figure went up to 59. It is not difficult to forecast future trends in this regard.
(c) The proportion of working women has increased dramatically and the trend is upwards.
(d) The percentage of smokers is decreasing.
(e) The percentage of people going abroad for their holidays has increased from nine to 23.
(f) Significant changes have taken place in the children population and of course it is possible to project the breakdown of the 0–15 population fairly accurately until year 2000.
(g) The number of homeworkers, outworkers and freelance labour has increased substantially during the last few years. They currently stand at around 1.7 million as against 1.1 million in the late 1960s. The trend upwards is discernible.
(h) Evidence is available to show that many consumers are developing an 'Inward directed' life style. Such individuals are less likely to want to save and/or insure their lives....

Such facts, figures and observations together with many other relevant statistical data provide the insurance marketer with a valuable insight into the kind of product policy that could be developed for the future. Marketers have to cope with surprises but in fact many of the 'surprise zones' can be reduced if one bothers to introduce a systematic approach to a more proactive planning process.

(4) Differentiated or undifferentiated marketing: The large proportion of insurance companies in the UK tend to drift into an 'undifferentiated marketing' posture. They simply take the view that they have 'products' that meet the needs of most people and/or organisations. The concept of 'segmentation', 'nichemanship' and/or 'positioning' is seldom explored and applied. The important point to remember is that in many situations a company could benefit from having a large market share of a limited segment than a small market share of the total market. BMW in the car business have recognised this truth and have developed a powerful penetration of a small albeit most attractive market segment. Many insurance companies could benefit from a similar strategy. Clearly it is not being suggested that every insurance company should redirect its

attention to micro-parts of the market-place. Nevertheless insurance companies are being advised to reflect upon what is better for them: to achieve a dominant position in one or two segments for which they are particularly well-suited or continue to maintain an 'all things to all men' approach.

In this connection two interrelated techniques are available for marketing analysis and planning: 'mapping' and 'positioning'. The former aims to identify the role which the company is currently fulfilling in the market-place vis-à-vis its competitors. A firm often operates in a certain corner of the market-place without realising that such a position has taken place. Figure 1 illustrates the type of analysis that can be carried out. It seeks to produce a 'map' of the market-place showing where the company and its competitors are operating. Different parameters can be selected for analysis. The aim here is purely to illustrate the way this technique can be used.

FIGURE 1
A 'MAP' OF INSURANCE COMPANIES OPERATING IN THE COMMERCIAL BUSINESS
(EXAMPLE ONLY)

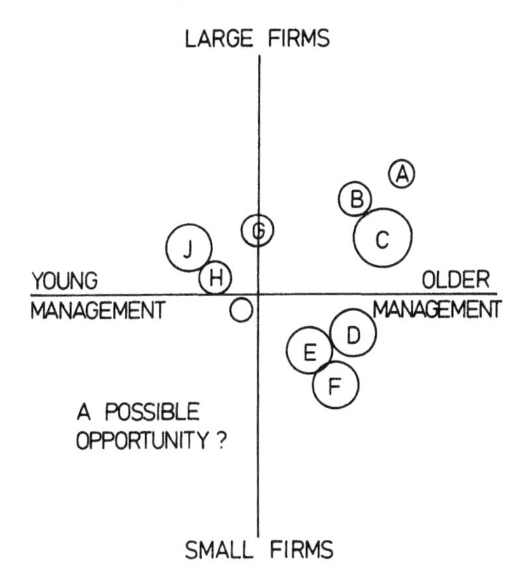

Once the 'mapping' exercise has been completed the marketing strategies can explore a 'positioning' plan aimed at:

a) developing a marketing programme for those segments which appear less crowded;
b) ensuring a high market share in such opportunity areas (once the validity of such sectors has been verified and quantified).

This approach can be a very exciting one in the hands of marketers who understand fully what is happening in their market-place and are anxious to escape from the rigours of pernicious competition.

(5) Marketing innovation: By and large the insurance industry suffers from 'tunnel vision'. Most insurance executives believe that it is a unique industry and that the only individuals capable of making a useful contribution to its success are those who grew inside the industry. The result is that very few companies in the insurance world manage to derive benefit from the cross-fertilisation of ideas from different industries and/or service organisations. This is a challenge that the more enlightened organisations in the industry must attempt to face. Whilst insurance encompasses a tremendous amount of specialised knowledge it is not outside the competence of an intelligent and creative marketer to absorb the main rudiments of this knowledge.

It is useful to remember that 'innovation' can be derived from the injection of ideas from different industries, activities and companies. As long as a company relies entirely on ideas emanating from people who have never been exposed to such influences the risk is that the level of innovation will be fairly low. Moreover, it is worth mentioning that in the competitive battle which insurance companies have to face it is not sufficient to strive for 'productivity'. The winners of the next decade will be those who will manage to combine high productivity with high innovation. Figure 2 illustrates the four options open to a company. Undoubtedly it is the company that reaches the top/right corner which will be the high flier of the industry. In order to achieve this status a company will need to ensure that its innovation is based on more than efficient and productive but incestuous managerial cadre.

(6) Marketing organisation: Having observed the way a large number of insurance companies are organised I feel that there is considerable scope for developing more effective organisational patterns for the marketing function. This is particularly true of composite companies who operate in a number of areas such as life, health, general insurance, pensions, etc. It is mostly the composite companies that find the management of marketing a most difficult task.

The dilemma of 'centralisation' and 'decentralisation' poses a severe challenge to top management of insurance companies. The extreme organisational options in this regard are:

(a) the development of a marketing department in each operating unit;
(b) the establishment of a central marketing department entrusted with the task of performing the marketing activities of all the operating business units.

The advantages and disadvantages of each of these options are numerous. The supporters of a centralised approach to marketing planning and practice could make a strong case for the former. The advocates of decentralisation would find a sufficient justification for the latter.

FIGURE 2
THE PRODUCTIVITY/INNOVATION DIRECTION – THE FOUR OPTIONS

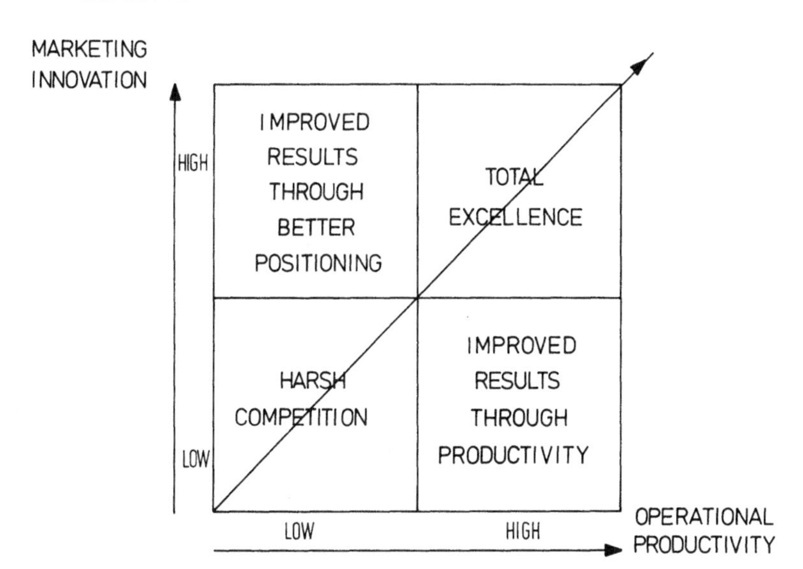

In truth both solutions suffer from a major weakness inasmuch as in a composite insurance company there are various marketing tasks which must be performed at the centre and others which are best carried out in the operating units. Thus the establishment of a corporate image strategy and guidelines is a matter for the 'centre' – the application of such guidelines to specific 'products' and marketing opportunities is clearly a prerogative of the commercial operating units. None the less there is a strong case for having a centrally-located monitoring and controlling function in this connection. 'Product'-design is normally best carried out by the operating units. However, someone at the 'centre' must ensure that such products are consistent with the overall firm's objectives, strategy and image. 'Selling' is often planned in a decentralised fashion and it is probably wise to do so. On the other hand, there is little doubt that a composite insurance company can often derive considerable 'synergy' from being able to sell all the firm's products to very large buyers and organisations. The absence of a central organ in this regard can easily mean that the firm misses a number of important 'package deals' with large and powerful clients.

Communication and promotional activities planned and executed in a totally decentralised fashion without some co-ordination from the centre may mean that the company is not deriving the full benefit of the multiple exposure generated by the various businesses. Marketing research activities can be much more cost-effective when they are planned in unison among the decentralised units. After all, it is often the same people who insure their cars and houses as those who insure their own life with the ABC Insurance company.

A combination of a decentralised structure with a 'light-touch' central co-ordination is probably one of the attractive solutions to this dilemma. The aim of such a person or a department is to attempt to obtain the full benefits of decentralisation whilst insuring that maximum logic and synergy is maintained to the benefit of all. The success of such an organisational compromise depends on:

a) The ability to select a person or persons who are capable of exercising their co-ordinative role in an empathetic and 'low key' profile.
b) The clarity with which a 'job description' has been prepared. There must be no doubt either in the 'centre' or in the operating units as to the responsibilities and authority of the incumbent.
c) The skill with which the so-called 'marketing co-ordinator' has managed to 'market' his role among the marketers in the 'line'.

   Failure on his or her part to perform an effective marketing task in this regard is very often the proof that the wrong person has been selected for this important task.

In practice this co-ordinative task represents a good example of 'matrix' management which is illustrated in Figure 3 and which, hitherto, has been used in very few insurance companies.

FIGURE 3
MATRIX MANAGEMENT AS A TOOL OF CO-ORDINATION IN INSURANCE MARKETING

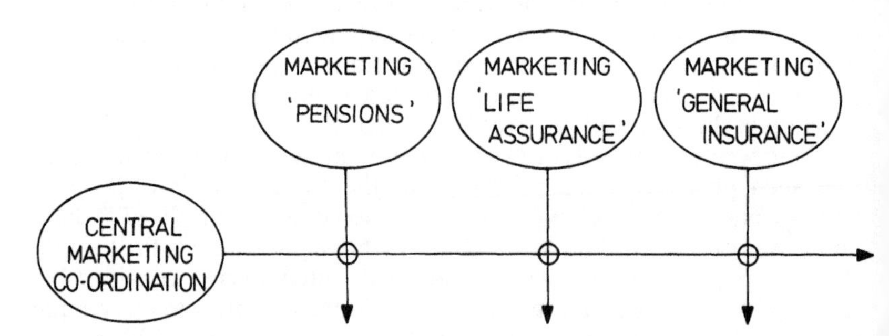

Insurance companies have been flirting with marketing concepts and principles during the last decade in a half-hearted way. 'Marketing departments' exist in an increasing number of firms. However, in many companies 'marketing' only represents a part of the activities that a fully-fledged marketing function entails whilst the rest are performed by non-marketing personnel who have very little feel for the customer and his needs.

How to organise a marketing function in an insurance company is probably one of the greatest challenges that senior managers in such firms have to face. They often do not know where to start and consequently it is not unusual to encounter marketing departments which operate with a total lack of direction and purpose. It is therefore useful to list the number of sub-activities that an effective marketing function should encompass. Figure 4 shows in a diagrammatic form all these activities. They fall under four headings: '*Input*'-gathering activities; '*Objectives*'-setting (planning); '*Operations*' – the 'doing' activities and '*Control*'.

The conscientious company strategist should determine:

1) who should perform each one of the tasks thus listed;
2) which of these tasks should be best performed in the 'centre' and which best left in the operating units.

It is only then that the marketing task could be performed in an effective and well-integrated way to the advantage of the individual businesses and the corporation as a whole.

FIGURE 4

THE SUB-ACTIVITIES OF A MARKETING FUNCTION IN AN INSURANCE COMPANY

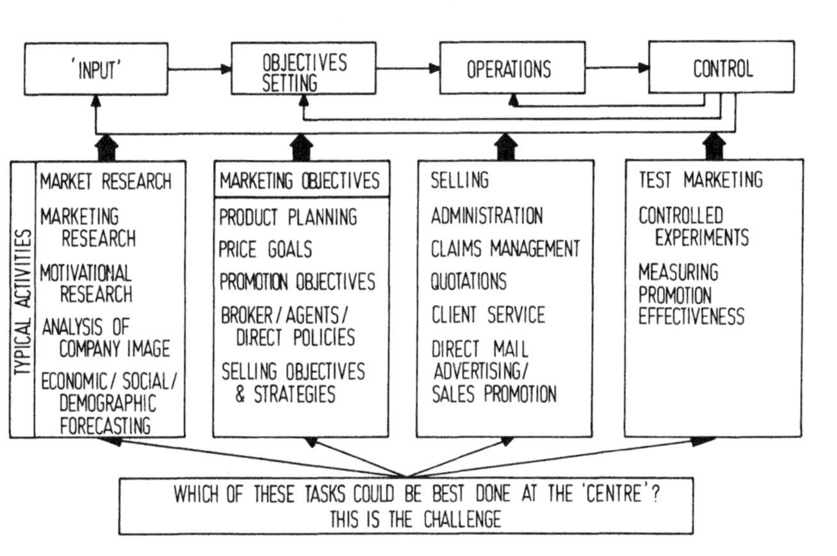

REFERENCES

Bateson, E.G., 1977, 'Do We Need Service Marketing?', *Marketing Consumer Services: New Insights*, Marketing Science Institute, Report Nos. 77–115.

Goodfellow, H., 1983, 'The Marketing of Goods and Services as a Multi-dimensional Concept', *The Quarterly Review of Marketing*, Vol. 8, No. 3.

Lovelock, C., 1984, *Services Marketing*, Englewood Cliffs, NJ: Prentice Hall.

Majaro, S., 1982, 'Insurance, Too, Needs Marketing', Chapter 15 of *Marketing in Perspective*, London: George Allen & Unwin.

Shostock, G., 1977, 'Breaking Free from Product Marketing', *Journal of Marketing*, Vol. 41, No. 2.

Wilson, A., 1972, *The Marketing of Professional Services*, New York: McGraw-Hill.

Estate Agency: A Marketing Challenge

by

John Driver

The application of marketing by estate agencies has been influenced and generally restricted by professional considerations, but dramatic changes are occurring as new types of competitor specialise in aspects of the agent's traditional work. The situation of local oligopoly is likely to change, especially in urban areas, but the advent of a new structure in house transacting paradoxically should enhance the professionalism of agencies as they transcend the role of information intermediary and pursue their distinctive competences in property assessment, buying and selling. Their marketing mix, however, must be better aligned to the needs of institutional and individual segments.

INTRODUCTION

Whatever the precise understanding of the nature and applicability of marketing, there has been in recent years a 'marketing revolution' which has extended marketing philosophy and technique into sectors previously oblivious or deliberately abstaining from this influence. Both the spread of this influence and the results have not, however, escaped critical comment, especially where the marketing approach, equated with commercialism, has been in apparent conflict with professionalism and/or the provision of services as of right (social services) or custom (religious organisations and charities). Whilst certain overtly commercial services have succumbed only recently to the influence, the assertion that service marketing is underdeveloped has some validity both in general, and especially, in the cases of the professions, for example, solicitors, opticians and architects. This is not the place to discuss the full relationship between such professional practices and marketing but the case of estate agency does highlight a variety of interesting issues which have a wider relevance.

The significance and topicality of the interrelationships between marketing, commercialism and professionalism in the case of (some) estate agents is indicated by the following opinions:

> Is it not extraordinary that the single most expensive purchase made by most people, namely a house, remains virtually untouched by the

> modern skills of marketing? ... Estate agents are, of course, the people who should be providing such a service; but they too are woefully lacking in any skill other than the eager pursuit of the fast buck [Murray, 1982: 27].

> The estate agents like to think of themselves as professionals, but have not been giving a professional service. They've been content just to handle the mechanics of the transactions.[1]

> Professionalism, in terms of codes of method and conduct, an alert quality of service and a high standard basic qualification and subsequent range of practical experience is the only answer to contemporary conditions (*Estates Gazette*, 1984: 1081].

In order to examine the interrelationship it is necessary to briefly review the salient aspects of marketing – both as a subject and a practice.

The core concept of marketing (the marketing concept) holds that a customer- or client-orientation is both desirable as an end in itself and as the means by which an organisation can fulfil its own objectives. The 'revolution' has reflected no more than a shift in perception that the customer has equivalent – or greater – importance in the focus of operations involving some realignment of the interests of other stakeholders in the organisation. The possibility that marketing permits the enhanced achievement of organisational objectives may obviate any conflict of interest between customers and, for instance, employees and shareholders; some can benefit and no-one loses. The point is contentious whether the adoption of marketing, in line with the marketing concept, is an enlightened and altruistic view of the consumer's rightful place or is in response to a set of factors which enable or compel such a stance – an issue which is clouded by the difficulty in distinguishing the mere utilisation of marketing technique and tools from their deployment in line with the concept. There are, inescapably, aspects of any organisation's relationship with clients/customers ('market') that are loosely describable in the vocabulary of marketing. Thus the dimensions of product/service, place, communication aspects and price (if charged) are relevant to the conduct of an organisation whether or not it espouses the marketing concept. Prevalent alternative operating philosophies which reflect non-marketing biases, though using the vocabulary, are the production and selling orientations; however, these descriptions have not typically been applied to the professions.[2] Indeed, one of the issues at the heart of the professionalism/marketing debate is a belief by the professions that marketing technique, so *apparent* in the case of branded fast-moving consumer goods, is fundamentally *inappropriate* in their cases. This has been cast not so much in terms of the degree to which marketing is applicable but of its applicability at all.

Professionals themselves, whilst eschewing the terminology of marketing, have equally typically maintained an apparent customer-orientation in their codes of conduct and acquired/customary ethical standards. Might it then be the case that they are indeed marketing-orientated to the extent that their practice is to offer a service subject to fee? Is it only the question of promotion – especially advertising (of prices) and certain forms of personal selling techniques, for example, canvassing, touting, soliciting and supplanting that professions typically restrict – that really is the impediment to viewing the professions *essentially* as marketers? Can it be that their service is meeting both customers' needs and their own? In order to clarify these questions in the case of estate agents it is necessary to consider customers' needs and the practice of estate agency.

ESTATE AGENCY PRACTICE

If the practice of estate agency is examined and the procedures of a marketing appraisal are adopted it is necessary to analyse the product, price, place and communication (marketing mix) decisions that are taken in relation both to their market, competitors and context, the latter being a blend of legal, cultural, environmental, technological and historical constraints and determinants.[3]

For the majority of agents for most of their time and for the vast majority of the market of house transactors, estate agency is concerned with the selling of houses. However, the product/service of the agent is not confined merely to the selling of houses and his activities typically include the roles of:

- information intermediary – providing information for both buyers and sellers;
- financial intermediary – providing assistance with mortgage advice and insurance in particular;
- service professional – offering advice/expertise on planning and procedures, as well as valuations, surveying, etc.;
- selling agent – for example, auctioneering;
- property manager – arranging lettings and property supervision and possibly services such as house clearance;
- property entrepreneur – subject to a declaration of interest in line with the Estate Agents Act 1979 the agent may act on his own account as a developer.

The term 'estate agency' also refers to more specialised activities in essentially separate markets in the agricultural, commercial and industrial sectors. Attention here, however, is confined to the residential sector, and to the market for used houses.

The way in which estate agents in their residential marketing deploy the elements of the marketing mix may be *generally* described because a broadly similar pattern is adopted reflecting the experience accumulated over many years, the emulation of others and a comparatively limited conception and scope. The elements feature: strategically sited shops/offices in or just off busy streets; window displays of property which are also promoted in (primarily local) press advertisements. Advertisements appear also in the agent's own property papers or in more general free-sheets – where available – and these are a further important form of information dissemination. Flagboards are also available for display on or adjacent to a property for sale which communicate the agent's name and address but give no information about the property itself. In qualitative terms there is a uniformity in the way the printed advertisements are constructed. The emphasis is primarily towards the individual properties which are featured with either photographs or artist's impressions and/or descriptions. In the promotion of the agency itself there is typically a listing of some, but rarely all, of the following services: free valuations for sellers without obligation; surveys and auctioneering; organisation of advertisements; compiling of particulars; free mortgage advice; free marketing advice; personal service; no sale, no charges; free advertising; 100 per cent mortgages available; no deposit terms; colour photographs; daily updating and printing; computerised mailing service; scale fees; sole agency discount; open seven days a week; open evenings; accompanied viewing where required.

In addition to these service elements, the agents make specific statements about themselves, for example: established; local; membership of ...; connections with ...; specialists in all types–higher price property, etc.; friendly service; reliable/trustworthy; and more ambiguously 'a real estate agent'.

In respect of the price dimension of the mix estate agents' advertisements do not feature price directly. There may be references to scale fees, without articulating what these imply, and 'free' is used with advertising (sometimes) valuations (typically) and to advice of various kinds. Also a *discount* may be given for sole agency status. Some agents, moreover, also may be engaged on the 'no sale, no fee' basis.

This brief review of the general characteristics of the marketing mix of estate agents warrants some comment and further description. Arising from the nature of the market, itself determined by the behaviour and preferences of consumers, the core of the agent's business is local (one survey showed that on a national average 40 per cent moved less than five miles and only 25 per cent moved more than 20 miles),[4] thus historically estate agencies have been confined to one or two offices with a large chain being in the order of a dozen offices. This emphasis on local, and to a lesser but increasing extent regional, coverage where the chains increase in size, means that the agent's own communication about his capabilities is not restricted to impersonal advertising but is significantly supplemented, even dominated, by forms of interpersonal communication beyond the marketer's direct control. Indeed, the agent's reputation is his prime business asset.

It follows that the agent's advertising needs only to demonstrate his existence and his capacity to match his local competitors' service and it is this which leads to the uniformity described above. On the other hand, the advertisements do include more subtle clues which help determine the agent's image. Thus the size of advertisment, which may even run to several full pages, is itself indicative of the agency's characteristics implying size (possibly prestige) and success since many people have independently chosen to instruct them. However, size can convey some less positive features, including impersonality, less effort, lower turnover of property, and too much choice for buyers working against the marginal vendor's interest. Further study of the structure of local advertisements reveals that there are tiers of competition (crudely) amongst the larger and the smaller, although both groups are, of course, also competing against each other.

Noteworthy features of the agency's communication in advertisments are the references to the dates of their establishment, qualification and to their membership of various associations. These are clearly to reinforce reputation and take several basic forms. Some, but by no means all, agents belong to professional institutions which, subject to qualifications obtained by examination and experience, entitle them to practice as registered surveyors, valuers and auctioneers. This is the case with the Royal Institution of Chartered Surveyors (RICS) and the Incorporated Society of Valuers and Auctioneers (ISVA). There are, however, other associations, the National Association of Estate Agents and the Corporation of Estate Agents and a variety of local associations (often including members from the above associations) which have membership requirements based on practice alone.

The scale fees, to which advertisements refer, arise primarily from the recommendations of the various associations and these are basically ad valorem fees, depending on the price of the property sold. Both the precise scale of fees and whether the particular scale is totally inclusive of such services as advertising, and the basis on which the fee is chargeable vary both between agencies and by area. The reference to sole agency discount relates to the use of a lower scale of fees when a single agent is instructed than would apply with multiple agency terms. However, there are marked regional differences (particularly between the North and South of England) in the prevalence of the use of multiple agencies, it being more common in the South. Likewise, the term 'no sale, no fee' is distributed by region and is common only in the South. The degree of charge when the 'no sale, no fee' basis does not apply is not uniform either. In some areas, particularly the North, where the vendor gives his agent sole selling rights, he is liable for the scale fee whether the agent actually sells or not. In other cases – again regionally distributed – even in the absence of sole selling rights there may be some fee and usually a charge for expenses incurred.[5]

The foregoing brief account of the marketing posture of agencies must be seen against the characteristics of the market.

MARKET CHARACTERISTICS

Agencies deal primarily in the transfer of used, as opposed to new, houses

– although in the latter case agents are often instructed by builders to handle the transaction. The factors which determine their market are varied and complex but an increased disposition to move because of 'trading up' or 'trading down', a desire for house ownership at all, a reduction in the proportion of public housing, an increase in the housing stock, rises in people's disposable incomes, and the availability of mortgages are perhaps the most significant. It should be noted that the agent has extremely little influence over these basic determining factors. Indeed, the relevant factors for the agent are firstly, whether a potential vendor wishes to instruct an agent or to conduct the transaction on a DIY basis and if the former, what are the determinants of the choice of agent, and secondly, the influencing of buyers.

The more macro factors are indirectly relevant, however, since they define the aggregate turnover of the property market which by definition must be apportioned between the various parties. The cyclical nature of the economy and its effects on the turnover and profitability of agencies are important influences on the viability of individual agencies. For although it is a relatively easy 'industry' to enter, requiring initially low capital investment, (perhaps) little formal experience (as a non-professional) the cyclical pattern may prove disastrous if reserves are inadequate and the local competitive capability is not sufficiently attractive to vendors.

The market is predominantly composed of local transfers – although some areas for specific reasons or at particular times have net 'immigration' or 'emigration' due to such varied influences as industrial development, or a favourable retirement location. A consequence of the fact that most buyers are local is that the average vendor will (typically) have had experience himself of local agents when he bought his house and this might be expected to be a prime influence on his subsequent choice of agent for positive or perhaps negative reasons. This contact is the more important because estate agency as a service would appear to be an appropriate example of the *experience good*, whose characteristics can only be discerned in use rather than by prior inspection or through the accounts of others.

Those who have experienced contact with estate agents either as buyer or as a previous seller comprise a different segment from the novice house seller – who perhaps bought initially from a house builder or inherited his house – who may be presumed to be less informed of what is involved. Of course, the greater the period since a previous transaction so the information requirements of the two groups become less distinct. There are analagous segments in the case of buyers – those who are experienced in dealing with agents and the other professionals (usually) involved in a house transaction – and those who have perhaps little idea of what a contemplated house transaction would involve. Indeed, the experienced buyer might have a limited recall of the issues too, given that the average interval between moves is five to seven years.

There may be many descriptive bases to segments but a priori certain socio-economic, demographic and experiential factors would seem to be important.[6] Further examples in the current context are those electing to move compared to those who, for some reason, are compelled to sell and accordingly may have less time and discretion in the many decisions involved. Qualitative differences in the search procedure are demonstrated between the local and distance mover. It is not only the case that different people are in the market for different types of property, but that their needs in the process which lead to the acquisition and/or the disposal of property are equally varied. The strategy of market segmentation entails a different marketing approach to any identified and economically viable segments. Only coincidentally can substantially different consumer needs be met by a standardised approach.

In purely marketing terms the agent is *the* intermediary between buyers and sellers. Cognisance only of the institutional fact that he is instructed by the vendor (who pays his fee for selling the house) is to limit the scope for the agent's contribution in the role of intermediary. Clearly the art of selling involves a sensitivity to the needs of the buyer and it is by the (only recent) cases of seven-day, or at least, weekend opening and the availability of evening consultations that the agency business is attempting to meet some of the long-standing requirements of buyers in new ways (although there are typically still restrictions on opening on bank holidays). The process is taken to a limit when for a fee (one per cent of the eventual purchase price – half that for selling [*The Times,* 1984a]) some agents will act for the buyer in finding a property to match a particular specification. There is, then, a continuum between the agent acting exclusively for the vendor – with perhaps little regard to the buyer per se, and acting exclusively for the buyer – a continuum which defines a considerable marketing opportunity.

Subsequently this potential will be discussed but it is now instructive to examine the existing performance of agents as seen by consumers.

MARKETING PERFORMANCE

A number of surveys bearing in various degrees on consumer experiences and opinion of agents in house transactions – often in a wider concern with housing research – have recently been conducted.[7] It is important to realise that in marketing terms it is the public's perception of estate agents' performance and their 'image' rather than their 'reality' in fully documented objective terms, which is the basis of an assessment. Moreover, the investigation of such perceptions and their basis in consumer experience is fraught with many problems of representativeness and interpretation, for example, recorded shortcomings can be the result of unrealistic expectations, atypical events or inappropriate attribution to agents. Such considerations qualify the broad picture as available from the Price Commission/BMRB study from which the following facts emerge.[8]

For Vendors

- nearly two-thirds of sellers obtain their expected price through agents;
- only half of buyers sent through agents were 'serious';
- just over half thought the agents' description of their property was 'very accurate' (39 per cent 'quite accurate');
- 86 per cent had terms of business explained to them but only 11 per cent were offered a choice of terms;
- the proportion experiencing a longer time than expected before sale (33 per cent) approximates those who experienced less time (38 per cent);
- three-quarters were very/quite satisfied on agent's sales efforts, advice on price, effort after offer and overall services;
- 45 per cent were very/quite satisfied that the service was value for money;
- 60 per cent were very/quite likely to use an agent on next sale.

For Buyers

- one in three thought agents had: i) offered choice of properties, implying a good property for the money; ii) offered convenience in negotiation.
- about half thought they contributed to speed in finding a property;
- three-quarters thought property descriptions were very/quite accurate (20 per cent thought they were inaccurate);
- one-third had experienced offers falling though;
- about one in seven obtained services not related to property information from agents, for example, introductions to solicitors, mortgagers and surveyors;
- three-quarters were very/quite likely to use agents in the buying process in future.

A qualitative impression of the agent's role and contribution to the house transacting process requires a more detailed understanding of the time and effort that the agent 'saves' both buyers and sellers. It is in this regard that the quality of information/advice/liaison is important in preventing unproductive effort but perhaps more significantly in bringing the transactor to a more realistic appreciation of the prevailing circumstances. There are two aspects here. The role of the intermediary in reducing transaction costs for all parties is well established and is explicable, at its simplest, in terms of a physical reduction in communication linkages. The qualitative aspect is infinitely more complicated; one aspect that has received some academic attention is the role of the agent as a 'gatekeeper', matching people to areas so that there is social compatibility. For a discussion and further references see Williams [1976: 51–61].

House-moving is in itself a cause of stress but it typically coincides or is caused by other stress-inducing changes in people's lives [*Housing Research Foundation*, 1981: 21]. This is exemplified by the case of the first-time buyer where the coincidental event may be marriage and setting up a home for the first time. For others the move may be prompted by extension/contraction of the family or by the occasion of a new/lost job. In all these instances the physical and mental effort expended in the house transaction, either buying or selling, is unlikely to be pleasurable in itself (at least if the process is attenuated).[9] Research shows that the average time of search by buyers approximates seven months, with 27 houses being viewed from the outside and 10 from the inside. There is, moreover, a considerable degree of compromise typically to be achieved both between the individual and his aspirations and (typically) between the partners/participants in the decision making concerning the house.[10] Such compromises contribute to stress even to the extent that moves are taken to avert possible conflict.

Against this background it is significant that the Price Commission/BMRB study found agreement by buyers and sellers to the following statements.

	Agreed	*Don't know*
'The authorities should do more to provide advice'	73%	8%
'Buying is so difficult that everyone needs professional advice'	74%	4%

Indirect evidence that estate agents are not perceived as contributing significantly to this process of stress reduction – in addition to the proposed repeat usage of estate agents given above – is given by the proportions answering to the statements that 'the best way to buy is DIY' and 'estate agents are unnecessary in buying' are 44 per cent and 36 per cent respectively with 'Don't knows' seven per cent in both cases [Price Commission, 1979: 61].

Another potent source of stress is the delay consequent on an offer being accepted but prior to the exchange of contracts, final completion and moving in. The stress arising from such delay may be aggravated by uncertainties as to the successful outcome of this process. This is compounded by the circumstances of the so-called housing chain where a set of transactions involving many houses/people are mutually dependent, or where the post-offer inspection/surveying of a property reactivates the process of negotiations or searches unearth information material to a decision to buy. Agents, as intermediaries, are variously involved in such circumstances.

The stress that may cumulate as a result of being frustrated in chain situations, having offers fall through, the vicissitudes of various negotiations and the process of transacting in general may be supposed contributary reasons for the level of dissatisfaction that some people have with the house eventually bought. To isolate the effects of stress concerning a house move from any deficiencies in general decision making is obviously difficult and the perception of the degree of stress and how it affects households may be expected to vary widely as well (one survey found four per cent advising categorically 'do not move' [*Which?*, 1979]; in another five per cent contemplate moving again within a year, their dissatisfaction with the house recently bought overriding the adverse features of a move [Alliance Building Society, 1978]). Dissatisfaction with a house typically correlates with a more intensive search where many properties are viewed in a shorter period of time compared with those who purchased more successfully.

Another major aspect of market performance concerns the competitive structure of the industry and whether the conduct of agencies is in the public interest. This aspect may be condensed into a consideration of the prices charged and the services given and whether they represent value for money. [Monopolies Commission, 1969, and Price Commission, 1979]. These enquiries into prices have been supplemented by requirements that associations of estate agents' (usually local) agreements are registered with the Office of Fair Trading and that practice conforms with the Estate Agents Act 1979. This process of investigation, with the potential for rationalisation and improvement, has more recently continued with the establishment by the Attorney General of a committee (in response to the withdrawal of Austin Mitchell's House-buyers' Bill) to not only investigate the scope for non-solicitor conveyancing but also of the '... scope for simplifying conveyancing practice and procedure and *other matters* concerning the simplification of house purchase' [*Building Society News*, 1984]. Also a consultation paper is due shortly on the possibilities that other organisations besides banks and building societies could undertake conveyancing.

The market research evidence reviewed above shows some concern by a significant proportion of vendors with the value for money given by estate agents especially in the case of relatively expensive properties sold in a short space of time (where the ad valorem system has its apparently most undesirable features). There has also been concern about the lack of competition amongst local agencies although, as a consequence of the Monopolies Commission's recommendations, competition has significantly increased and there is variability in the structure of scale fees and in their implementation.

MARKETING POTENTIAL

The role of professional associations in maintaining a particular (and general) mode of conduct of estate agency has been considerable and their influence has affected all aspects of the agents' marketing mix from service definition to promotion. This in turn has determined the structure and degree of (intra-channel) competition amongst agencies, but the marketing task confronting estate agencies may be defined not only in intra-channel terms but also in inter-channel terms where alternative organisations comprise the competition. Moreover, in competing for custom any tendency for vendors to 'do it themselves' must also be addressed.

The intra-channel task may be divided into various market segments which at least, in principle, exhibit different consumer needs and therefore present different marketing opportunities. Taking a systems view, people's perception of the transaction may involve considerations of time, information, finance and risk [Fisk, 1967]. Potentially, it is the agent's role as an intermediary to provide services which meet these needs, but whether it is economic and/or practicable to treat such segments in different ways depends on the costs involved in relation to the substantiveness of the segments and the ease with which the various segments may be identified.

There is currently evidence that marketing activity in the generic field of estate agency is showing a greater recognition of the potentiality of market segmentation. The following examples are illustrative. First, it has long been the case that a few agents have operated on a national/up-market/prestigious/expensive property segment in contrast to the generality of agents who are local or regional and deal with the whole spectrum of property and client types. Second, the particular needs of the business mover and his employer may now be met. The recognition by some organisations that their staff and their families should have the potentially undesirable transactional consequences of their forced moves mitigated to some degree has led to the organisation of package deals which facilitate a quicker, smoother and certain move. This relocation scheme, in essence, enables the employee to sell his house instantly (subject to his acceptance of independent valuations) and thereby to finance his new purchase. This enables the employee to cost his uncertainties and stress, in a house sale, as the difference between his valuation of the property and that potentially advanced to him. It is one way of reducing the effects of the buying chain [*Sunday Times*, 1984a]. Third, for the inter-area distance mover the advent of computer technology facilitating the presentation of property information by Viewdata transmissions. Thus the local agent in such a participating network – for instance, National Homes Network [*Financial Times*, 1983] can contribute to the successful purchase in another area through a linked office.

The second case differs from the others above because it explicitly involves a financing operation, whereas the others are confined to specialisation in information. The attraction of specialising in the provision of property information, purely as an intermediary without offering additional services, has been noted by a variety of organisations some of which have been established to exploit the perceived gap in the market (so-called property shops) whilst others have merely had to adapt. Thus in the cases of High Street retailers and department stores the substantial customer flows generated by other goods and services and their prime locations confer economic advantages which they are prepared to pass on to clients in the form of flat rate fees which significantly undercut existing scale fees of estate agencies. Firms experimenting on various lines include Debenhams [*The Times*, 1984a], who are operating on their own account and Woolworths [*The Times*, 1984b], who are letting space on a concessionary basis. Another modification of the principle of using customer flow involves the display of property information at newsagents' premises – using free-standing boards, again for a flat fee [*Sunday Times*, 1984c].

The linking of an information service with financial benefits in a different form is provided to those with a common mortgager (for example, the Abbey National Property Service). Participating estate agents are able to offer reductions on their usual fees and associated survey, legal and mortgage arrangements fees are also reduced on transfer of properties amongst the mortgagees. The computerised records of large financial institutions facilitate such 'internal' transfers with obvious benefits to both buyers and sellers.

The computing matching facility need not be linked with a financial institution; however, there are a variety of specialised firms offering an information service alone. Another recent development is the move by one such firm, in conjunction with conveyancing expertise, to arrange the valuation of the house for mortgage purposes, check title, carry out searches and generally facilitate the transaction as soon as the property is on its list (for a flat fee). This eases the purchase formalities when a vendor is found and obviates, in the case of a deal falling through, the repeat of the process by the new buyer, thus significantly reducing time, effort and expense [*Sunday Times*, 1984b].

These evolving alternatives in the house transacting process involve existing estate agents to different degrees, so they demonstrate both inter- and intra-channel competitive features. Amongst agencies themselves, structural changes with marketing implications are under way, in part, as a response to the competitive pressures briefly described above, but also in an attempt to pre-empt further incursions into their traditional domain. There is an apparent tendency for estate agency chains to increase in size but this does not necessarily have any direct advantages for consumers unless additional services are forthcoming, although size alone and/or a national identify may contribute to reduce the risk that consumers may perceive in the choice of agent. However, the local reputation has traditionally been important and in recognition of this some chains, despite a unified ownership, have retained the local name of their component offices, for example, Lloyds Bank Black Horse Agencies – and so do such franchise operations as Property World.

Some existing agents are responding to the competitive threat, most manifest on price/value considerations, by offering discounted fees to affiliated members of horizontal marketing organisations (for example, Leicestercard for those investors in Leicester Building Society), whilst others extend money-saving vouchers to their clients (both buyers and sellers) [*The Times*, 1983a]. Price promotions may be supposed influential in local choice, where reputation and other considerations relating to competence and probity are equal, but in themselves are unlikely to affect the decision of the intending DIY vendor who probably will still consider the charge for agency services too great relative to the alternatives. Price promotions, however, are not widespread. Existing agencies are maintaining their historic aversion to overt price competition preferring instead various forms of competition in service offerings. This is most noticeable in terms of the opening hours and general availability of estate agents.

Intra-channel competition – such as exists – is conducted on a relatively narrow front with location and display features to the fore. The lack of more innovative promotional efforts is, however, explicable in terms of market and consumer characteristics. The numbers conceivably in the market for an estate agent, though great in relation to those potentially available to a particular agency, are absolutely small (about one to one-and-a-half million per annum, which is reduced by the DIY segment of perhaps 30 per cent). Moreover, the degree of consumer involvement with estate agency selection, especially prior to the event, is likely to be low, so for an advertising campaign, for instance, to have a significant impact by providing information when the client is responsive, it would need to be sustained and, therefore, relatively expensive. Conventional thinking holds that television is the medium which has the greatest potential impact; it may be more cost-effective too in reaching a large population. For estate agency both market and media properties are not favourable. The demographic characteristics of home buyers do not correspond to the profile of 'heavy' commercial television watchers and providing opportunities to receive the (or any) message to a largely inappropriate audience reduces its cost effectiveness in terms of any realisation – communication for its own sake is not the objective. Moreover, the reasons that justify extensive television campaigns for branded, fast-moving consumer goods (which predominate in that medium) are to be found not only in the initial information provision phases – which are of strictly limited relevance to repeat buyers – but as a means of offering reassurance and reminders of satisfaction received. There is in the estate agency product little that commends it in *positive* terms; its basic utility stems from the avoidance of negatives – undue time, inconvenience and risk – which may in the event be incapable of delivery. The operation of post-purchase dissonance which frequently prompts a consumer to seek justification for his actions, particularly in the cases of relatively large expenditures, is recognised by advertisers in their provision of reasons to justify purchase and thus they provide the means by which the consumer is reassured.[11] Such messages are particularly appropriate when *tangible* benefits are to be seen and the consumer's dissonance is in terms of their perceived relative values, hence appeals to the status connotations of expensive goods or allusions to quality. Estate agency services, however, are commonly perceived to be expensive but there is generally no scope for social cachet in incurring their fees. The reassurance objective, if appropriate to assuage doubts about the value of agency services for those who have employed them, may be of limited value to the advertiser because of the typically long elapse of time before the recipient is likely to move again. There is some justification, however, in the case of the frequent mover segment, but this is small and mainly restricted to business movers – with the consequence that it involves inter-area moves thereby reducing its relevance to any but large national claims. Perhaps for this reason, despite the generally adverse factors associated with national television promotion, as shown above, there has been some experimentation with such an approach by National Homes Network [*National Homes Network News*, 1982]. Significantly national press advertising has not (as yet) been a feature of estate agency marketing.

To the extent that existing agencies are viewed primarily as information intermediaries by both their customers and the new competitors it is apparent that their existing scale fees are vulnerable to significant undercutting by alternative retailing approaches – at least in urban, populous situations. Although there is scope for an expansion of their role as financial intermediaries this is likely to be pre-empted by the clearing banks and/or the larger building societies both of which have the retail premises, large computer systems and 'captive' clients. Indeed the possibility of their further combining the information intermediary and financial intermediary/principal roles is probably the greatest threat to existing agencies.

There is, however, their area of distinctive competence [Blois, 1983: 251], the agents' core role as an expert in property – assessment, surveying, valuation, planning and building aspects – and given the complexities involved a further counselling role in the provision of *independent* advice/information on the whole transaction. As a true intermediary this kind of service is of value to buyer, seller, mortgager, insurer and the various public (service) authorities. This role may in some respects impinge on the traditional spheres of other professions, for example, architects and solicitors. Moreover, the agent can still offer as a separate service expertise in buying and selling in ways that significantly extend the role of information intermediary.

In these professional roles there is a continuing economic justification for the existence of the agent, but his marketing task is to organise, communicate and provide his service in ways appropriate to client needs (both institutional and individual) at prices they are both willing to pay and which give perceived value. This will inevitably require a sensitivity to heterogeneous market conditions and the adoption of the strategy of market segmentation. At present there may be some conflict between the requirements of professional uniformity – conceived in a non-marketing environment – but marketing and professionalism are not necessarily incompatible.

CONCLUSIONS

In many ways the marketing of the estate agency service is a challenging task exacerbated by an increasingly changing context. The historic marketing strategy of offering a broadly defined service consisting of information, and in some cases, professional expertise to the general house-moving public with little price competition, promotion and limited distribution has become increasingly vulnerable to both intra- and inter-channel influences. Increasing size of agency chains, to the extent that these can achieve cost-reducing efficiencies and offer a better service within existing parameters, will threaten the smaller agencies for they cannot achieve the economies of scale in management, advertising, central services and visibility. This concentration, however, is logically little more than a rationalisation of existing structures and procedures.

A more significant development, with greater long-term consequences, is the increasing separation of information provision from the professional services associated with housing matters. Thus the agent's traditional product is being unscrambled and parts of it offered at significantly lower charges and increasingly by established marketing organisations with substantially greater resources than existing agencies. The coupling of information provision, separately or in combination with financial and legal services, holds the prospect of profound structural change in estate agency as currently ordered. These structural changes wrought by economies of organisation and technique will themselves be limited and may polarise between urban and rural areas, although electronic information technology may well reduce the significance of distance and space. Despite these potential changes and the simplification of the process of house-transacting the functions of buying and selling still remain. Economic logic may justify the role of an independent specialist intermediary in this regard and the heterogeneity of property further justifies a place for specialist knowledge and expertise. In this sense the role of the agent – possibly in a new guise – is assured, but a logical justification alone is insufficient. Its efficacy must be demonstrated to a possibly sceptical public and, above all, the service must offer value for money which is universally perceived. This is indeed a marketing challenge.

NOTES

1. Clive Thornton when Chief General Manager of the Abbey National Building Society as quoted in Murray [1982: 27].
2. Further discussion of these alternatives and a more detailed account of marketing and services is available in Foxall [1983: 279–95].
3. For a wide ranging discussion of the relationship between the context and the mix with an emphasis on legal aspects and competition policy see Driver [1983: 108–25].
4. Extensive research on a variety of housing matters is reported in six reports by the Alliance Building Society Housing Research Unit, 1978.
5. A summary of the structure and distribution of the scales is available in Price

Commission [1979: Ch. 6 and 7].

6. For an account of the potentiality, problems, techniques and examples of market segmentation see Wind [1978: 317–37].
7. See, for example, *Which?*, April 1984 updating *Which?*, 1979; also 'Britain on the Move' for Polycell Products referred to in *The Guardian* [1984]; A Mintel survey referred to in *Sunday Times* [1984a] and a MORI poll conducted for Black Horse Agencies referred to in *Accessability* [1984: 22–5].
8. British Market Research Bureau Study for the Price Commission reported in Price Commission [1979].
9. It should be pointed out that there are many possible hypotheses which may be appropriate for different categories of people and for people at different times. Hypotheses which would involve fundamentally diverse concepts, for example, attitudes, personality traits, socio-economic and demographic determinants and be couched in different disciplinary terms, for example, psychological, economic and sociological. Our use of stress here is pragmatic – an insight into the alternatives is provided by review texts of consumer behaviour, for example, Engel, Blackwell and Kollatt [1978].
10. Survey evidence to this effect is contained in 'Aspirations and Achievements in House Buying', Alliance Building Society Housing Research Unit [1978], especially p. 44. For academic research on decision making see Park [1982].
11. The interrelationships between hypotheses of consumer behaviour, advertising content and the characteristics of particular audiences are imperfectly understood. For a descriptive account see, for instance, De Losier [1976]: an analytical discussion is available in Driver and Foxall [1984: Ch. 4 and 5].

REFERENCES

Accessability, 1984, Spring, No. 13, Lloyds Bank plc.

Reports, Alliance Building Society Housing Research Unit, 1978, Department of Psychology, University of Surrey:

Report 1: 'House Buying Chains';
Report 2: 'Purchasers Options of House Buying';
Report 3: 'Descriptive Statistics on House Buying';
Report 4: 'Searching for and Buying a House';
Report 5: 'Buying for the First Time';
Report 6: 'Aspirations and Achievements in House Buying'.

Blois, K.J., 1983, 'The Structure of Service Firms and their Marketing Policies', *Strategic Management Journal*, Vol. 4.

Building Society News, 1984, Vol. 4, No. 3.

De Losier, M.W., 1976, *The Marketing Communications Process*, New York: McGraw Hill.

Driver, J.C., 1983, 'For P's in a Context not a Pod', in M. Christopher, M. McDonald, and A. Rushton, *Back to Basics: The 4 Ps Revisited*, Cranfield.

Driver, J.C., and G.R. Foxall, 1984, *Advertising Policy and Practice*, London: Holt, Rinehart and Winston; New York: St. Martin's Press.

Engel, J.F., Blackwell, R.D., and D.T. Kollatt, 1978, *Consumer Behaviour*, 3rd ed., Hindsdale, Illinois: Dryden.

Estates Gazette, 1984, 'Opinion: Seal of Approval', Vol. 269, 24 March.

Financial Times, 1983, 21 October.

Fisk, G., 1967, *Marketing Systems*, New York: Harper and Row.

Foxall, G.R., 1983, 'Can the Public Sector Provision of Leisure Services be Customer Oriented?', *The Services Industries Journal*, Vol. 3, No. 3.

The Guardian, 1984, 21 April.

Housing Research Foundation, 1981, *Why Now? The Motivations for House Purchase*.

Monopolies Commission, 1969, *Estate Agents*, London: HMSO.

Murray, L., 1982, 'Where Estate Agents Miss the Point of Sales', *Marketing Week*, 5 March.
National Home Network News, 1982, Vol. 1, No. 5.
Park, C.W., 1982, 'Joint Decisions in Home Purchasing: A Muddling Through Process', *Journal of Consumer Research*, Vol. 9, No. 2.
Price Commission, 1979, *Charges, Costs and Margins of Estate Agents*, Cmnd. 7649, London: HMSO.
The Sunday Times, 1984a, 29 April.
The Sunday Times, 1984b, 6 May.
The Sunday Times, 1984c, 13 May.
The Times, 1983, 9 March.
The Times, 1984a, 22 February.
The Times, 1984b, 1 May.
The Times, 1984c, 11 May.
Which?, 1979, 'Moving Home', May, Consumers Association.
Which?, 1984, 'Estates Agents', April, Consumers Association.
Williams, P., 1976, 'The Role of Financial Institutions and Estate Agents in the Private Housing Market: A General Introduction', Centre of Urban and Regional Studies, Working Paper, No. 39.
Wind, Y., 1978, 'Issues and Advances in Segmentation Research', *Journal of Marketing Research*, Vol. 15, August.

Advertising and the Professions

by

Stanley Siebert*

This article aims to assess the consequences for prices and consumer protection of permitting professional advertising. The need to protect consumers given their lack of knowledge in the buying of professional services is seen as explaining the role of professional self-regulation particularly with respect to entry standards. But the case is not so strong for advertising restrictions, and it is shown that there are logical reasons to expect such restrictions to raise fees without much protecting the consumer. Empirical studies are surveyed confirming the favourable effect of advertising on prices. The conclusion reached is that specific advertising of fees and specialism would not necessarily be costly to monitor and would bring benefits in terms of increased price competition.

INTRODUCTION

Some occupational groups are composed of persons with advanced training in a systematic body of knowledge which they sell to individual members of the public. These occupations are sometimes called the 'learned professions' or the 'self-regulating professions'. Craftsmen are not professionals in this sense, because their body of knowledge is not complex, nor are academics since they do not in general have individual clients. The classic examples of the self-regulating professions are the doctors and lawyers, but there are other groups such as architects and accountants which also meet the definition. A list of such professions is given in Table 1.

The self-regulating profession generally has a statutory monopoly of providing its particular services (for example, only solicitors certified by the Law Society can issue a writ). Typically it lays down strict entry qualifications including the passing of an examination set by the profession (see Table 1). The typical profession also restricts members' business decisions, for example, by fixing common fee scales, banning advertising, and banning certain forms of business organisation

* I am grateful to S.C. Littlechild for comments on an earlier draft but retain responsibility for errors and omissions.

TABLE 1
THE MAIN SELF-REGULATING PROFESSIONS

	Date of Registration[a]	Date Examinations Initiated	Number of Advertising Restrictions[c]	Number of Practitioners (000)
Barristers	No statute; rights date from fourteenth century	Pupillage fees only until 1853; compulsory examination 1872	8	4
Solicitors	1729 (England and Wales)	1836/7; taken over by the Law Society in 1877	14	27
Stock Exchange	1802	1971	3	3
Pharmacists	1852	1925	7	30
Medical Practitioners	1858 (General Medical Council)	1858; Royal College of Physicians, sixteenth century	10	119
Dentists	1878	1844	10	17
Patent Agents	1888	1889	7	1
Midwives	1902	1902	n.a.	102
Architects	1931	1863	10	22
Accountants	b	1880	10	87
Surveyors	n.a.	1881 (Royal Institute of Chartered Surveyors)	11	78
Veterinary Surgeons	1844	1844	10	8
Opticians	1958	1896 (British Optical Association)	9	8

Notes

(a) Registration denotes state licensing of practitioners generally involving the fulfilment of tests of competence to standards set by the registering authority, and the requirement to observe certain standards of practice after registration.

(b) Accountants are not registered, but by the Companies Act only members of certain associations are allowed to audit accounts of incorporated companies.

(c) As identified by the Monopolies and Mergers Commission [1970: Appendix 19].

(solicitors cannot share fees with non-solicitors; barristers cannot form partnerships).

The purposes and effects of the activities of the self-regulating professions are disputed. Control of entry and restrictions on business activity are defended as protecting the consumer by reducing the risk of poor quality service. Those services which the consumer cannot easily evaluate and consequently where the vendor decides largely what the buyer buys can, of their very nature, be said to require more consumer protection than unrestricted competition and *caveat emptor* provides. It might be for this reason that we observe that the professions of medicine and law, for example, in all countries have restrictions on advertising [Monopolies and Mergers Commission (MMC), 1976, Apppendix 1]. On the other hand, some of the activities of the professions might have a more selfish justification. The effect of restricting price competition and other competition between members might raise the price of the service and so improve the average pay and conditions of the members.

In this paper we focus on professional activities with respect to advertising. The aim is to investigate the effects of restricting advertising on the price and quality of professional services.[1] This is an area of current policy interest. For example, in December 1983, an amendment to the Opticians' Act of 1958 was published which required that the opticians lift their advertising restrictions. Moreover, in the United States the Supreme Court has deemed some advertising restrictions as being contrary to the First Amendment, which protects the right to freedom of speech and of the press. Accountants, lawyers, doctors, dentists, pharmacists in America are all therefore having to consider permitting advertising. In the next section some arguments for and against professional advertising are discussed. The following section reviews the main empirical studies. The article concludes with a discussion of recent legislative changes in Britain and America.

THEORETICAL ISSUES

Much of the argument about advertising revolves around issues of consumer protection. Let us first consider how the nature of professional services causes special problems for consumer decision making, then assess the role of advertising.

The Nature of Professional Services

Where the quality of goods can be assessed, and where there is competition among producers a firm cannot gain sales by making fraudulent claims. Rivals will expose these claims and consumers can, by assumption, judge the evidence. In such a market consumers will have the quality of service they choose at a price that reflects the least cost method of production. Firms will adopt higher standards of product (or of care) to the extent these bring about an increase in revenue greater than the cost of the improvements. This is because higher prices can be charged for higher quality (or safety). There are also legal sanctions: the courts attempt to hold firms liable for product malfunctions, the expected loss of which is greater than their expense of prevention [Posner, 1977: 119]. However, in the market for professional services quality is very difficult to assess. The client knows much less about the commodity being bought, and how much of it to buy, than does the vendor.

The consumer's ignorance is extensive not only as a consequence of the typical profession's arcane body of knowledge. It is also a consequence of the fact that the service is often highly personalised (making it difficult for one client to compare his treatment with another), and infrequently bought (thus learning is slow). Moreover, what 'would have' happened if the advice had not been followed, or if different advice had been followed, is hard to determine. Professional services (like repairs) have effects which are difficult to assess even by experts, let alone laymen.

Remedies do develop in markets in which consumers find product quality difficult to assess, but these remedies tend to be inapplicable to professional service markets. Some of these remedies result from the fact that it pays buyers and sellers to come to an arrangement whereby sellers assume liability for faults, for example, with a guarantee. However, this is not appropriate in the case of professional services because of the indefinite nature of what is promised, and the expense of proving fault.

An analogous way of shifting liability to the seller is the action for damages. However, this method of deterring losses is 'excessively costly and cumbersome' [Veljanovski and Whelan, 1983: 703] for the same reason as the guarantee method, the difficulty of proving fault. Another remedy is to separate diagnosis of a problem from treatment as when, for example, an insurance broker provides independent advice on the wares of insurance companies. This acts as a check on the supply of unnecessary service. However, in the case of professional services it is generally cheaper to have diagnosis and treatment carried out at the same time (although admittedly second opinions can be obtained, at a price). Still another remedy is the building up of a reputation for quality with the use of brand names or franchising. Although a franchising plan has recently been put forward for dentists [McIntyre and Weinrauch, 1981], one difficulty with this type of remedy is that it falls foul of professional ethical restrictions such as restrictions on splitting fees with non-professionals.

Insurance can in principle also reduce consumer uncertainty, but there are problems again in the professional services area. While insurance can reduce consumer uncertainty arising from the unpredictability of expenditures for professional advice, it is more difficult to shift the burden of uncertainty due to possible failure to benefit from advice because of the problem of defining such failure. In medicine the difficulties for insurance of adverse selection and moral hazard have been described by Arrow [1963]. These difficulties are presumably even greater in the legal field (that is, legal insurance would lead to litigation), which explains why consumer legal insurance is not widespread.

Certain institutions based on professional self-regulation have nevertheless developed which protect the consumer. Most important, the system of professional examinations certifies minimum levels of competence. All professions appoint a body which oversees standards of competence and conduct. This system reduces uncertainty over quality for the consumer. (Admittedly it is also necessary to explain why the public typically do not have the option of using unqualified practitioners at their own risk. This is another matter, but it can occur – for example, with surveyors.)

Second, there is the 'client relationship'. Trust and personal ties are emphasised in professional ethics. Personal recommendations are the chief method of competition. Stable ties themselves protect the client because the expectation of future business ('goodwill') encourages the practitioner to satisfy the client rather than manipulate him [see Darby and Karni, 1973]. Friendship, or acquaintanceship, is itself a protection. Admittedly in large towns, and for newcomers to an area, the reputation of the various practitioners will not be well known, so this protection is weaker. But the initial cheap (or free) consultation allows an acquaintance to be struck up if the parties desire.

Third, to protect the consumer there are rules regulating business practices such as the limitations on advertising which we now consider in detail. What our discussion up to this point has shown is that special entry and marketing requirements are inevitable given the nature of professional services.

Advertising Restrictions – The Arguments

Advertising restrictions in the self-regulating professions are wide-ranging and detailed. The Monopolies and Mergers Commission has identified 16 categories of restriction, that is, rules regulating: the supplanting or undercutting of colleagues; general advertising; the size of nameplates; the type of stationery; the type of premises; social contacts; the use of agents; direct mailing; advertising for staff or change of address; 'card' advertising; directories; advertising for clients; advertising by clients; outdoor advertising; broadcasting [MCC, 1970: Appendix 19]. Professions generally have a detailed code covering most of these subjects minutely, with a disciplinary committee to enforce the code. The Law Society has rules under 14 of the headings, the opticians under eight, the dentists under 10, as shown in Table 1. Similar behaviour occurs in other countries.

Many arguments have been advanced to explain these rules. It is convenient to identify four sub-headings for clarity of discussion: a) the misleading nature of professional service advertising; b) the effects of advertising on 'professionalism'; c) the effects of advertising on quality; and d) effects of advertising on price and industry structure.

(a) The misleading nature of professional service advertising: The following statement by the Law Society emphasises mainly this point:

> The relationship between solicitor and client is based on trust. The client should have the right to select his solicitor freed from any outside pressure. Professional skill can seldom be evaluated by the client. The practice of 'shopping around', which may save money or yield improved quality in the case of commercial products, is of no relevance when professional services are sought. Legal services are rendered to an individual, they are not 'impersonal' like the supply of a commodity through a retailer. Advertising can have little or no effect upon the supply of the service, since it does not increase the

> number of solicitors or change the system so that more clients can be 'served' more rapidly. To permit advertising would be to increase the cost of legal services to the public, since the cost of advertising, which is heavy, would have to be passed on to the client. To permit individual solicitors or firms to advertise would favour the rich and well-established firms at the expense of the small and newly established, and thus entry into and establishment in the profession would become harder [MMC, 1976a: 1vii].

Analysing the above statement, the main point seems to be that the professional service is so unstandardised, so personal, that there is nothing to advertise except the bare fact of a practitioner's existence. A professional has no wares to display. To say anything about the available services would be speculation potentially more harmful than secrecy. In what this harm consists we are not told specifically. According to the Canadian Bar Association the harm is that any advertising could 'arouse unattainable hopes and expectations resulting in the distrust of legal institutions and lawyers' [MMC, 1976a: xv]. Any information except that tailored to the specific case would be misleading. On this view it seems that there is no way of judging between practitioners. Moreover, such an important thing as specialism can only be appraised from within the profession; fields of interest cannot be advertised without being misleading. The United States Supreme Court has said that:

> Physicians and lawyers, for example, do not disperse standardised products; they render professional *services* of almost infinite variety and nature, with the consequent enhanced possibility for confusion and deception if they were to undertake certain kinds of advertising (Virginia Pharmacy Board v. Virginia Consumer Council [1976], cited [Supreme Court, 1977: 824, note 17]).

Or again, as Chief Justice Burger has said, 'In the context of legal services, [such] incomplete information could be worse than no information at all. It could become a trap for the unwary' [Supreme Court, 1977: 838].

To the argument that advertising of professional services is inherently misleading, we might respond firstly that not *all* advertising need be misleading. There are some relatively standardised services such as uncontested divorces, or routine medical check-ups, or a practitioner's hourly charge. Admittedly there is a problem of deciding what is 'routine', and also the fact that some people will think they have a routine problem which turns out in fact to be complicated. Nevertheless, there is such a thing as a routine service.

Second, deceptive or misleading advertising could be punished (via liability for damages) or prevented (by some regulatory body). The difficulty with the first approach is that errors in judicial assessment of the fact of an advertisement being misleading, or the extent of the injury attributable to it, could be too great to make liability much of a deterrent.

The other possibility is regulation by some body such as the Advertising Standards Authority advised by the relevant profession. Such a regulatory body would be expensive, and would face similar problems to the courts in defining the boundary between misleading and non-misleading advertising.

A case for society benefiting from a blanket restriction on advertising, that is, for allowing one practitioner to stop advertising by another, could be made to rest on the expense of distinguishing between informative and deceptive advertising. It might well be that the costs of making such a distinction are high enough, relative to the benefits, to justify allowing a complete ban. A complete ban is more economical (simpler) on this view. On the other hand, if we were to believe that the public were sophisticated enough to realise the limitations of advertising, and if deceived could bring the offender to book, the decision to advertise or not would be a matter for the individual practitioner to decide. Individual remedies rather than one blanket remedy would then suffice. Society seems to be behaving 'as if' a blanket ban is more efficient than individual remedies.

(b) The effects of advertising on professionalism: Professions have a certain 'dignity' which it has been contended would be infringed by the commercialisation of advertising (see the Code of Ethics of the International Bar Association [MMC, 1976: iii]). Arrow has argued, in connection with physicians' advertising restrictions, that since medical services are so hard for the consumer to evaluate the practitioner has to be given a 'social obligation' to live up to his position of trust [1963: 965]. He has, as it were, to be put on his honour. Arrow pointed to psychology as playing a part in this. He said: 'As a signal to the buyer of his intentions to act as thoroughly on the buyer's behalf as possible, the physician avoids the obvious stigmata of profit maximising. Purely arm's length bargaining behaviour would be incompatible, not logically, but surely psychologically, with trust relations' [1963: 965]. Thus if the practitioner avoids the 'obvious stigmata of profit maximisation' he can build up the client's trust. As we have seen, this might be advantageous for the client in that the practitioner has more goodwill to lose and so has an incentive to take more care. (It is advantageous for the practitioner, too, because the client is less likely to move to a competitor.) A certain 'ceremony' in the relations between practitioner and client assists in the building up of a personal tie. Honourable behaviour is thereby encouraged.

It is easier to accept that professional dignity is a good course for the individual practitioner to follow than that it justifies preventing a practitioner advertising if he wants to. Does a given practitioner losing 'dignity' have affects beyond his practice? True, the effect of more commercial behaviour might be more fraud. The matter would end there if the consumer had his own remedies, but it is generally thought that these are not effective because of the nature of professional services. In place of individual action we therefore have a regulatory mechanism (for example, the professional ethics committee). It might be that this mechanism can work more cheaply and certainly with no commercialisation, and this outweighs the advantages of a wider dissemination of price information that advertising could bring. The size of these costs and benefits are unknown (although surveys show that people generally greatly overestimate the possible costs of legal services – see, for example, Freedman [1977: 68] – so the advantages of more price information could be considerable). But an argument such as this would have to be made to justify the public's interest in 'no commercialisation' in addition to their clear interest in minimum standards of competence.

(c) Advertising and quality: It is sometimes said that allowing the advertising of professional services will reduce the quality of service that the average client obtains (presumably given price). The simplest argument is that preventing advertising 'protects the public from unscrupulous practices' (Justice Rehnquist, quoted in Coase [1977:24]). Against this we might say that unscrupulous or fraudulent advertising is only a small part of the whole and might be prevented as noted above. More convincing is the idea that advertising will cause quality to fall because advertising is most easily undertaken with regard to price, not quality [Kwoka, 1984: 211–12]. Quality is too difficult to specify and judge. If there is much advertising it is possible therefore that the low price/low quality practitioners will gain business because consumers are attracted by low prices and low quality is not fully recognised. High quality practitioners will have to follow suit by lowering both price and quality or else lose business.

However, a recent model put forward by Chan and Leland [1982] suggests the price advertising could increase the average quality of service (given price) that ignorant consumers are offered. They assume that some consumers are well informed. These consumers will patronise practitioners who give clients a utility maximising price/quality combination. Now take the case where price advertising is allowed so that uninformed consumers know a practitioner's price, but not his quality (they know the distribution of quality conditional on price). The uninformed search randomly among practices. If they are lucky and happen upon a practice catering for the informed they receive the informed person's price/quality package. If they come upon a practice not patronised by the informed they will be charged the same price but receive a lower quality service. Now assume price advertising is disallowed. In this case establishments catering for the uninformed can charge a higher price as well as provide lower quality. This means more practitioners will be attracted to serving the uninformed, so lowering the chances of their finding a high quality service. Also the turnover of the average firm will fall, raising unit costs. Average quality of service, given price, therefore, rises when price advertising is allowed in this model.

What this discussion shows is that it is by no means certain that the price/quality combination available to the average uninformed person will deteriorate consequent on price advertising. It might be inferred that permitting advertising could result in a greater diversity of practice. Some firms will go for high advertising, high volume, low price and less individualised service. Others will specialise in a high price service emphasising testing. This diversity would contrast with a restrictive advertising environment favouring the smaller practices.

(d) Effects on price and industry structure: The discussion above suggests that advertising will be associated with lower prices, given quality, and will also cause a rise in the market share of large firms. Considering these points in more detail, one consequence of increasing the flow of price information is that each practitioner is less insulated from competition by others. If there are fewer advertising restrictions it is less costly in terms of time and effort to sample the market. Where less time has to be spent on each search, more searches will be made *ceteris paribus*. Customers become more price sensitive in their demands; in other words, the demand curve for each practitioner becomes more elastic. A more elastic demand curve means that a lower price can be charged. The implication is that fewer advertising restrictions would lead to lower prices for the reason that they reduce monopoly power.

A further reason to expect advertising to be associated with lower prices is related to economies of scale. To the extent that low cost production is brought about by high volume, low cost production implies the need to draw consumers from a wide area. This would require advertising. Liberalisation of advertising would mean that the necessary sales to maintain low prices could be generated more easily.

Looking at industry structure, the Law Society (quoted above) believes that advertising would favour the rich and established firms because they are more able to bear the cost. So entry into the profession would be more difficult. The United States Supreme Court comes to the opposite conclusion:

> In the absence of advertising, an attorney must rely on his contacts with the community to generate a flow of business. In view of the time necessary to develop such contacts, the law in fact serves to perpetuate the market position of established attorneys. Consideration of entry-barrier problems would urge that advertising be allowed so as to aid the new competitor penetrating the market [Supreme Court, 1977: 832].

In fact advertising has advantages and disadvantages for both established firms (if they are big) and small (new) firms. The advantage for the big firm is that advertising would enable it perhaps to generate larger economies of scale. For the small firm publicity assists in the building up of a practice. The disadvantage for the big firm is that, as noted by the Supreme Court, it will have to change its methods of promotion. It will require more vigilance to guard its market share against innovations by newcomers. The newcomers as well face a disadvantage, that is, that advertising might well bring with it lower fees. However, surveys (discussed below) show that younger practitioners are more likely to favour advertising than older which indicates that for the new firms the advantages are held to outweigh the disadvantages. In sum, advertising would lead probably to a somewhat greater range of sizes of practice, with output more concentrated in larger practices and smaller firms supplying specialist skills.

Summarising, the arguments that price advertising would have adverse effects on price, quality or professional dignity are not clear. However, price advertising would be difficult to monitor. It is necessary to weigh these difficulties against the advantages to the consumer of more information.

EMPIRICAL STUDIES

Advertising and Price

The best-known study is that by Benham, who found that as of 1963, states which had advertising restrictions had average eyeglass prices 25 to 100 per cent higher than states which did not, *ceteris paribus* [1972: 344]. In a later study he found that eyeglass prices were 39 per cent higher in states which had over 70 per cent of opticians in membership of the American Optical Association compared to states which had less than 50 per cent membership [1975: Table 4]. The Federal Trade Commission in 1980 found the price of an eye examination plus spectacles to be 11 to 36 per cent lower in the least advertising restrictive cities compared to the most restrictive, other things being equal. There was not found to be a significant difference in quality of eye examinations as between more and less restrictive cities (see Office of Fair Trading (OFT), 1982: 124]. Kwoka found a similar result for the price of eye examinations, holding the length of the examination (a measure of quality) constant [1984: Table 2]. Feldman and Begun found that price of an examination for presbyopia was about 15 per cent lower in states which allowed both optometric and optician price advertising, holding many measures of quality constant (for example, examination length, a 1–8 scale for procedures, a 0–6 scale for equipment) [1978: 257]. Moreover, since the FTC moved against opticians' advertising restrictions with its Final Regulatory Order of June 1978, eyeglass prices have been increasing much more slowly than the price of other commodities. In 1979 eyeglass prices increased at half the rate of the consumer price index, and one-third of the rate for other health-related goods [Boddewyn, 1982: 34]. The evidence that advertising reduces prices therefore seems strong in this profession.

It is interesting to note that Kwoka [1984] finds that firms which choose not to advertise much in areas where advertising is allowed, appear to offer more thorough eye examinations than firms which do advertise a lot. This is indicative of the greater diversity in a free market suggested earlier. Several price/quality packages are available instead of a standard package. The big firm's type of service differs from that of the individual practitioner and the consumer chooses what he or she wants.

Empirical results in other professions are not so clear-cut because there is less variability in advertising restrictions. Nevertheless, in the case of lawyers in the United States there is evidence pointing the same way. It appears that the price of routine legal services such as wills and uncontested divorces has fallen since 1977 when the Supreme Court ruled that price advertising was permissible.[2]

A study of the price of a routine doctor's consultation might also have implications for advertising. Taking a cross-section of 92 large metropolitan areas in the US in 1972, it was found that the price of an office visit was higher in areas with a higher proportion of households resident in the area less than five years, holding measures of physician demand (for example, proportion of aged people in the city) and supply (physicians per head) constant [Pauly and Satterthwaite, 1981: 494–95]. The authors interpret the result as picking up the effect on price of lack of information; a recently arrived family does not have relatives or trusty neighbours to recommend a doctor. An objection to this interpretation is that newcomers could have more serious medical problems, which would account for the higher fee. Restricting the inquiry to 'routine' visits, and holding other determinants of price constant is meant to control for this. If we are prepared to accept these controls, then the study does indicate a weakness in the word-of-mouth dissemination of information about medical services.

Advertising and Industry Structure

In the US eyeglass market, permitting advertising seems to have made for a more concentrated industry structure. In Benham and Benham's study the proportion of eyeglasses supplied by large commercial firms was only 22 per cent in states which restricted advertising. However, in non-restrictive states the proportion was 45 per cent [1975: Table 1]. It should be noted, however, that even in non-restrictive states the majority of eyeglasses were supplied by independent optometrists or physicians, so advertising does not spell the death-knell for the independent practitioner.

Looking at the smaller practitioner, we have noted that advertising has the advantage of appealing to a wider clientele, so assisting entry, but on the other hand, has the likely disadvantage of reducing fees. In this context it is interesting to note that younger practitioners, when questioned, are more likely to be pro-advertising than older practitioners whose practices will typically already be well established. In a survey of dentists, for example, to the statement 'I favor the use of advertising by dentists to attract new patients', 81 per cent of those who had been in practice over 20 years responded negatively, compared to only 42 per cent of those in practice less than ten years (Shapiro and Majewski, 1983: 37]. In a study of lawyers, it was found that those who intended to advertise tended to be 'younger, practice by themselves or with a small firm, and focus more on the legal affairs of individuals rather than businesses or institutions' [Shrimp and Dyer, 1978: 80]. A study of accountants has also shown that young practitioners are more likely to wish to advertise [Traynor, 1984: 37]. These studies suggest that on balance advertising would help young practitioners (as assessed by themselves) and thus assist entry.

Advertising and Consumer Attitudes

Some studies have been made of consumer attitudes towards advertising in the professions. These are of interest since it is the consumer (as voter) who gives the profession the self-regulating status from which advertising bans develop. It is of interest to see if the consumer feels these bans are a protection. In fact they do not appear to. Thus in response to the question on whether dentists should advertise quoted above, while half the total sample of dentists responded negatively, only nine per cent of the sampled consumers were negative, and 34 per cent were strongly in favour [Shapiro and Majewski, 1983: 37]. In a study of attorney selection criteria, though the respondents in fact mainly used personal acquaintance or friend's recommendation as the selection criterion, it was found they would have preferred to use other criteria including area of speciality and cost of service which can be specifically advertised [Smith and Meyer, 1980: Table 1]. A UK survey of spectacle wearers found that 68 per cent were either interested or very interested in having spectacle prices advertised [OFT, 1982: 11.72].

Moreover, it seems that consumer groups generally range themselves against the professions on the question of advertising. The Consumers' Association, giving evidence to the Monopolies and Mergers Commission inquiries into professional restrictions on advertising, said that veterinary surgeons should be 'free to advertise facts about the services they offer for a fee' [MMC, 1976b: para. 59]. The Association has made similar statements with regard to other professions such as accountants [MMC, 1976c: para. 68]. Similarly, in the *Bates* case consumer organisations filed briefs as *amici* urging that advertising restrictions be lifted [Supreme Court, 1977: note 35].

Some regulation of professional standards of practice is supported by consumers given their lack of knowledge of professional services. It is inevitable that this regulation be self-regulation since only members of the profession have the expertise. The consequence is that a certain monopoly power is conceded to the professional association. It is possible, therefore, that certain aspects of professional organisation will not be to the consumer's benefit, even though the professions, as presently run, on balance benefit the consumer. Advertising could be a case in point. Consumers seem to feel that while retaining most other aspects of self-regulation, a move towards advertising would be to their benefit.

DEVELOPMENTS IN BRITAIN AND AMERICA

Britain and America are interesting countries to compare. While in both countries the self-regulating professions have had a history of similarly restrictive rules, recently certain forms of advertising have been permitted in the United States. There might be some lessons to be learned from the American experience.

In both Britain and America moves against anti-competitive activities in the professions began in the mid-1970s. The way was opened in the United States in 1975 in the case of *Goldfarb v. Virginia State Bar* where the Supreme Court ruled that the setting of a schedule of minimum legal fees was a violation of the Sherman Anti-Trust Act (see Werner [1982]). At about the same time in the United Kingdom the Benson Commission was appointed to consider changes 'desirable in the public interest' in the structure, organisation, training and regulation of the legal profession [Benson, 1979], and the Monopolies and Mergers Commission issued a series of reports on advertising restrictions among accountants, vets, barristers, solicitors, and stockbrokers. The reports of these bodies were generally critical of the restrictions on publicity adopted by the professions (see, for example, MMC [1976: para. 118]; Benson [1979: para. 27.32]). But while the 1975 Supreme Court decision presaged other decisions, and has resulted in an increased volume of professional advertising, in Britain the various Commission reports have caused less action.

The main legal decision in America was in 1977, in the case of *Bates and O'Steen v. State Bar of Arizona*. Here the Supreme Court laid down the principle that the organised bar's ban on advertising prices of routine services controverted the constitutional right to free speech.[3] It is interesting to note that Bates and O'Steen were two young lawyers engaged in establishing themselves in the profession. They had set up a 'legal clinic' with the aim of providing routine legal services at low cost. Only routine cases were accepted, and costs were kept down by extensive use of paralegals and standardised procedures. The Supreme Court upheld price advertising because 'Commercial speech serves to inform the public of the availability, nature, and prices of products and services, and thus performs an indispensable role in the allocation of resources in a free enterprise system' [1977: 823]. The Court also noted that 'many persons do not obtain counsel even when they perceive a need because of the feared price of services or because of an inability to locate a competent attorney' [1977: 827].

The 1975 and 1977 Supreme Court decisions helped the Federal Trade Commission to pursue some professions for unfair methods of competition in terms of the Federal Trade Commission Act. Dentists, optometrists, pharmacists, lawyers, and even doctors have been ordered not to ban price advertising (the Final Order for doctors coming in June 1982). In practice, for the marketing of medical services the FTC Order is probably overshadowed by the rise of the 'Mediglomerate' employing salaried physicians [Wright and Allen, 1983: 48]. By advertising and offering standard packages (for example, emergency, maternity, elderly person) these corporations are stimulating the independent physician to compete. On the other hand, in the case of legal services the Supreme Court judgements have had a noticeable effect. Lawyers now even appear on television [Middleton, 1983]. Their advertisements have useful content; they include information on fees, and (since a further ruling by the Supreme Court in 1982) details of field of specialism so long as these are not false or misleading [Andrews, 1982].

By contrast the pace of change has been slow in Britain. There is the fact that opticians can now advertise, and spectacles can be bought from other sources (subject to safeguards). Minimum commissions on the Stock Exchange are being abolished. Some rules such as the 'two-thirds rule', whereby a junior barrister has to be paid two-thirds of his leaders' fee have been dropped (not that it has made much difference [see Zander, 1979: 493]. Moves are afoot to remove the solicitors' conveyancing monopoly. On the other hand, there is little evidence of much more advertising being undertaken. In the medical field, the client in the NHS has little effective choice. His place of residence largely determines his general practitioner, who places him in the hospital system as necessary, so publication of individual doctor's characteristics via advertising is less relevant. Perhaps by extension advertising is rarely mentioned either in regard to the private health care sector. As for other professions, lawyers and accountants have made small changes in their advertising regulations. For example, the Law Society now allows local newspapers advertisements (at specified intervals), but the vital information regarding fees and area of specialism is not yet allowed.[4] American lawyers were allowed to reveal more than this even before *Bates* [Supreme Court, 1977: 825, note 18]. The other professions – barristers, dentists, vets, architects, stockbrokers – are still considering their positions.

The professions in Britain are smaller and probably more socially homogeneous than in the US – there might be successful informal pressures to prevent advertising even if it becomes illegal explicitly to ban advertising using professional codes. In the British context, although once an occupation is organised it quite quickly moves to set up examinations, the time elapsing before publishing a code is much longer, and many associations do not even have a written code. For example, of the 160 qualifying associations surveyed by Millerson, only 20 per cent had a written code of conduct [1964: 148], and the gap between foundation and code publication averaged 57 years [1964: 185 note 3]. As a member of the Institute of Chartered Accountants of England and Wales explained, disciplinary decisions based on a written code had the disadvantage that they could be upset by the courts [Millerson, 1964: 160].[5]

Even in America, despite the *Bates* decision, not many practitioners have moved to advertise. For example, 94 per cent of dentists questioned in one survey said they had no intention of advertising [McIntyre and

Weinrauch, 1981: 99], and similar high figures have been found for lawyers [Benson, 1979: para. 27.25]. Against this, however, it does seem that certain types of practice such as the 'legal clinic', which relies on simple work and high volume, have benefited from the opportunity to advertise [Bernacchi and Koro, 1981: 75].

It seems likely, therefore, that permitting advertising will have a gradual effect. This is to the good, since the changes in the structure of the industry, and the tendency towards lower fees consequent on price advertising will impose costs on some practitioners. A slow adjustment will make these costs less onerous.

CONCLUSIONS

Our aim has been to assess the possible effects on the price and quality of professional services of permitting advertising. To argue for the derestriction of advertising involves the weighing up of costs and benefits. On the one hand, we have seen that professional judgements are hard for the layman fully to evaluate. The prime defence of blanket advertising restrictions then rests on the utility of preventing 'misleading' advertising claims. On the other hand, there are logical reasons to suppose that advertising would result in reduced fees and easier entry, and there is empirical evidence to support this. Moreover, it is not clear that allowing modest, specific advertising of fees and specialism would be so costly to monitor.

The weight of the argument therefore seems to be in favour of disallowing professional advertising bans subject to safeguards. Both the Monopolies and Mergers Commission and the United States Supreme Court can be said broadly to have taken this position. Further, judging by American experience only a fraction of practitioners take advantage of their freedom to advertise, so there is not likely to be an upheaval in the professions.

NOTES

1. For an analysis of entry restrictions in the case of the medical profession see Siebert [1977].
2. This evidence is given by S.R. Cox, 'The Price Effects of Attorney Advertising Regulations' cited in Littlechild [1982: 27].
3. Banning advertising prices also infringed the Sherman Act. However, in the Bates case this infringement could not be used to strike down the bans, due to the doctrine that state laws such as that of the Arizona Bar displace Federal anti-trust laws.
4. See *Financial Times*, 'Mixed Reception for Easing of Ban on Lawyers' Advertising', 19 November 1983.
5. There is a parallel here with the international Brotherhood of Teamsters which keeps its grievance procedures 'informal' – decisions are not formally explained and so there is no development of case law [Levinson, 1980; 128–29].

REFERENCES

Andrews, L.B., 1982, 'The Model Rules and Advertising', *American Bar Association Journal*, 68, July, 808–11.
Arrow, K., 1963, 'Uncertainty and the Welfare Economics of Medical Care', *American Economic Review*, 53, 941–73.
Benham, L., 1972, 'The Effect of Advertising on the Price of Eyeglasses', *Journal of Law and Economics*, 15, 337–52.
Benham, L., and A. Benham, 1975, 'Regulating Through the Professions: A Perspective on Information Control', *Journal of Law and Economics*, 18, 412–47.
Benson, Sir H. (Chairman), 1979, *Report of the Royal Commission on Legal Services*, Vol. 1, Cmnd. 7648, London: HMSO.
Bernacchi, M., and K. Koro, 1981, 'Attorney Advertising' in J.H. Donnelly and W.R. George, *Marketing of Services*, Chicago: American Marketing Association.
Boddewyn, J.J., 1982, 'Advertising in the 1980s: The Underlying Global Forces', *Journal of Marketing*, 46, Winter, 27–35.
Chan, Y., and H. Leland, 1982, 'Prices and Qualities in Markets with Costly Information', *Review of Economic Studies*, 49, 499–516.
Coase, R.H., 1977, 'Advertising and Free Speech' in A. Hyman and M.B. Johnson (eds.), *Advertising and Free Speech*, Lexington: Lexington Books.
Darby, M.R., and E. Karni, 1973, 'Free Competition and the Optimal Amount of Fraud', *Journal of Law and Economics*, 16, 67–88.
Feldman, R., and J. Begun, 1978, 'Effects of Advertising – Lessons from Optometry', *Journal of Human Resources*, supplement, 13, 247–62.
Freedman, M., 1977, 'Advertising and Solicitation by Lawyers: Legal Ethics, "Commercial" Speech, and Free Speech', in A Hyman and M.B. Johnson (eds.), *Advertising and Free Speech*, Lexington: Lexington Books.
Kwoka, J.E., 1984, 'Advertising and the Price and Quality of Optometric Services', *American Economic Review*, 74, 211–16.
Levinson, H.M., 1980, 'Trucking', in G.G. Somers (ed.), *Collective Bargaining Contemporary American Experience*, Industrial Relations Research Association.
Littlechild, S.C., 1982, *The Relation Between Advertising and Price*, London: Advertising Association.
McIntyre and J. Weinrauch, 1981, 'Opportunities and Challenges of Franchising Dental Care', in J.H. Donnelly and W.R. George (eds.), *Marketing of Services*, Chicago: American Marketing Association.
Middleton, M., 1983, 'The Right Way to Advertise on TV', *American Bar Association Journal*, 69, July, 893–97.
Millerson, G., 1964, *The Qualifying Associations*, London: Routledge & Kegan Paul.
Monopolies and Mergers Commission (MMC), 1970, *Report of the General Effect on the Public Interest of Certain Restrictive practices so far as they Prevail in Relation to the Supply of Professional Services*, Cmnd. 4463, London: HMSO.
Monopolies and Mergers Commission, 1976a, *Services of Solicitors in England and Wales*, HOC 557, London: HMSO.
Monopolies and Mergers Commission, 1976b, *Veterinary Services: A Report on the Supply of Veterinary Services In Relation to Restrictions on Advertising*, Cmnd. 6572, London: HMSO.
Monopolies and Mergers Commission, 1976c, *Accountancy Services: A Report on the Supply of Accountancy Services In Relation to Restrictions on Advertising*, Cmnd. 6573, London: HMSO.
Office of Fair Trading (OFT), 1982, *Opticians and Competition*, London: HMSO.
Pauly, M.V., and M. Satterthwaite, 1981, 'The Pricing of Primary Care Physicians' Services', *Bell Journal of Economics*, 12, 488–506.
Posner, R., 1977, *Economic Analysis of Law*, 2nd ed., Boston and Toronto: Little, Brown.
Shapiro, I.A., and R.F. Majewski, 1983, 'Should Dentists Advertise?', *Journal of Advertising Research*, 23, June/July, 33–37.
Shrimp, T. and R. Dyer, 1978, 'How the Legal Profession Views Legal Service

Advertising', *Journal of Marketing*, 42, July, 74–81.

Siebert, W.S., 1977, 'Occupational licensing: The Merrison Report on the Regulations of the Medical Profession', *British Journal of Industrial Relations*, 15, 29–38.

Smith, R.E., and T.S. Meyer, 1980, 'Attorney Advertising: A Consumer Perspective', *Journal of Marketing*, Spring, 44, 56–63.

Supreme Court, 1977, *Supreme Court Reports*, Lawyers edition, 53, 810–50.

Traynor, K., 1984, 'Accountant Advertising: Perceptions, Attitudes, Behaviour', *Journal of Advertising Research*, 23, December/January, 35–40.

Werner, R.O., 1982, 'Marketing and the US Supreme Court 1975–1981', *Journal of Marketing*, 46, Spring, 73–81.

Wright, R.A., and B.H. Allen, 1983, 'Marketing and Medicine: Why Advertising is not an Issue', *Journal of the American Medical Association*, 250, 7, July, 47–8.

Veljanovski, C.G., and C.J. Whelan, 1983, 'Professional Negligence and the Quality of Legal Services – An Economic Perspective', *Modern Law Review*, 46, November, 700–18.

Zander, M., 1979, 'Promoting Change in the Legal System', *Modern Law Review*, 42, 489–507.

Marketing Freight Transport: The Need for Customer-orientation

by

Norman E. Marr

The use of marketing is relatively new in most areas of freight transport operations. The idea that the industry has a 'product' to offer is discussed. Why freight transport companies adopt the marketing concept is reviewed. To help this the techniques used in promotion and market segmentation are explained.

INTRODUCTION

'Marketing is useful for firms manufacturing consumer or industrial goods. It is no use for service companies such as transport or distribution'. This is the kind of statement which is often uttered by executives of distribution service companies. The idea that the marketing concept only applies to companies with a physical product to offer has been slow to die. The idea that the companies carrying a physical product for profit, that is, distribution companies, can do so without applying any marketing principles may, in part at least, account for the high failure rate among such companies.

This article describes briefly the basic concept of marketing and examines why companies in the international freight transport industry need or even adopt marketing techniques. The product of the industry is examined in the context of product life cycle. The market is described briefly before the state of marketing in the freight transport industry is discussed.

MARKETING – THE BASIC CONCEPT

Perhaps one of the most practical definitions of marketing is: 'the process whereby the firm, regardless of its area of operation, seeks to identify, quantify and anticipate the needs of its markets both present and potential, and develops the product to satisfy such wants'. Confronted with this definition most businessmen will say, 'We do this normally'. However, there is a series of questions which when answered would indeed show just how little marketing the average freight transport operator actually does. A full list of questions is shown at the end of this article. In common with many industries, the freight transport industry, until very recently, has spent very little time investigating customer needs.

Why Marketing in a Freight Transport Company?

What leads companies to discover marketing? Broadly speaking, there are five sets of circumstances which may initiate an interest in marketing:

(1) Declining sales – this is perhaps the most common cause. The demand for transport and its related services is a derived demand, that is, the demand is derived from industrial activity. Therefore, the world recession has brought with it a drop in the movement of products and a consequent drop in the demand for transport and its related services.
(2) Slow growth – some companies reach the limits of growth in their industrial sector and start to look around for new markets or new products. There is a recognition that they need marketing know-how if they are to successfully identify, evaluate and select new opportunities. Recently the development corporation of a well-established city commissioned research into the feasibility of the provision of certain new facilities which were totally new to the traditional industries of that area.
(3) Changing buying patterns – many companies are experiencing increasingly turbulent markets, marked by rapidly changing customer wants. In the past five years there has been an ever-increasing awareness of the costs involved in the distribution of products. This in turn has brought about greater demands on companies supplying distribution services.
(4) Increasing competition – the complacent companies in the distribution industry have suffered disastrous results. Those companies which survived did so by learning the fundamental principles of marketing to combat the increased challenge.
(5) Increasing sales expenditures – the cost of a company's advertising, sales promotion, marketing research, and customer service may increase without any rhyme or reason. This may bring management to the conclusion that there is a need to control these marketing functions.

There is still the inherent unwillingness to accept the need to move into the modern highly competitive environment a firm needs to employ modern techniques such as marketing. This results in a very slow learning curve in the freight transport industry generally.

THE PRODUCT

The notion of 'product' in the context of a service industry such as transport has in the past presented a problem. However, if one thinks of a 'product' as something which is capable of satisfying a want then the problem should be resolved. A simple example will serve to illustrate this point. A manufacturer of a large piece of capital equipment has a need to transfer the equipment from point of manufacture to the point where it is to be used. The product which will satisfy this need is a service to convey the equipment. Therefore, a transport company providing such a service will be providing a need satisfying product. The 'product' in the case of transport and distribution normally has no shape or utility of form. The shape or colour of the vehicle used to move the above article is of no consequence to the customer. What is of importance is what the service purports to achieve. Over a number of years the various utilities provided by the product in the freight transport industry have changed either through technological advances, or changes in customer needs.

There have been changes in the attitudes of manufacturing companies to the 'necessary evil' of moving the goods from place of manufacture to place of need. Many have taken the view, 'what business am I in?', and therefore prefer distribution to be undertaken by those people with specialist expertise. This attitude has led to the development of the 'through transport' offering. This is the idea that the manufacturer can form a contract with a haulier to carry the company's product. This contract will make the haulier responsible for all documentation, both transit, and where necessary, Customs and Excise. Thus the responsibility for one of the areas which causes most concern to exporters is passed on to a third party. The 'through transport' concept is not something that applies solely to road freight. It applies equally to all modes of movement. Many would-be customers demand more than just the transportation of product. They demand warehousing, order assembly, packing, documentation and shipping.

Other developments in the product have been brought about by the need to achieve a competitive edge. The concept of product life cycle is well understood amongst marketing personnel and a detailed description of such a concept is outside the scope of this article. However, a product will usually have a five-stage life, the *introduction* where the level of the awareness of its existence is low. This stage will be followed by the *growth* stage, where service acceptance is rising through the results of: (i) promotional effort; (ii) satisfied customer recommendations. Obviously the expertise used in the promotional effort in the transport industry in the past has been operational expertise in many cases, rather than marketing expertise. Perhaps the air cargo industry, owing to its links to air passengers, has benefited from the availability of marketing expertise. The incidence of customer satisfaction has considerably increased in recent years due to the fact that companies are more and more using market research techniques to find out the needs of customers and prospective customers.

The third stage is the *mature* stage, where revenue may grow slowly but new customers are hard to come by, and competition is increasing. This is a familiar stage in transport service offerings. In many cases the simple provision of a means of conveying a physical product is not a very profitable operation because of the ease with which competition develops. It is relatively cheap to enter the transport service industry in terms of capital outlay. The persistence with the mature product leads to the final two stages in the product life cycle – *saturation*, with heavy competition and *decline*, where newer and better services have started to replace the existing product. The simple carrier has suffered the fifth stage of decline. This is applicable whether one is considering land, sea or air movement of cargo.

THE PRESENT MARKET

The demands of the customers in the market-place have become greater and greater with the onslaught of the recession in world trade. Many customers, for instance, are no longer willing to undertake the documentation required for the exporting of products. They recognise the limitations in their expertise or the need to employ specialist expertise with the accompanying costs. The majority of customers/potential customers do not have the throughput of exports to economically justify the employing of full-time expertise. In many ways these are a large ready-made market for the 'total package' offering. This number is also an increasing number as more and more companies have been forced into exporting to survive the domestic recession.

The companies which have been exporting for a long time are also looking at changes in philosophy concerning the distribution part of their operations. The development of sophisticated cost monitoring systems is bringing about a greater realisation of the actual costs of distribution as a proportion of sales value. In many ways, the market demand for distribution services as a total package has grown in contrast to the demand for simple transportation, which has declined in line with the recession. The market for the 'distribution service package' is very largely untapped in so far as there has been until recently little marketing effort with, perhaps, the exception of the air cargo sector.

MARKETING – STATE OF THE ART

Promotion

This ingredient in the Marketing Mix is an essential part, creating awareness that such services are available among potential users, generating detailed knowledge of the firm's services, improving the firm's image amongst existing and potential customers, eliminating misconceptions, and advising the market-place of new channels and product special offers/modifications. Recently there has been an increase in the promotion efforts of companies providing the 'all-in service package'. Such adverts as '. . . brings the world to your door', advertising the door-to-door services offered by a particular company, '. . . offers complete range of services to West Africa'. These examples come from 1981 and the trend in advertising has continued upwards into 1984.

A recent example of the need to correct a misconception involved the partial closure of the Manchester Ship Canal. The author, whilst conducting a short course for the ports industry, was surprised to find amongst the delegates four commercial staff of the Canal company. The surprise was as a result of a certain media headline 'Manchester Ship Canal to Close'. In fact only part of the Canal is to close and the remainder is very much a commercially viable proposition. The best service offering lacks utility unless its availability is communicated effectively to prospective customers. Much promotional activity is centred around transport/distribution trade papers. Whilst these have obviously very good connections should there not be consideration given to the thousands of companies which do not have any in-company expertise and, therefore, may not be part of the readership of such papers.

Competition

The changing face of competition has been accelerated by the increased incidence of deliberate inventory reduction policies both on the side of the manufacturer and the customer. Much has been published about the pros and cons of air freight compared with sea freight, etc. However, this has recently been changed considerably with the high cost of maintaining inventory. On the other hand, a recent extensive study carried out for an international distribution company amongst 'high technology' manufacturers showed that the two major requirements of a service package were reliability and documentation expertise. However one views the transport and distribution industry, competition is fierce for all types of freight to all parts of the world. However, it can be divided into three possible types of competition which the marketing department of a transport company must recognise.

The customers, firstly, will look at the alternative sources of supply of a particular service. This is operational competition. The second type of competition involves a type of brand loyalty in so far as once a customer has used a transport company which has provided him with reliability, no problem transit, good information, etc., it is going to take further innovation to move that customer. On the other side, a supplier who has failed to supply the required service levels will attract less and less loyalty as the word is spread. The third area of competition which the customer comes up against and therefore suppliers of services need to recognise is the limit of cash, budgets, which the customer has available. This may mean a manufacturer may opt out of distribution in areas of the world where it would be excessively expensive to carry out deliveries. This may mean the market available for the third party operator may exclude, as far as this particular manufacturer is concerned, the more populated areas.

Market Segmentation

The size of the freight transport/distribution market is such that no one supplier can be all things to all users. Therefore, it is of paramount importance that a supplier, be it an established company or a new entrant, recognises this fact and establishes the market segment(s) to which its resources are best applied to bring the most satisfactory results in terms of corporate objectives. The idea of market segmentation has become more important with the increasing demands of potential customers. In the previous section mention was made of the attributes of a service package which are the most influential in the purchase decision. The important attributes vary considerably over the different types of customer and with the same customer serving different situations with his manufactured products.

Since the mid-1970s much research has been carried out and, indeed, much has been written about the important factors of distribution service in the purchase decision. The only concrete findings with an overall influence are, first, the confirmation of the statement above in respect of the variability of important attributes and second, an obvious need to obtain the details of customer needs from the customer. The market segments chosen will be those in which your unique selling points match most closely the requirements of prospective customers.

Marketing Opportunities and Threats

The involvement of the marketing concept in freight movements means there is a need for companies to develop a marketing plan. Whilst the detailed description of market planning is outside the scope of this article, the first stage of such a process is considered an important link in the development of marketing of freight transport. The analysis of marketing opportunities is something that is receiving more and more attention from suppliers of distribution services. The evaluation of marketing opportunities process may be broken down into a series of questions:

(a) What are the major operating characteristics of each type of market?
(b) What are the main environmental trends, opportunities, and threats facing the industry and the firm?
(c) How is the purchase decision made?
(d) What are the different major segments of the maket?
(e) What are the trends in the market size?

The questions above are based on the acceptance, by the freight transport industry, of the need to involve market research. This acceptance is slowly gaining credence in an industry which has undergone great changes in the last ten years.

Recognising the fact that the demand for freight transport and associated services is derived from industrial activity, it is no surprise that there is a need to investigate trends and forecasts in areas not necessarily connected closely to transport, for example, trends in world interest rates, and unemployment.

The forecasting of trends in freight transport services demand may be carried out in several ways. One of the newest ways as far as transport is concerned is *expert opinion*. Here knowledgeable people are selected and asked to study various possible future developments. The most refined version, the Delphi method, puts experts through several rounds of event assessments, where they keep refining their assumptions and judgements. Other more traditional methods may be used. The recognition of the opportunities in a market must also be accompanied by the identification of the threats that actually exist or are likely to exist. The failure to recognise threats may result in a firm being ousted from its position. This is particularly applicable in the freight transport industry where innovation by firms not traditionally involved in a particular market segment may result in a traditional company losing market share. The emergence of the all-in service package offered by international hauliers means greater competition for freight forwarders.

Threats that are recognised can be countered in one of three ways:

(a) the firm can try to fight, restrain or reverse the unfavourable development;
(b) the firm can try to improve its fit within the existing environment by changing its customers with which it deals or one or more elements of the Marketing Mix;
(c) the firm can shift to another market segment where it can produce more value.

In the environment of international freight movement companies must always be looking for threats and opportunities. It must not become a bundle of obsolete attributes. It must be prepared to adapt creatively to the changing environment.

SUMMARY

This article has by no means exhausted the span of a subject such as marketing freight transport. However, it has brought to light the idea that marketing principles can be applied to the service of freight transport in very much the same way as the application to a physical product. The *product* in this industry is a series of attributes put together in a certain combination under the title of 'a service package', or 'a service offering'. The *price* in this industry is the same as for any physical product. The *promotion* factor in the Marketing Mix serves very much the same function as in the case of a physical product. It creates awareness about the existence of the product. The final factor in the Marketing Mix, *the place*, is perhaps one of the factors which has seen the greatest developments over the last ten years. The channel of distribution is very much a growing part in the international freight transport industry, with the increase in freight forwarding activity. The freight forwarder is very much the 'wholesaler' in the international freight transport industry.

Many companies whose traditional area of operations is in decline are moving in very competitive ways towards pastures new. This is compounded by the demands from customers whose in-house expertise is also improving with the ever-increasing director representation on company boards.

APPENDIX

Checklist

A manager, in the field of transport and distribution who is able to answer 'yes' to all the following questions, is probably in possession of most of the marketing inputs that a firm requires:

1. Are you able to state with some accuracy what your market share is in each segment in which you operate? (Yes/No).
2. Do you know why your customers use your service in preference to competitive products? (Yes/No).
3. Are you able to assess how many more years your product or service is likely to last? (Yes/No).
4. Do you know what level of satisfaction exists among your customers? (Yes/No).
5. Do you know the price elasticity of your service? (Yes/No).
6. Are you sure that your sales force is adequate? (Yes/No).
7. Do your salesmen cover the best opportunity areas? (Yes/No).
8. Do you know how many potential users of your service are aware of your existence and the type of service you offer? (Yes/No).
9. Do you promote your service by objectives? (Yes/No).
10. If yes, are you able to say how effective your promotional effort has been? (Yes/No).
11. Do you experiment with new ideas which might help you to improve the service and level of satisfaction of your market? (Yes/No).
12. Do you control your marketing effort in such a way as to learn what to do or not to do in the future? (Yes/No).

(*Source*: *Marketing in Perspective* by Simon Majaro, London: George Allen & Unwin, 1982.)

Development of the 'Travelcard' Concept in Urban Public Transport

by

Peter R. White*

Traditionally, urban bus operators have collected fares in cash for each trip. Some limited mechanisation has occurred in ticket issue at stations. Partly for reasons of operating convenience, there has recently been a shift to simpler fares and prepayment, notably through the introduction of 'Travelcards', that is, tickets or passes permitting unlimited use of the network (or zones thereof) for a defined period. These cover both all-bus systems, and bus/rail networks (such as the West Midlands PTE system). They are now used in all main British conurbations, following introduction of the London Transport bus/rail Travelcard in May 1983. The Travelcard in effect redefines the 'product' being sold. Instead of the public transport service being perceived as a series of separate journeys, payment is made periodically for use of the network as a whole. Cost perception is thus put on a similar basis to that for the private car. The marginal money cost for each trip becomes zero. Interchange penalties associated with re-booking are eliminated. Payment may be made by cheque or credit card, rather than cash, further changing the perception of costs. Product quality is also enhanced through speeding up of services (one-person-operated buses), and enabling the user to select the quickest and/or most convenient route in a network by removing the interchange penalty.

INTRODUCTION

Until recently, urban public transport operators paid relatively little attention to marketing. Some traditional timetable and route map information was given, but little effort was made to 'market' services even in the very simple sense of greater advertising and passenger information.

* Evidence in this article is drawn from many sources. In addition to those shown in references, many operators have kindly provided data as part of continuing work at PCL in urban public transport. Particular thanks are due to Werner Brög of Socialdata Brög, Munich; Peter Collins and Malcolm Fairhurst of London Transport; and Phil Haywood and Ernest Godward of West Midlands PTE. However, responsibility for conclusions drawn is the author's own.

The extent of this is now greater, as most operators realise the need to make their services known to potential users; even where total use is static or declining a high 'turnover' of users occurs as people change home, workplace or place of education. As many as 20 per cent of passengers in recent surveys have been found to be users of less than one year's standing, joining the service they now use mainly as a result of change in location, rather than in mode.

The interest in marketing has extended to greater research in users' trip purposes, and attitudes. In particular, the Market Analysis Project of the National Bus Company (and its parallel in Scotland, 'Scotmap') has in recent years covered much of Britain. Detailed passenger surveys have enabled market sectors to be identified, both geographically and by time of day, trip purpose, and so on. These have led to revised networks, matching supply and demand more closely, and innovations in pricing, such as peak/off-peak discrimination, and promotional offers.

Within the local authority bus sector – including over 40 urban operators under district councils (England and Wales) or regional councils (Scotland), London Transport, and the seven Passenger Transport Executives in the metropolitan counties and Strathclyde – a somewhat different approach has been taken. Comprehensive networks remain, without such pressure to match specific costs and passenger revenue as the companies have experienced. However, in changing the nature of the product offered, there has in some respects been more radical innovation in the larger cities. This takes the form of the 'Travelcard', a ticket or pass permitting unlimited use of a public transport network (or zones thereof) within a given time period (typically one or four weeks, or a year). The name 'Travelcard' as such is used in London and the West Midlands, with similar titles elsewhere (such as Travelticket in Tyne and Wear). Here, it is used also as a generic term. The travelcard consists of a photocard, identifying the holder, and a renewable portion, the latter often purchased through local agents, such as shops, as well as the operator's own outlets.

Together with an expansion of the use of passes by pensioners and disabled, the travelcard represents a major shift from the traditional form of fare collection and ticket issue, in which a cash fare is paid for each ride on a bus or train, often with a separate payment needed each time a transfer takes place between buses, or bus and train. About 50 per cent or more of all passenger journeys in London Transport, West Midlands and Tyne and Wear systems no longer involve cash payment for each trip. A substantial proportion, around 10 to 20 per cent, is also comprised of travelcard users in Strathclyde (the network centred on Glasgow), Merseyside and Manchester. Pre-paid multi-ride tickets (a strip of which is cancelled for each trip and/or zone crossed) supplement travelcards in West Yorkshire, Greater Manchester and some other areas.

This change represents more than a different method of payment. In effect, it redefines the 'product' being sold. The public transport user perceives a payment for the use of the system as a whole (or substantial part thereof), with individual journeys at zero marginal cost. By eliminating financial penalties of interchange, use of the fastest or most convenient combination of modes and routes is encouraged. Boarding times of buses (now almost all one-person-operated, except for parts of London and South and West Yorkshire fleets), are reduced, improving service speed and reliability (both for travelcard holders and others). Perception of cost is placed on a similar footing to that of the private car, that is, a periodic substantial payment (akin to weekly refuelling for local trips, and/or annual tax, insurance and servicing).

In this article the history of travelcard development is described briefly. An analysis of user/price response is then given, showing how an approach based on price thresholds rather than the economists' elasticity curve is more appropriate. It is illustrated by case studies, notably that conducted by the author on behalf of the West Midlands Passenger Transport Executive [White, 1983a], and recent innovations in London.

HISTORICAL DEVELOPMENT OF THE TRAVELCARD

Station-to-station season tickets were adopted by railways in the mid-nineteenth century. With a substantial discount from ordinary fares, they encouraged a rapid growth in commuting, especially around the largest cities such as London. Queuing delays at booking offices were reduced, and fewer booking clerks required. The railway companies gained in that revenue was received when the ticket was first sold, rather than as each trip was made. Deliberate stimulus to commuting was given, as the new residential areas thereby established helped to generate all-day traffic. However, a somewhat rigid approach came to be adopted, with unduly large discounts given on standard fares, and certain low rates institutionalised (for example, in the early morning 'workmen's seasons' which can be traced to the 'Parliamentary trains' introduced in the 1840s). This, coupled with the high marginal costs of peak-only capacity has led economists to stress (with some justification) the dangers that may result from such a pricing policy, while perhaps ignoring the marketing and operational benefits from such forms of ticket.

Local, road-based public transport began with horse omnibuses and tramcars from around 1870 in many urban areas, but did not grow rapidly until after the adoption of electric tramways from about 1895. With numerous kerbside stops, a 'station to station' ticket system was impractical, and most British systems came to adopt a graduated fare system, in which fares were based on the number of stages traversed, each stage usually comprising a section of route with several stops. Virtually all fares were collected in cash by a conductor, although some variations were found. This system of fare collection changed little with the switch to trolleybus and motor-bus operation. Even as one-person-operation of buses expanded in the 1970s, operators were slow to change. Most applied the conductor-based system to the driver, including change-giving. As a result, the boarding time per passenger rose from about 1.5 seconds with conductor operation, to four to five seconds or more. This had particularly serious effects on urban services (with an average of five to seven passengers boarding per bus mile), both on average speeds, and reliability (since running time varies with loadings, aggravating the tendency to 'bunch'). The cost-saving through eliminating the conductor was thus offset in part through additional buses and drivers that might be needed to maintain the same frequency with greater running times, and also through revenue losses resulting from the lower quality of service offered. Requiring passengers to present the exact fare cuts boarding time down to about 2.5 seconds, but with the risk of further patronage loss due to the inconvenience caused.

In contrast, urban operators elsewhere in Europe and North America tended to adopt flat fares from an early stage, together with one-man-operation. Tickets were often not needed (since over-riding was not a problem) or were fairly simple. Interchange between routes, and/or modes could be covered by a simple 'transfer' ticket, either at the same flat rate, or with a small supplement. Boarding times were thus kept fairly low, although cash payment was still needed for each trip. The retention of tramways (as in many medium-sized European cities) or growth of rail rapid transit systems, with bus feeders, created a greater need for easy interchange than in Britain, where much less investment in rail took place, and even conurbations of over one million were served largely by all-bus networks.

A shift from single fare cash payment to some form of travelcard began in the 1930s and 1940s with simplification of existing structures, notably in Germany [Engelbrecht, 1981]. The use of such tickets remained relatively small, although growing in importance in the 1950s. A similar ticket was adopted by Edinburgh City Transport in 1957, although with a very small market penetration for many years.

The present extensive use of travelcards dates from the Stockholm 'monthly card' introduced in 1971, followed by many other European cities in the early 1970s, notably West Midlands in 1972, and the Paris 'Carte Orange' in 1975. This rapid growth was, to begin with, because the concept became politically fashionable, and as levels of public expenditure rose, low fares could be offered. This led to some scepticism from the operators themselves, and from economists already critical of the effects of season ticket discounts. However, as will be shown below, the *long-run* effects of travelcards are often more beneficial, and do not necessarily require more financial support than conventional fare systems. *Greater* levels of partronage may be attained for a given level of financial support, due to the improved product being offered.

USERS' RESPONSE TO PRICE CHANGES

Economic theory has traditionally represented response to price changes through price/demand curves of the form shown in Figure 1. A smooth concave curve is shown, demand falling (horizontal axis) as price rises (vertical axis). The rate of change (elasticity) may be assumed constant, or changing as price level changes. Aggregate elasticities derived from such curves have been found in the past to give fairly good predictions for price changes, at any rate for traditional cash-based fare systems. A value of −0.3 (percentage change in trips for a percentage change in real average revenue per trip) has been found remarkably robust.

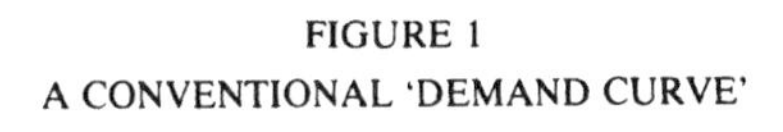

FIGURE 1
A CONVENTIONAL 'DEMAND CURVE'

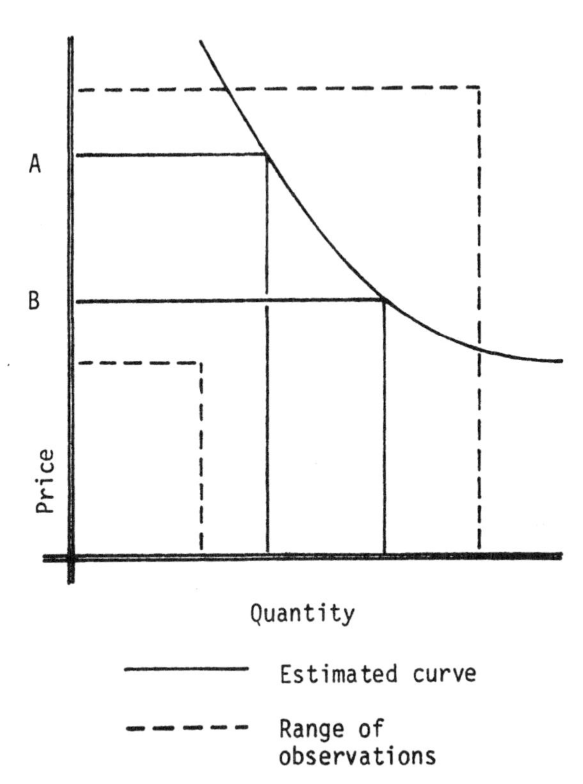

But does such a form, however convenient in aggregate, really represent user behaviour? The response of an individual user to a price change may also be presented as a switch at a critical threshold value at which behaviour changes. For example, in Figure 2, a critical point occurs at which further price increases will cause a change in behaviour. For example, a rising public transport fare could cause a change in mode (to walk/cycle for short trips, car for longer journeys). For some types of trip, this 'all or nothing' switch could be appropriate – for example, the work journey. For other types, such as shopping trips, the change could be more gradual, as trip frequency is gradually reduced, rather than a change of mode occurring. Note that in Figure 2, conventional scientific labelling of axes is adopted, that is, the cause (price change) is shown on the horizontal (x) axis, the effect (change in demand) on the vertical (y) axis.

FIGURE 2
NOTIONAL INDIVIDUAL PRICE RESPONSE

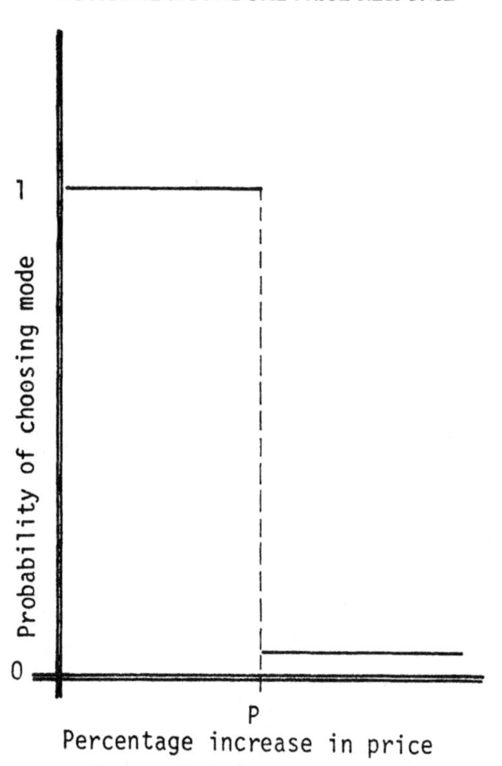

The same distinction might be drawn by form of payment. A travelcard might continue to be purchased up to a certain price level, at which a sudden change in behaviour would occur, with either a switch to another mode, or to a much lower level of trip-making, at single cash fares. Note that frequency of travel would not change as travelcard price rose, until the critical point was reached, since each trip has a zero marginal cost. Applying this concept to a whole market sector, we may postulate a distribution of threshold price levels around the mean shown in Figure 2. This would lead to an aggregate price-response curve of the form shown in Figure 3. If, for example, the values were normally distributed around the mean, an S-shaped curve would result. A similar curve is already adopted in disaggregate models of mode choice (in which price may be one of the variables). However, time-series work (from which most price elasticities are derived) has tended to adopt the traditional form shown in Figure 1 almost without question.

FIGURE 3
NOTIONAL AGGREGATE PRICE RESPONSE

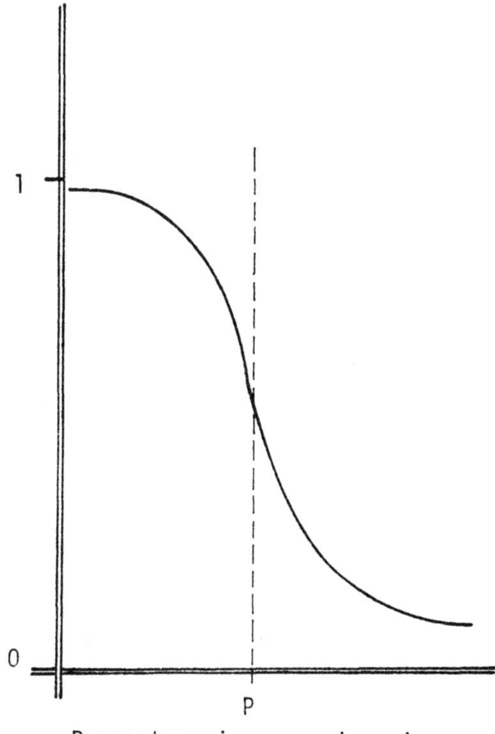

Further analysis of this concept is provided by the author elsewhere [White, 1984], including application of the 'catastrophe theory' concept, to cover a wider range of conditions. The essence of the S-shaped price response curve is that it should be possible to increase travelcard prices from a relatively low level up toward the threshold value with little effect on sales. Hence revenue could be raised without losing traffic, or the operational benefits (notably quick boarding times) that travelcard gives in comparison to cash-paid systems.

Support for the S-shaped curve (as representing demand from one group of users at one point in time) comes from surveys in Munich by Brög [Brög and Förg, 1980]. For evidence in practice, over a period of time, it may be inferred from sales/price changes for selected operators. For example, given a very low initial price (corresponding to an asymptotic part of the S-shaped curve), increases might take place with little effect on sales, until the critical threshold range was reached, in which a rapid change would occur. Movement along the asymptotic part of the curve would be associated with a negligible price elasticity, and probably one that could not be distinguished satisfactorily from other effects such as the cross-elasticity between travelcards and single journey fares, where the latter rise more quickly (as in the West Midlands case, described below).

Two stages in travelcard use may be proposed:

1. Introduction at a low price, with a substantial discount *vis-à-vis* the cost of equivalent single journeys. Apart from the obvious transfer effect to those who gain, benefits may be ascertained in terms of time savings, reduced operating costs, and possibly diversion of car users to public transport. Cost-benefit analysis may be used to evaluate the net benefit or cost resulting – for example, in work on Greater Manchester by Tyson [Tyson, 1978]. Disaggregate modelling techniques may be employed to explain user choice between travelcards and cash fares [Doxsey, 1984], although this in itself does not provide an evaluation of costs and benefits, and may lead to a naive interpretation that schemes are not worthwhile, due to the net financial loss which must result in the short term. Another recent example of initial benefits being appraised in cost-benefit terms is the London Transport Travelcard, described below.
2. Subsequent real price increases, in line with general trends (to cover rising labour costs, etc.) and to offset the initial loss due to discount offered. If single, cash-paid fares rose less rapidly, and the same elasticity applied as in the first stage, then changes would simply be reversed, with a gain in real revenue (since public transport demand is inelastic), but loss of the benefits due to faster boarding times etc. as listed above. If, however, the effect is *not* symmetrical, then we may be able to retain the user and operational benefits, while improving financial performance. The analysis of the S-shaped curve described above supports this concept, which is examined in the West Midlands case study.

   Another long-run factor is a 'learning curve' process in which knowledge of the Travelcard gradually becomes more widespread, both among existing public transport users who may be slow to switch to pre-payment (although response to the London Travelcard has been very rapid) and others (such as car users). This may produce an underlying growth, quite apart from effects of fares changes. In Britain, conversion of urban bus operations to one-person-operation during the 1970s has been another factor. The relative convenience of the travelcard is increased when cash has to be paid to the driver on boarding, especially on 'Autofare' systems in which exact change is required. This is likely to have been an underlying element in growth in use of the Lothian Region 'Ridercard' [White, 1981] and West Midlands Travelcard.

CASE STUDY 1: THE WEST MIDLANDS

The West Midlands conurbation, centred on Birmingham, offers the most extensive example of Travelcard use in Britain, apart from the recently introduced London scheme. As such, it has provided the opportunity to study in greater depth than elsewhere, the long-run impact of such a scheme [White, 1983a], described briefly in this paper. The conurbation contains some 2.6 million people, covering Coventry, Birmingham, the 'Black Country', West Bromwich, Walsall and Wolverhampton. Since 1973 almost all buses have been operated directly by the Passenger Transport Executive, following the takeover of formerly separate municipal fleets, and the extensive 'Midland Red' (National Bus Company) services in the area. The Travelcard is available also on local rail services, operated by British Rail on behalf of the PTE, and other bus operators in the area, but these account for only six per cent of all public transport journeys and 12 per cent of passenger mileage.

The Travelcard was first introduced in 1972, providing unlimited use of the bus network over the whole metropolitan county from late 1973. Weekly and four-weekly versions have been offered throughout this period, with a 13-week version since 1979. In June 1975 a bus/rail Travelcard was introduced, at a slightly higher price. Its use grew rapidly, and since August 1980 the distinction has been abolished, with the standard Travelcard covering both bus and rail services. Bus/rail integration has been encouraged by new interchanges. Local Travelcards were introduced in March 1980, for the fairly self-contained Coventry and Wolverhampton areas, followed by a similar card for Walsall. However, most cards continue to be for the county as a whole. An off-peak only card was introduced in August 1982. The number on issue has risen from about 20,000 in 1973 to 120,000 in 1980, and is currently around 160,000. Journeys made by Travelcard holders average around 20 (unlinked) per week, and account for about 30 per cent of all trips on the network. A further 23 per cent of all trips are made by holders of free concessionary travel passes (mostly pensioners). 'Market gearing' may be estimated: the Travelcard holders comprise about seven per cent of the adult population, yet make about 30 per cent of all bus trips.

Until 1975 a general 'fares freeze' was applied to the West Midlands network, with the Travelcard introduced at a low price, but not changing relative to other fares. From 1975 a series of real fare increases took place, which have continued apart from a period of low fares in 1981/82. The steady rise in Travelcard sales *since* 1975 is thus striking. As Figure 4 shows, a falling real price correlated with rising sales up to 1975, as would be expected, but the steady growth in sales continued thereafter *despite* substantial real price increases. The apparently absurd phenomenon of a positive 'price elasticity' may be explained by the fact that cash-paid single fares rose more rapidly in real terms, the resulting transfer to Travelcard explaining much of the sales growth. Figure 5 includes a price ratio for Travelcard to single journey fares, rising from 100 in 1974 to 129 in 1982. However, even when this ratio displayed little change (for example, in 1977 and 1978), Travelcard sales continued to grow. Although the shift may explain a substantial part of the growth, it does not explain the continued retention of Travelcard use as such, while the price rose substantially in real terms. No meaningful 'own price' elasticity for the Travelcard can be derived.

FIGURE 4

TRENDS IN 'TRAVELCARD' SALES AND PRICE IN THE WEST MIDLANDS

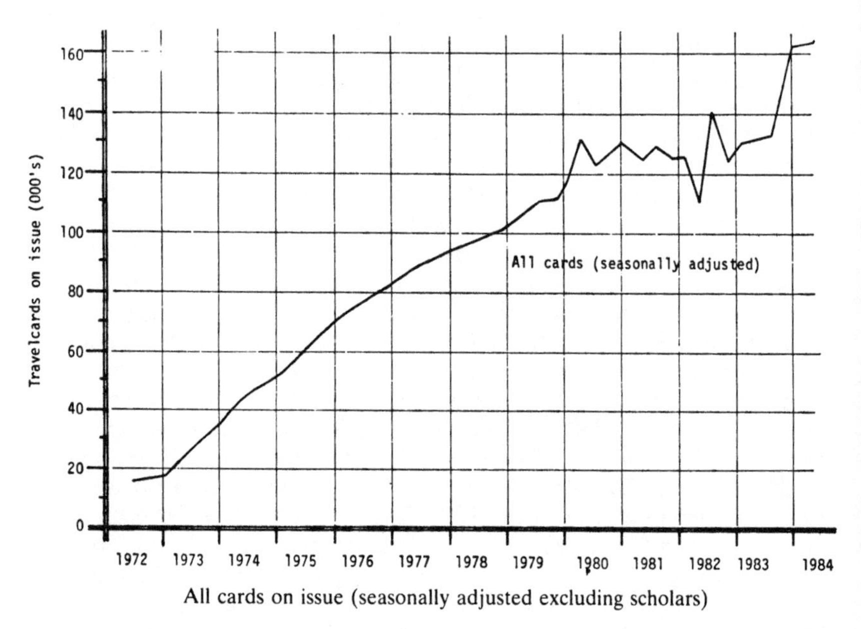

All cards on issue (seasonally adjusted excluding scholars)

Source: White [1983a]

The growth of Travelcard use was associated with a high level of bus use in the West Midlands during the 1970s, especially in comparison with other Passenger Transport Executives (apart from South Yorkshire, with extremely low real fares). An attempt to estimate Travelcard's contribution to this difference was made by applying a simple time-series model of the form generally used for urban bus forecasting:

$$\Delta T = -1.5 - 0.3\Delta RF + 0.4\Delta BM$$

in which Δ represents the percentage change between successive years, T total passenger trips, RF the average 'real fare' (that is, revenue per trip, adjusted for inflation), and BM bus miles run (a proxy for the level of service). The constant of -1.5 is a trend factor, representing the underlying decline in bus travel that would be associated with rising car ownership, and falling population density. Such models have been found to give

FIGURE 5
TREND IN REAL PRICE OF FOUR-WEEKLY ALL-COUNTRY ADULT TRAVELCARD, AND PRICE RATIO WITH CASH-PAID TRIPS

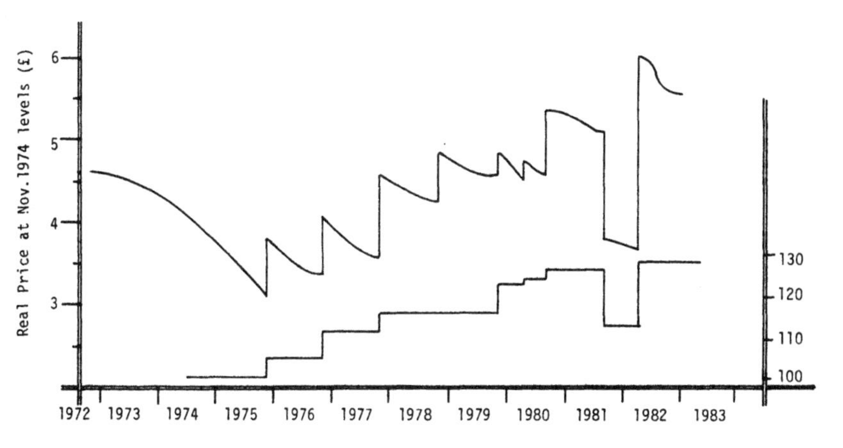

Source: White [1983a]

a good fit to data for many operators, albeit with higher trend factors in some cases.

In the above equation −0.3 and +0.4 are elasticities of demand with respect to real fares and service level. Using such an equation, 1974/5 was taken as the base year, and changes in the PTE's own bus trips were replicated using known annual changes in fares and bus miles. Given a virtually stable level of service to 1980, changes in fares were the main factor, leading to an 'expected' decline in trips from 1974/5 such that the 1979/80 observed total was about 7.5 per cent higher than that estimated from the model. Allowance was made for the need to raise fares further in order to obtain the same revenue as that actually received, had all fares remained cash-paid. Sensitivity tests for the trend factor (taking −1.0 per cent) were also made, revealing again a significant difference between estimated and observed totals. Pensioner's free travel was excluded entirely from the model, which was based on fare-paying groups (adult and child) only.

From 1979/80, unemployment rose steeply in the West Midlands, after a gradual rise in the late 1970s. This has had severe effects on bus patronage. Not only are work trips lost (and the types of worker becoming unemployed are more likely to have been bus passengers), but reduced household income hits other types of bus trip. Where a car-owning worker becomes unemployed, his car becomes available for other trips by household members, again causing fewer bus trips.

Based on work in West Yorkshire [Fisher, *et al.* 1982] a drop in bus travel of about 1.4 per cent for each one percentage point rise in unemployment was assumed (a rise from five to ten per cent unemployment thus causing a seven per cent drop in trips). As a sensitivity test, a 1.0 per cent patronage drop for each one percentage point rise was also tested. Extension of the time-series model to 1981/82, including the unemployment factor and effects of service cuts from 1980, confirmed that patronage was substantially higher than expected, by seven to ten percent, although Travelcard sales were fairly static during this period (as one would expect, given the journey to work as the main rationale for purchase).

Growth of Travelcard use in the West Midlands has also enabled costs per bus mile to be reduced, as a result of faster boarding times. This is particularly valuable at peak periods, enabling a small reduction in the number of buses and crews needed, as scheduled journey times can be cut. Conversion to 100 per cent one-person-operation has been made possible, even on the heaviest routes. In terms of cost-benefit analysis, allowance must be made for the fact that at least some of the patronage 'retained' through Travelcard use requires greater peak capacity than would otherwise be needed. On the other hand, time savings to passengers through quicker boarding times (reducing journey time for *all* users) may also be included, in line with the evaluation methods used for road improvements. A sensitivity test was applied to the assumed extra capacity costs, showing a net benefit at all values applied.

The introduction of the Travelcard, with its low initial price, and associated revenue loss, followed by improved financial performance in later years, may be viewed as a form of investment. A negative cash flow is followed by a positive flow, to produce a net benefit over the whole period. Timing of costs and benefits may be incorporated by use of discount cash flow. In the West Midlands case, taking passenger trips made (as a proxy for user benefit), and net deficit (allowing for operating cost savings), both were discounted at five per cent per annum from a base year of 1974/75. Compared with a situation based on 'expected' patronage using the time-series model, trips per £ deficit were about 13 per cent higher over the period to 1981/2 with the Travelcard in use. Most of the net benefit arises from a greater level of traffic retention. With a more cumbersome cash-paid fares system than the rapid 'Autofare' used by WMPTE, a substantially greater operating cost saving could have applied.

Recent development of the West Midland travelcard has focused on the off-peak market. An off-peak only Travelcard was introduced in August 1982, valid countywide from 0930 to 1530 and 1800 to 2215 Mondays to Fridays, and all day until 2215 at weekends, initially priced at £5 for two weeks, and reduced to £3.50 in October 1983, when the cash-paid off-peak fares were cut to a maximum of 32p. This has proved popular, and about 25,000 are currently on issue (at April 1984). About 20 per cent of users are part-time workers, 25 per cent housewives, and over 40 per cent are unemployed. Further analysis is now being made of price elasticities in the West Midlands by the Transport Studies Unit, University of Oxford. This includes further examination of relative

Travelcards: cash-paid journey price effects, and also turnover of the Travelcard market over time (about twice as many photo identity cards have been issued as there are Travelcards currently in use).

CASE STUDY 2: LONDON TRANSPORT

In many respects, London is one of the areas with the greatest potential for travelcard use, given its complex networks of bus and rail services creating extensive interchange. Heavy loadings lead to substantial savings in operating costs and passenger queuing/boarding time from simplified fare systems. The high proportion of regular journey-to-work trips also creates a favourable market for the travelcard. Yet not until the present Travelcard was introduced in May 1983 did these benefits – as described below – at last become apparent. Explanations for the delay lie in managerial conservatism, institutional factors and political instability.

Season tickets have long formed a major part of rail demand in London, for reasons explained earlier in this paper. Journeys to work are the largest single trip purpose: in 1971, some 72 per cent of the London Transport (LT) rail ('underground') journeys were to/from work [GLTS, 1971]. Yet, on LT railways, only 37 per cent of passenger trips in 1976 were made by season ticket holders. Even those travelling to work and making other frequent trips continued to buy daily, rather than season, tickets. One factor in this was probably the restriction of seasons to specific routes and stations, making them unattractive for someone whose travel pattern involved frequent variations from a set route. Each season ticket holder made about 11 single linked trips per week, suggesting relatively little use additional to the five return trips to work.

On LT buses, virtually all fares were paid in cash in the early 1970s. However, extension of free off-peak travel to all GLC pensioners from 1973 resulted in a substantial proportion of the market (currently around 20 per cent of all bus passengers) shifting to this form of pass, instead of cash payment. A 'bus pass' was introduced in 1972, following the general fashion for travelcards at that time. All fares were frozen until March 1975. The bus pass price was initially held down, leading to a rapid growth in sales, to over 100,000 by the end of 1976. However, subsequent price increases appear to have caused a shift back to cash-paid trips, together with a general decline of bus patronage, such that sales fell to about 50,000 by early 1981 [Collins, 1982].

Appeal of the bus pass was limited by the fact that a single price was set for the whole GLC area, without zoning. A relatively high price was thus set, and only users with a very high trip rate, and/or making long trips, would find purchase worthwhile. Since bus use is generally for short, local journeys, predominantly non-work, the great majority of users would not find purchase attractive. Initial purchase, and subsequent renewal, was made difficult by the poor access to sales outlets, mainly LT's own bus depots. A further problem was that the bus pass was relatively cheap *vis-à-vis* rail fares. Although reflecting the higher elasticity of bus travel, it had the unfortunate effect that some rail users were encouraged to shift to bus at peak periods, despite the higher marginal operating costs and longer journey times which resulted.

The shift from Labour to Conservative control of the GLC, from 1977 to 1981, resulted in further fare increases, although it was accepted that break-even operation was unlikely. Although they were not opposed to new fares structures as such (Travelcard use in the West Midlands continued to expand during the corresponding period of Conservative control), the general reduction in financial support made it more difficult to take the risks involved in a radical change. None the less, some important changes did take place during this period, resulting from a shift in management attitudes rather than political views. LT management had tended to see the traditional graduated fare system as the best form of maximising passenger demand for a given financial target, as indeed a conventional interpretation of elasticities would suggest. One-person-operation ('opo') had been slow to develop in London, due in part to the cumbersome forms of ticket issue used, and also the poor mechanical reliability of the rear-engined buses needed for opo compared with the front-engined 'Routemaster' type. Due to the high price, bus pass penetration remained low, and did not influence significantly the case for further opo conversion.

Management views changed after experimental flat fare schemes in the Harrow and Havering areas in 1980 [Fairhurst, 1981]. Although still based mainly on cash fares, these showed a different response to that which would have been expected on traditional elasticities. A loss of short-distance trips occurred, but less than expected, while medium- and longer-distance trips grew. Fare evasion was reduced, as those who previously paid the minimum fare then over-rode, were charged the same flat fare. Following these experiments, a general suburban flat fare (on buses only) of 25p was introduced in April 1981. This covered over half the total operating area and patronage, but excluded inner suburbs and the central area. A 'suburban' bus pass was introduced, as well as the all-London form, but was purchased mainly by existing bus pass holders, rather than new customers.

In May 1981 a Labour council was elected, with a commitment to a 25 per cent fares reduction. The exact form this was to take was not specified but four options were put forward, including a 25 per cent cut on all existing fares, and a flat fare. With LT management encouragement, a simplified zonal scheme was introduced from October 1981, under the title 'Fares Fair'. Four bus zones were set up – the existing suburban zone, two zones within the central area (West End and City), and an inner suburban zone, with weekly and monthly passes for each. A similar cut was also made in underground fares, but except in the two central zones, these did not match the bus flat fares.

'Fares Fair' is best known for the complex legal disputes which followed, culminating in a judgement from the House of Lords in December 1981 [White, 1983b]. A 100 per cent fares increase took place from March 1982. However, the effects on patronage were not as bad as might have been expected, probably due to the attractions of the simplified structure and some increase in bus pass penetration, to give sales of about 80,000 [Collins, 1982] and about 18–20 per cent of peak passenger boardings. The GLC subsequently reformulated its policies in a manner acceptable to lawyers, and under its 'Medium Term Plan', a new 25 per cent fares reduction came into force in May 1983. This was combined with a further shift toward zonal pricing and, at last, the introduction of bus/rail Travelcards. The West End and City zones were merged into a single central zone for both modes, and additional concentric suburban zones introduced for rail travel to discriminate more finely by trip length along the major rail corridors into central London. All existing rail seasons were replaced by the Travelcard, as were most bus passes, although some bus-only passes remain in use within suburban areas.

The impact of the bus/rail Travelcard has been immediate and dramatic. By the end of 1983, passenger journeys had risen by 11 per cent and passenger miles by 16 per cent. A total of almost 600,000 people held Bus Passes and Travelcards, compared with 450,000 holders of rail seasons and bus passes 12 months before. They took advantage of the additional 'free' trips to make about 60 per cent more trips each, offsetting a decline elsewhere in single trip sales. Despite increased traffic, queuing times at stations, and total boarding times on buses did not increase, due to the greater use of pre-paid travel. The regular October cordon survey of peak travel by all modes into central London showed car use down by nine per cent, and bus and underground combined up by seven per cent, suggesting a substantial shift from car to underground. Using LT's criterion of passenger miles generated per £ spent, a figure of 8.3 was observed, more than double the conventional return expected. On a cost-benefit basis, a benefit to cost ratio of 2.3 was observed [London Transport, 1984].

Such effects have caused some financial loss, although far less than estimated, due to high sales. Even within the first stage, as defined earlier in this paper, the LT Travelcard displays most encouraging performance. The experience of the 100 per cent fares increase after 'Fares Fair' suggests that even with the low bus pass penetration at that time, more patronage was retained for a given fares increase. For the present, the GLC intends to keep fares fixed, while working toward a logical extension of the Travelcard to BR services within London, and some through ticketing for single journeys. Some fares increase may become necessary, especially under the central government takeover of London Transport (renamed London Regional Transport) from 29 June 1984. Provided that the fare increases do not pass the critical threshold level, this should provide a further illustration of the theories in this article, and enable an improved financial performance while retaining the user and operator benefits of Travelcard.

OTHER SYSTEMS

West Midlands and London have been selected to illustrate two aspects of Travelcard use, one in which long-run effects can be appraised, the other in which a large initial benefit is clear. Elsewhere in Britain, Travelcard use continues to grow, although not as yet subject to such detailed analysis. Most other PTEs, notably Tyne and Wear, and Merseyside, offer similar tickets, but with a greater degree of zoning to reflect the complex urban structure.

Many other British urban areas have travelcards, including most district council and regional council operators, and many areas served by the National Bus Company (such as the Bristol city 'Rovercard'). However, market penetration is often weak, due to relatively high prices being charged. Such operators generally operate much closer to 'break even' (after contributions for concessionary fares to pensioners, etc.) and although this may be held traditionally to stimulate marketing innovation and operational efficiency, it does limit the degree of risk which can be taken in the short run. The initial discount given is thus small, and relatively few users will find purchase worthwhile. Market penetration remains limited to about five per cent or even less, often insufficient to have any significant effect on total boarding times or overall patronage trends, although individuals with a high trip frequency clearly benefit.

Elsewhere in Europe a much higher penetration is found, associated with a history of flat fares and transfer tickets mentioned earlier in this paper. Given a flat fare, once a discount is given, a large proportion of regular users will probably switch to Travelcard. Total public transport use has often grown, assisted by high levels of investment and operating subsidy, in which the travelcard is one element. Examples such as the 'Carte Orange' of Paris, and the Stockholm monthly card account for over 50 per cent of all passenger trips in systems on which they apply. There is evidence of a low elasticity of demand for price increases from a low initial level for such travelcards [White, 1981], but fuller analysis has yet to be undertaken.

North America offers many travelcards, which have developed as part of general low price strategies. Extensive analysis has been undertaken of the relationship between price discount and market penentration, for example, Mayworm and Lago [1983], but there appears to be little evidence of the appraisal of long-run benefits. Coupled with present concern about operating deficits, this could lead to a somewhat short-term view being taken.

The 'Carte Orange' offers an interesting contrast with London, in that it covers SNCF (national railways) suburban services, as well as the bus and metro network of RATP (equivalent to London Transport). This more extensive coverage gives it not only a bigger market share, but also a much higher number of holders (1.5 million at May 1982).

CONCLUSIONS

This article has aimed at setting out an approach to public transport marketing in which a changed form of pricing and ticket issue affects not only the average cost per journey, but the entire perception of system quality. This change has been initiated not, in most cases, by marketing specialists within the public transport industry (whose role has remained closer to that of selling existing products) but by politicians and senior management. Almost all the operators are in any case within the public sector, and substantial financial support from public funds has often been necessary to initiate such schemes. However, their subsequent effects may be analysed in the same terms as other marketing initiatives – on sales, revenue, consumer benefits, and production costs. In the long run, financial performance is not necessarily worse than for conventional pricing structures, while other benefits can be retained.

Experience in Britain is of particular interest, since travelcards have been introduced against a background of generally lower financial support than elsewhere in North America or Western Europe, and thus the effects of subsequent real price increases can be analysed, instead of travelcards simply forming one component of a general low fares level.

REFERENCES

Brög, W. and O.G. Förg, 'What Public Transportation Management Should Know About Possible User Reactions', Transportation Research Record, 746, *TRB*, Washington.

Collins, P.H., 1982, 'The Effect of Recent London Transport Fare Changes', *Proceedings of PTRC Summer Annual Meeting, Seminar M: Public Transport*, pp.41–54 (PTRC, London, 1982) and report in *The Transport Economist* (London), Issue No. 2.

Doxsey, L.B., 1984, 'Demand for Unlimited Use Transit Passes', *Journal of Transport Economics and Policy* January (see also forthcoming 'Comment' by P.R. White).

Engelbrecht, P., 1981, Paper at Confederation of Passenger Transport Annual Conference, Eastbourne, September 1981.

Fairhurst, M., 1981, 'Why Simplify? The Case for Simplified Fares', Economic Research Report R244, London Transport Executive.

Fisher, R., F. Grimshaw and R. Tebb, 1982, 'Analysing Bus Patronage – The Effects of Fares, Services and Unemployment', *Proceedings of Seminar on Public Transport*, pp.55–66 (PTRC, London, 1982).

GLTS, 1971, Greater London Transportation Survey 1971, Greater London Council.

London Transport Executive, 1984, Memorandum to the Greater London Council (LT Sub 575), 'The May 22 Fares Revision: Results and Impacts', January.

Mayworm, P.D., and A.M. Lago, 1983, Transit Fare Prepayment: A Guide for Transit Managers, Report by Esometrics, Inc. for Urban Mass Transportation Administration, Washington DC.

Tyson, W.J., 1978, 'The Economic Effects of Bus Season Tickets', paper at Tenth Annual Seminar on Public Transport Operations Research, University of Leeds, July.

White, P.R., 1981, 'Travelcard Tickets in Urban Public Transport', *Journal of Transport Economics and Policy*, January.

White, P.R., 1983a, 'An Evaluation of the long-term effects of the West Midlands Travelcard', West Midlands PTE, Birmingham.

White, P.R., 1983b, 'Further Developments in the Pricing of Local Public Transport', *Transport Reviews*, Vol. 3, No. 4.

White, P.R., 1984, 'User Response to Price Changes: Application of the "Threshold" Concept', paper at World Conference on Transport Research, Hamburg, April (to be published in *Transport Reviews*, 1984, Vol. 4).

Local Authorities and the Marketing of Leisure Services

by

David Yorke

In the past, local authorities have attempted with varying degrees of success to fill a need for leisure activities amongst the community each serves. Of late, there have been two significant trends facing the operation of these activities – first, the increasing competition, particularly from the private sector, in the provision of leisure services and second, a reduction in public resources to provide them. This article shows how, by adopting a more customer-orientated approach, the twin problems may be tackled to the benefit of both the authority and the community.

INTRODUCTION

From a marketing point of view, there is no such thing as 'the general public' because, theoretically, every customer is an individual, displaying wide-ranging characteristics in each purchasing situation. However, in most cases, supplier organisations, particularly those providing consumer goods and services, cannot treat their purchasers as individuals and so are forced to group those of similar habits and characteristics into 'market segments', where each is sufficiently discrete to warrant separate treatment either in the form, or the perceived form, of the product or service being offered, or in the manner in which communication takes place in order to motivate them to buy.

Furthermore, very few organisations possess the resources to be able to supply the whole range of market segments and, therefore, some form of priority list has to be drawn up, with a concentration of resources on those segments which yield a return in line with corporate objectives, both current and those in the defined future. The problem of resource attraction and allocation is even more pressing for local authorities in trying to meet the needs of the community each is trying to serve. Quite clearly there are statutory obligations which have to be met, for example, the provision of education, housing, roads, social services, security and waste disposal but, following these, there are other 'discretionary' needs which may be met, principally those associated with leisure-time activities.

How, then, might local authorities seek to provide a range of activities which meets the leisure needs of the community they exist to serve, together with an organisation structure which is capable of deriving the best possible use for them?

LEISURE

A number of national statistical indicators continue to forecast a rapidly changing demographic and social environment in the 1980s where practically all elements of the population will be faced with increased spare time. In certain areas of the country, notably those with a large number of retired persons and those where unemployment continues to persist at a high rate, the amount of available spare time will assume even greater proportions. For those in work developing technology will mean less manual and more sedentary work; this work will be done increasingly by females, particularly married females, and the balance of the traditional household will change as a result. Finally, people are seeking more 'active' ways in which to spend their leisure time, not necessarily by the expenditure of physical effort but by performing 'worthy' activities.

Against such a background, there have been, and will continue to be, marked economic changes. Real incomes for those in employment, and also in particular parts of the country, will rise, and expenditure on 'leisure activities', as a percentage of disposable income, is expected to grow. In addition, increased affluence generally brings greater mobility, particularly by private means of transport and the opportunity to indulge in a wider range of leisure activities will subsequently increase.

Expenditure by consumers in 1980 on leisure and recreation activities, together with percentage changes from 1970, can be seen from Table 1.

Only the cinema has suffered a major decline over the period and is unlikely to see the trend substantially reversed in the 1980s. However, as a result of the major social and demographic changes, referred to above, which began at the end of the last decade, it is likely that real expenditure on the various other leisure activities shown in the table will accelerate during the current decade.

LOCAL AUTHORITIES

To help serve these consumer needs, local authorities have become major suppliers and operators of facilities. Table 2 shows the increasing amount spent, even in recent years, by local authorities on some such activities.

Local authorities may thus be said to be well and truly in the leisure business but, unfortunately, they do not have a monopoly of the consumer's time or purse in this growth area as the competition from commercially orientated organisations in the private sector is intense. Such competition may not, at first sight, seem obvious, as there does not appear to be a large number of private sector organisations involved in operating libraries, and recreation centres. There is, however, some

TABLE 1
PERCENTAGE CHANGE IN LEISURE EXPENDITURE IN REAL TERMS (1971–1980)

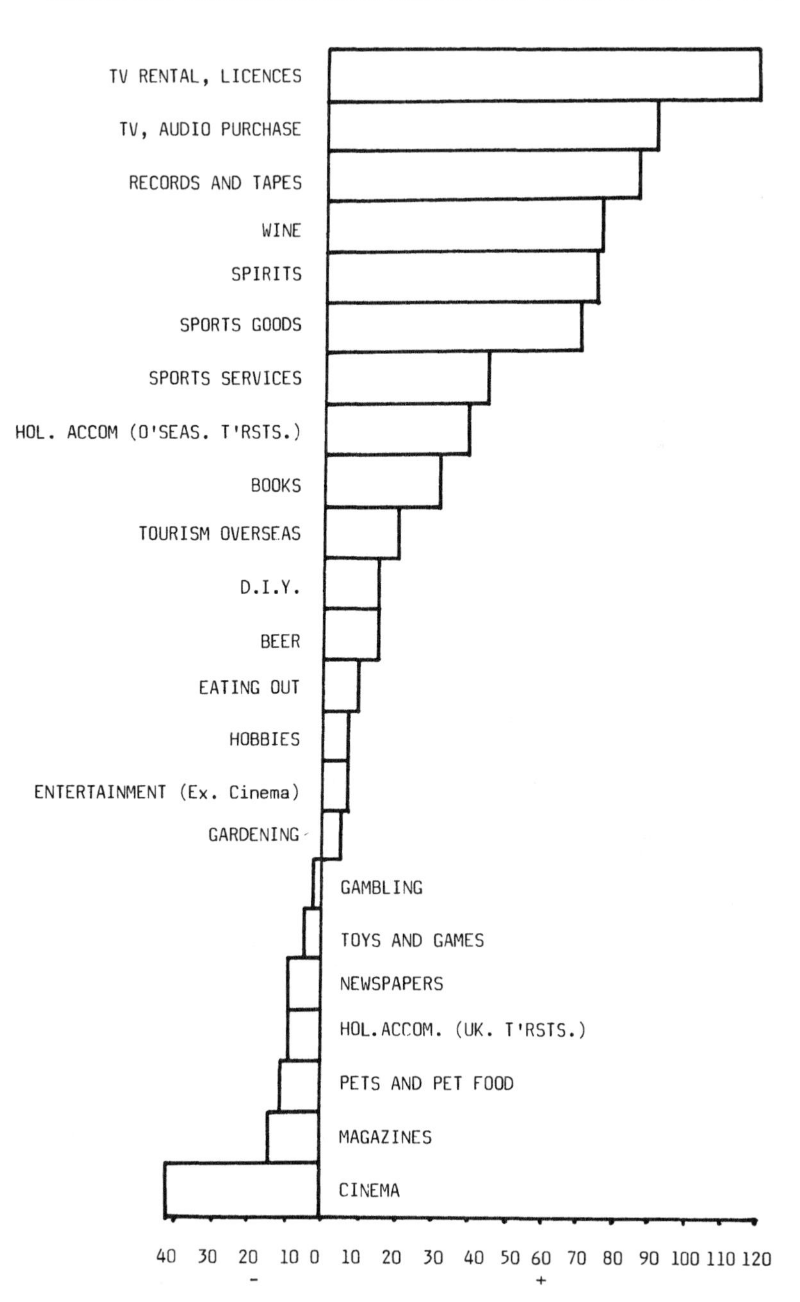

Source: Sport in the Community, The Sports Council, 1982.

TABLE 2

ESTIMATED LOCAL AUTHORITY EXPENDITURE ON LEISURE AND RECREATION
(England and Wales)

	£'000		
	1980–81	*1981–2*	% *increase*
Parks and open spaces	219,260	241,570	10
Swimming pools	83,262	89,979	8
Indoor sports halls and leisure centres	70,047	83,935	19
Theatres, etc.	34,781	47,033	38
Art galleries/museums	36,388	44,073	21
Community centres and public halls	27,037	30,814	14
Outdoor sports facilities	19,462	21,151	8
Country parks/amenity areas	15,166	13,980	(8)
Libraries*	298,000	320,000	7

*(Great Britain)

Source: Social Trends 1983

overlap in the case of theatres, museums, parks and gardens and swimming pools and, at the other end of the spectrum, local authorities, in the main, do not concern themselves with the direct provision and operation of cinemas and the many varied sports clubs and interest societies. Nevertheless, all these activities are competing for the consumer's time and purse and what would seem to be required, therefore, is a strong realisation by local authorities that a more customer- or market-orientated approach is required for the successful operation of any leisure-based activities in which they are, or might become, engaged.

At this stage it may be interesting to state what the objectives of local authorities are, in general, and also, in relation to the provision of specific leisure activities. Writing in 1967, Maud said that the purpose of local government action is 'human happiness' but, undoubtedly, local government policy makers face a multiplicity of potentially conflicting and, perhaps, irreconcilable demands on their limited resources in their attempt to achieve this.

There is a wide disparity both in the quantity and quality of services provided by local authorities as national legislation normally gives wide powers of discretion by only laying down the maximum and minimum 'levels' (often described qualitatively) of service provision. For instance, in 1964, the Public Libraries and Museums Act stated that the Minister was to 'superintend and promote the improvement of the public library services provided by local authorities and secure the proper discharge by the local authorities of their functions in relation to libraries conferred on them as library authorities by or under the Act'. Nevertheless, it may be that it is this very discretion, coupled with the democratic basis of government, which actually ensures the effective provision of consumer services within a context of accountability, control and redress of grievances.

However, it is not only legal guidelines which condition the quality of services provided by local authorities. Whereas before 1975 it was expected that local authority expenditure would exceed forecasts both in total and on individual services, thus leading to a situation of incremental budgeting, that year saw the imposition of cash limits on expenditure and local authorities were faced, probably for the first time since the Second World War, with a critical review of services. There were, inevitably, disproportionate reductions in individual service budgets as resources were transferred within authorities to support the 'key' services of education, housing, roads, etc. Further controls and penalties have since followed, with the resulting deceleration of the development of 'non-key' services such as leisure and recreation.

The fundamental problem, therefore, facing local authorities, particularly in these 'non-key' areas, is how best to meet the needs of the community they purport to serve. Whilst they are expected to operate 'in the public interest' where 'public' is a synonym for 'community', quite clearly, given the problem of limited resources, such an ideal becomes manifestly difficult. Nevertheless, they must operate, and be seen to be operating, 'efficiently', where maximum output is being effected with given inputs and, in this respect, they are no different from profit-orientated organisations. Difficulties arise with respect to the measurement of 'output' but perhaps, more importantly, it is not the simple measurement of 'output' which is required, but that of the 'desired' or 'planned' output which can be achieved given the limited resource inputs available. Such measurement would form part of the marketing concept for a profit-based organisation.

MARKETING AND LOCAL AUTHORITIES

Is the concept of marketing, however, relevant to local authority operations? In the main, local authorities aim to provide a service and the above question presupposes, firstly, that marketing can be applied to any service industry. Much has been written on this subject [see, for example, Stanton, 1967: 572–5; Blois, 1974; Shostack, 1977; Thomas, 1978; Cowell, 1980; Shostack, 1982; Lovelock, 1983]. However, there still remains the problem of its application to a service, the objective of which is something other than profit. The dialogue on this subject was initiated in the late 1960s in the USA [Kotler and Levy, 1969; Luck, 1969] and has continued during the 1970s and early 1980s [Shapiro, 1973; Kotler, 1975; Capon, 1981]. More recently, doubts have been expressed anew [Foxall, 1983, 1984]. The argument would seem to depend on the definition of the term 'marketing' and if the argument is to be resolved it is to this problem that an answer must be found. Perhaps an acceptable, even if broad, definition might be 'The matching of corporate resources to the needs of customers in order that each may achieve defined objectives', but this definition still begs a number of questions, namely, 'What do we mean by "resources"?' 'Can market "needs" be identified?' and perhaps, most important of all, 'Can "objectives" be defined in such a way that they become operational from the point of view of the supplier's management?' Each of these questions has implications for a local authority.

Firstly, resources. For any organisation, resources usually mean manpower (and the necessary skills which it holds), money (to pay for both the manpower and the fixed or intangible assets) and the time available to do things. Typically, local authorities have been large employers of semi-skilled or unskilled labour on the one hand and 'professionals' on the other. 'Management' skills, it is suggested, have been relatively lacking, particularly in outward-looking activities such as marketing. However, manpower, in all its forms, is becoming expensive and the accent is currently being placed on the most efficient matching of inputs and outputs. This feature, together with the reduction in the number of hours worked by most employees is probably leading to a reduction in the total time available to do things. The repercussions for community leisure-based activities which, by definition, cannot take place in full during 'normal' working hours, are obvious. Finally, reference has already been made to the stricter controls being imposed on the traditional fund-raising activities of local authorities which now, in theory, are no longer able to obtain incremental financial resources from the rates. All in all, 'resources' are now at a premium and new ways will probably have to be devised both to raise income, and to ensure their efficient use.

The identification of market 'needs' is a perennial problem facing any organisation. Crucial to the issue is the answer to the question 'What business are we in?' and it has already been suggested that local authorities are, for the purpose of this article, in the 'leisure' business. Nevertheless, a person's 'leisure', or more correctly, 'leisure time' can be filled with innumerable activities ranging from doing nothing to virtually anything for which financial reward is not sought and from which a degree of pleasure is experienced. (For a discussion of the meaning of 'leisure' see Kaplan [1961]; Parker [1971]; Rapoport and Rapoport [1974].) The possibilities thus facing a local authority in providing services to meet this need are almost limitless but, as of now, in practice, are limited by financial constraints, resulting in a decision process which must, of necessity, lead to the provision of certain services to the exclusion of others. The mechanism of actually identifying 'needs' again presents problems. Market researchers in general know only too well the difficulties in establishing and measuring needs; the problem is compounded for local authorities by the lack of resources for the conduct of such research, a situation far from incomprehensible as the decision to sanction public expenditure on something so intangible as market research must be hard.

Objective-setting has, in the marketing sense, never been easy for local authorities. Profitability can, and should, never be the sole criterion for performance, but the question of what should replace it, and at the same time provide measurable yardsticks for management control, has never been satisfactorily answered. 'Number of users' of a particular service is a possibility, but this gives no indication of the degree of satisfaction obtained, or the costs involved in supplying it. Nevertheless, it is argued that quantifiable objectives should be set, particularly in the interests of taxpayers who are the principal providers of the resources.

The challenge facing local authorities in this area of leisure is, therefore, one of giving the 'best possible' service to as many members of the community as possible and as frequently as possible given the potentially limited resources available. Taking the above three variables, namely 'services', 'community' and 'frequency', a possible eight combinations present themselves at the macro level.

FIGURE 1
A TYPOLOGY OF STRATEGIES

	Services ('Things')	*Community* ('People')	*Frequency* ('Time')
1.	All	All	All
2.	All	All	Some
3.	All	Some	All
4.	All	Some	Some
5.	Some	All	All
6.	Some	All	Some
7.	Some	Some	All
8.	Some	Some	Some

By definition, the first combination (to be all things to all people all of the time) is currently (and likely to remain) out of the question. At the other end of the scale, a local authority is clearly not trying very hard if it adopts the last-named limited objectives (although some would argue that, in reality, this is their enforced present position). Six other possibilities would seem to present themselves and the question of which strategy to follow is essentially the crux of this article.

The marketing concept dictates that 'people' (market needs) should be paramount, whilst a strong body of opinion within any organisation (and traditionally within local authorities) would argue that it is the 'range of services' which should dominate, believing that their provision is a social responsibility, often filling gaps which private sector organisations will not fill, prime examples being the public library and museum services. However, even at the micro level, that is, within a given service, such as that of public libraries, there still remains the problem of trying to be all things to all people all of the time. Notwithstanding the fact that many people have never used a public library and are probably unaware of its range of services, lack of resources precludes sufficient attention being given to the many minorities within the community (such as ethnic groups, the housebound, the retarded, etc). Thus, resource allocation remains essentially subjective and 'service-based', perpetuating the essentially inward-looking strategies which have been the dominant feature of local authorities in the past.

A local authority is attempting to serve the whole community and it would seem, therefore, that any of the six strategies which clearly concentrates on 'some' of the people (to the permanent exclusion of others) should not be adopted, whether such concentration is for all or for some of the time, with or without a 'full' range of services. To take an extreme case, to pour all the available resources into the provision of a mobile library service for the housebound or, alternatively, to erect a sports centre for the physically active would satisfy the individuals involved, but would do little or nothing to meet the needs of large numbers of others. Thus strategies three, four and seven, whilst being perhaps theoretically desirable from a marketing point of view, would not conform to present-day local authority objectives and would be socially disastrous.

How, then, to repeat the question posed at the end of the Introduction, might local authorities seek to provide a range of activities which meets the leisure needs of the community they exist to serve? Which of the three remaining strategies previously outlined should be followed?

An answer to these questions is perhaps to be found in the concept of market segmentation.

MARKET SEGMENTATION

The 'community' is made up of a large number of individuals, each of whom has varying leisure needs both in terms of the activities sought and the frequency with which each is pursued. In any competitive situation, a supplier should attempt to identify those individual members of the community (or market) whose interests he thinks he can best serve, whilst simultaneously achieving the objectives he has set himself. Quite obviously, such service on a personalised basis is usually impossible and resort has to be made to combining as many individuals as possible into viable groups in order that an effective response is obtained. Such groups are called 'segments' and the concept of market segmentation should be the cornerstone of any marketing strategy, whatever the objective set. Yet the concept is largely misunderstood, particularly in local government but is, in the author's view, one which could and should be used by local authorities in facing their current problems.

Market segmentation analysis should satisfy three criteria [Kotler, 1980: 205–6]. Segments should, firstly, be measurable. Statistics giving demographic and socio-economic profiles of the community should present few problems for a local authority, but more recent bases for segments using 'personality' or user behaviour variables are less easy to quantify and are relatively expensive to obtain from field surveys. The second criterion is that each segment should be accessible, not physically, but in a communication sense. Consideration should be given to reaching the target groups(s) in as cost-effective a way as possible, but again the more qualitative, the less quantitative the segment, the more difficult such cost-effectiveness becomes. Thirdly, each segment should be substantial, that is, large enough to be worthy of consideration. For a local authority, this last criterion might be unacceptable; a segment does not have to be 'large' to be worthy of consideration.

The advantages to be gained from adopting the concept of segmentation are many [Engel, Fiorillo and Cayley, 1972: 2–3]. First, the organisation should be able to spot opportunities in the market-place more rapidly. Second, as a result, the whole ethos of an organisation will become outward-looking, attempting to achieve its own objectives by giving customer satisfaction and developing customer loyalty. Finally, and most importantly, from the point of view of organisations in general and of local authorities in particular, limited resources are being committed efficiently, not only by the provision of assets, physical and human, to meet market needs but also in choosing the means of communication by which potential customers or users can be informed of their existence.

The question now arises as to how the total market for local authority leisure activities may be subdivided into segments and what bases might be used to distinguish meaningfully one group of people from another. There is no standard answer to this problem – indeed regional variations in the population structure will preclude any simple solution. Nevertheless, it is argued that there is a small number of meaningful bases which may be adapted and used by local authorities in their quest to identify discrete target markets. The combination of such bases could result in the following segments being identified:

Stage in family life cycle
Employment (or otherwise)
Neighbourhood type

– and the resulting three-dimensional grid being established (see Figure 2.)

It is stressed that these variables or bases are purely hypothetical but may, nevertheless, provide useful starting points for the purpose of illustration. Perhaps some explanation of the subdivisions of each variable should be made. From the point of view of a number of organisations, prospective customers may well be sought, not simply by age, but by the stage they have reached in the life cycle. Thus, single persons, notwithstanding their age, may have differing leisure needs and interests from young marrieds, or from marrieds with children or married persons, whose children have left home to establish themselves. The second dimension: student, working (full or part-time) retired/not working, has obvious implications for leisure activities as a result of the amount of spare time available. Thirdly, 'neighbourhood type'. In recent years, an alternative method of classifying persons, other than by 'social class' (which is based on the occupation of the head of the household) has been developed and is based on the existence of 11 neighbourhood types, that is, the type of residential area in which persons live. The system, known

FIGURE 2
A THREE DIMENSIONAL APPROACH TO THE IDENTIFICATION OF MARKET SEGMENTS

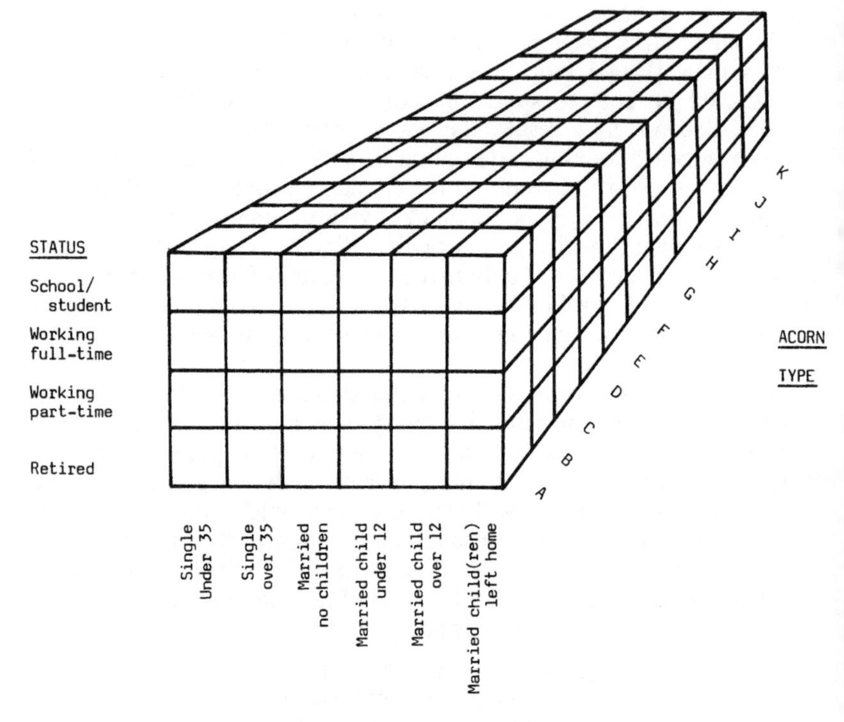

STAGE IN FAMILY LIFE CYCLE

as ACORN, 'A Classification of Residential Neighbourhoods', applies published census statistics, using 40 different variables, encompassing demographic, housing and employment characteristics, to produce 11 distinctive groups of neighbourhood, which may be further subdivided to form 38 neighbourhood types in all [CACI, 1983]. It is argued that different neighbourhoods produce different lifestyles for their inhabitants. Lifestyle may thus be a relevant factor in a person's or a family's quest for leisure activities.

Theoretically, therefore, there exists, using these three dimensions, 6 x 4 x 11 = 264 identifiable segments, each of which differs from another along at least one dimension. In practical terms, some segments quite clearly do not (or rarely) exist (for example, retired, single, aged 35 and under) and the number of actual segments is, therefore, correspondingly reduced. In addition, it may be possible to combine a number of segments making the ultimate total more meaningful and actionable.

The next question to arise is 'what are the leisure needs of each identifiable market segment?' Results from previous research [Yorke,

1984] has revealed differences, as one might expect, in the leisure needs of different community groups, and in different areas of the country.

TABLE 3
LEISURE ACTIVITIES ENGAGED IN DURING THE PAST WEEK

	Married with children		*Married no children*	
	Area A	*Area B*	*Area A*	*Area B*
Playing Sport	12	2	4	1
Watching Sport	4	1	0	2
Going to cinema/theatre	1	0	1	0
Having a meal out	3	2	6	2
Going to a disco	5	2	1	0
Going for a drink	10	4	6	3
Attending an interest club	2	4	5	3
Attending an exhibition	1	1	1	0
Going to an evening class	0	0	1	0

Thus, for both these two groups, those in Area A seem to pursue more leisure interests of the type quoted than those in Area B. More particularly, more of these groups play sport in Area A than B. From another viewpoint, relatively more marrieds without children in Area A attend an interest group, whereas in Area B, it would seem to be relatively more marrieds with children who have a propensity to do so. Numbers are very small, but it is hoped that they serve to illustrate the point being made.

Further questions revealed that the communication process by which different groups in the community can be reached varies considerably. Whilst the local newspaper is a frequent source of information, marrieds, as opposed to young singles, can also cost-effectively be reached by carefully positioned posters in, for example, shopping centres and public libraries where the greatest number of the target group will see them.

STRATEGY

Quite clearly, therefore, the 'community' can be divided into meaningful groups or segments with differing needs and differing ways of reaching them. How may a local authority use this fact in the conduct of its leisure activities, given the three suggested strategies remaining, namely, to be:

all things to all people some of the time;
some things to all people all of the time;
some things to all people some of the time.

There are possible arguments for and against all three strategies, depending upon one's personal preferences and perhaps the resources which can be made available. However, it may clearly be argued that the third-named above is an inferior strategy to the second in that similar resources are being deployed to meet community needs, but at less frequent intervals and that their redeployment may result in increased customer satisfaction. Take a simple example within a particular leisure service (Figure 3).

FIGURE 3
INPUT/OUTPUT TABLE

Before Redeployment	*Activity A*	*Activity B*	*Total*
Costs (Units)	10x	12x	22x
Usage (Units)	15y	20y	35y
After Redeployment			
Costs (Units)	8x	14x	22x
Usage (Units)	15y	22y	37y

By redeploying some resource from one location to another, with no increase in total costs, the measured output (customer usage, etc.) has increased. Theoretically, there has to be an 'optimum' solution, but how many local authorities can honestly say that they have achieved it, particularly as the community is always in a state of change?

The choice between the first and second strategies above is difficult and must depend upon how one views the ability of each strategy to generate more custom and usage in the longer term. To offer 'some things all of the time' may alienate sections of the community who feel that their particular needs are unlikely to be met and, therefore, they perceive that there must be competing substitutes from the commercial sector better able to satisfy particular needs and resort to using them. Similarly to offer 'all things some of the time' implies that there will be periods during which certain services will not be offered, which again may alienate custom. The last-named also implies a deal of flexibility of organisation in that a list of priorities has to be drawn up and services offered in rotation over a given period of time.

My own preference is for the latter. In an ever-changing environment the former may result in an over-rigid approach with a given range of services being presented as a *fait accompli*. On the other hand, the latter at least offers a more flexible approach by adapting to the environment and to specifically changing needs as they occur, or even in advance of their occurrence, thus satisfying the advantages posed for the adoption of a market segmentation strategy (see previous section). Resources can be concentrated relatively more on those segments of the community which, it is currently thought, should need them. (Note that the market targets to be selected at any one time are not necessarily based on a high level of demand, but on criteria which the local authority chooses.)

It is important to emphasise, however, that this particular strategy – one of concentrating on different needs at different times – makes certain demands on any organisation which many may find difficult to meet. Above all, what is needed is flexibility – that of switching certain resources from one task to another, not necessarily with rapidity but in a planned and co-ordinated way. Such a strategy, therefore, demands both a flexible and a unified organisation structure to put it into practice.

ORGANISATION

The detailed consideration of local authority business cannot be done at full meetings of the Council, so committees are normally established to deal with specific areas. Some are devoted to a single service, for example, education (a vertical function); others to, for example, finance (a horizontal function). Committees are composed of elected members of the Council, but can include co-opted members with full voting rights providing they constitute less than one-third of the full voting membership. This process allows for the injection of specialist knowledge that, other than in education, unfortunately is rarely used.

The most evident drawback of the committee system is that committees are, by their very nature, introspective and tend to be swayed by the professional opinion of the paid officers (for example, the chief librarian). Likewise, there is a hierarchy of committees which vary in prestige, political power and, as a consequence, the financial resources which are controlled by them, together with the ability of individuals to administer them. 'Key' services, such as education, the social services, police, fire and highways, not unnaturally attract not only the young and able personnel, but also 80 per cent or more of the total financial resources, and it is hardly surprising that the development of 'non-key' services, such as the provision of leisure activities, is severely hindered. As stated earlier, of late, the withdrawal of central government support has seen greater pressure to reduce expenditure on what are considered to be non-key services, resulting in disproportionate cuts in these areas.

However, one of the problems which has probably beset the leisure-based services of local authorities is their own lack of co-ordination. Typically, there exists a Public Library Service, sometimes a Museums and Art Gallery Service (although on occasions the two have been combined to operate perhaps as 'Cultural Services'), departments covering the operation of leisure centres, parks and recreation grounds and occasionally, publishing. Each competes with the others for limited resources with little or no integration.

A corporate approach to the organisation of local authorities in general has been proposed [Lord Redcliffe-Maud, 1967; Bains, 1972.] Both urged the creation of a more senior or central committee which would formulate policy on major issues and manage the authority's activities, with Bains proposing its principal role as one of formulating a comprehensive plan to govern priorities in expenditure which would focus attention on the effectiveness of services (the output) relatively more than in the past when too much attention had been paid to expenditure (the input).

Bains emphasised the corporate approach, the essence of which is that few, if any, decisions can be made in isolation without having an impact elsewhere. The need to set objectives in the light of environmental change is paramount, together with a strategy for achieving them and a process for monitoring performance. What is also important is that whilst his proposals were aimed at the council or macro level they are also capable of implementation at the micro or committee/department level.

To date, such proposals have not generally been implemented by the local authority at the macro level, even with the tightening economic climate. There may, however, be a case at the micro level for a change of thinking and, in particular, where the range of leisure services is concerned. The creation of a department with a Director of Leisure Services embracing most, if not all, of such services would at the same time recognise both the growing importance which the provision of leisure activities takes within the work of a local authority, and also the need to develop more bargaining power for control of a greater proportion of the resources which may be made available. Indeed, this combined with a more market-orientated approach to meeting customer needs may result in not only the more cost-effective use of such resources but also in a more intensively used range of leisure services which can then be put forward as a very strong case for the appropriation of further resources.

The concentration on the provision of a range of leisure services to the community as often as possible (all or some things to all people some of the time) may then move a step nearer to the ideal where every member of the community, either as an individual or as part of a group, will be adequately provided with the services he or she needs.

REFERENCES

Bains, M.A., 1972, *The New Local Authorities Management and Structure*, London: HMSO.

Blois, K.J., 1974, 'The Marketing of Services: an approach', *European Journal of Marketing*, Vol. 8, No. 2.

CACI International, 1983, Market Analysis Division, London.

Capon, N., 1981, 'Marketing Strategy differences between state and privately owned corporations', *Journal of Marketing*, Vol. 45, No. 2.

Cowell, D.W., 1980, 'The Marketing of Services', *Managerial Finance*, Vol. 5, No. 3.

Engel, J.F., H.F. Fiorillo, and M.A. Cayley, 1972, *Market Segmentation*, New York: Holt, Reinhart & Winston.

Foxall, G.R., 1983, 'Can the Public Provision of Leisure Services be Consumer-Oriented?' *Service Industries Journal*, Vol. 3, No. 3.

Foxall, G.R., 1984, 'The Meaning of Marketing and Leisure: Issues for Research and Development', *European Journal of Marketing*, Vol. 18, No. 3.

Kaplan, M., 1961, *Leisure in America: A Social Inquiry*, New York: Wiley.

Kotler, P. and S.J. Levy, 1969, 'Broadening the Concept of Marketing', *Journal of Marketing*, Vol. 33, No. 1.

Kotler, P., 1975, *Marketing for Non-Profit Organisations*, 2nd ed., Englewood Cliffs, NJ: Prentice-Hall.

Kotler, P., 1980, '*Marketing Management*', 4th ed., Englewood Cliffs, NJ: Prentice-Hall.

Lord Redcliffe-Maud., 1967, *The Committee on the Management of Local Government*, London: HMSO.
Lovelock, C.H., 1983, 'Classifying Services to Gain Strategic Marketing Insights', *Journal of Marketing*, Vol. 47, No. 3.
Luck, D.J., 1969, 'Broadening the Concept of Marketing – Too Far', *Journal of Marketing*, Vol. 33, No. 3.
Parker, S.R., 1971, *The Future of Work and Leisure*, St Albans: Granada Publishing.
Rapoport, R. and R.N. Rapoport, 1974, 'Four Themes in the Sociology of Leisure', *British Journal of Sociology*, Vol. 25, No. 3.
Shapiro, B.P., 1973, 'Marketing for Non-Profit Organisations', *Harvard Business Review*, Vol. 51, No. 5.
Shostack, G.L., 1977, 'Breaking Free from Product Marketing', *Journal of Marketing*, Vol. 41, No. 2.
Shostack, G.L., 1982, 'How to design a service', *European Journal of Marketing*, Vol. 16, No. 1.
Stanton, W.J., 1967, *Fundamentals of Marketing*, 2nd ed., New York: McGraw-Hill.
Thomas, D.R.E., 1978, 'Strategy is Different in Service Industries', *Harvard Business Review*, Vol. 56, No. 4.
Yorke, D.A., 1984, 'The Definition of Market Segments for Leisure Centre Services – Theory and Practice', *European Journal of Marketing*, Vol. 18, No. 3.

The Marketing of Tourism

by

Arthur Meidan

The objectives of this article are to present the applications of marketing management in the tourism industry. The article discusses the various factors affecting the tourism market and its major sectors: (i) travel agencies and tour operators; (ii) hotel and catering; and (iii) transport. Any meaningful analysis of tourism marketing, should be based on: (a) market segmentation; (b) tourism marketing mix; and (c) marketing strategies. As the market for tourism services and products is dynamic and accompanied by rapid changes in the environment due to increased competition, technological changes and inflation, increased attention should be given to the employment of appropriate marketing management methods in this industry, as indicated in the present article.

INTRODUCTION

Tourism is one of the major industries in the world today. There are over 400 million tourists annually to all countries – large and small, socialist and capitalist. The total volume of sales in the industry is estimated at $500 billion per annum and growing at an average annual rate of between nine and 12 per cent. Tourism denotes temporary short-term movements of people to destinations outside the places they normally live and work [Burkart and Medlik, 1975: 17]. It is international in character depending particularly on living standards and incomes, transport developments, on entertainment and leisure provided. In tourism we can find involved three major industries: (1) passenger transportation; (2) accommodation (hotelling); and (3) travel agents and tour operators.

During the last decade, some critical factors have caused major shifts in the distribution and flow of the world tourism: (i) floating exchange rates have altered the relative position of various tourists receiving and generating in countries, based on the cost of tourism services; (ii) differential inflation rates in tourism countries, especially within the tourism components (hotel, labour, transportation), have drastically increased the tourism prices in some countries; (iii) rising energy costs have caused an increase in the cost of transportation and accommodation; this has resulted in a certain reduction in the international tourism towards regional and local tourism; (iv) political and social disturbances in some countries have reduced some tourist flows. Today, the tourism industry is of a major and increasing importance in the United Kingdom's economic life. A look at latest surveys confirms that holidays are certainly a major business, with over £1,000 million holiday sales, 60 per cent of the British population take a holiday each year, one-fifth of them abroad. On the other hand, around 13.5 million tourists have visited Britain in 1983, spending over £3 billion in this country.

The Tourism Industry

In tourism we find involved three major sub-industries: (i) tour operators and travel agencies; (ii) the accommodation (hotelling and catering) sector; and (iii) passenger transportation. In average, a tourist spends about 35 per cent of his total expenditure on transportation, about 40 per cent on lodging and food and the remaining 25 per cent on entertainment, recreation, shopping and incidentals. The people that influence most this expenditure are tour operators and travel agents.

Tour operators: These offer to tourists an *inclusive* tour, that is, they make sure the tourist product is properly packaged, standardised, quality controlled and mass produced. The tour operating marketing is susceptible to the same marketing techniques that are applied successfully for consumer goods marketing.

Travel agents: The importance of the travel agents is emphasised by the fact that over 68 per cent of all the holidays taken abroad, 84 per cent of all the holidays abroad *by air* and 90 per cent of all package holidays (tours) abroad, taken by Britons were booked through a travel agent (Meidan, 1979: 26]. And, although the industry has suffered a real decline in the last few years due to generally lower disposable income, inflation in holiday prices, and the relative devaluation of the pound, the future of the industry still looks very promising [Butlin, 1977: 278].

The hotel and catering industry: This is another major sub-sector in tourism. The hotel industry is one of the largest service industries in this country with an annual turnover in excess of £700 million [Kotas, 1975: 26], employing over 200,000 staff in about 34,000 establishments [Bosman, 1976: 48]. There are several ways of classifying hotels. G.W. Lattin [1977: 5] suggests a way which is perhaps more appropriate to the North American hotel industry: (a) the commercial or transient hotels; (b) the resort hotels; (c) the residential hotels; and (d) the motel-motor hotels. The automobile associations, amongst others, rate commercial lodging establishments according to their standard and quality of service. The nature of ownership (for example, public vs. privately owned company) forms another method of categorisation. Governments' publications indicate a recognition of a variety of ways, although the method which appears most frequently is that of classification in relation to location, namely, seaside, countryside, small town or large town hotel [Meidan, 1980: 19].

However, one way of distinguishing among hotels that is fast growing in significance is that of identifying and comparing hotels in relation to whether they belong to a group ('chain') or are being run independently. The independently managed hotel may be still the typical firm in the industry; however, the growth of the industry has been increasingly associated with hotel groups. Usually these groups operate hotels owned by them, but alternative arrangements are in existence, for example, the operations under franchise arrangements which are rising in popularity.

The major factors influencing the growth of tourism are: (i) greater *affluence* and more *leisure* time; (ii) *better, speedier, safer* and *cheaper* (in real terms) air transport facilities; (iii) enormous *growth* in international business; (iv) proliferation of conferences, exhibitions and meetings; (v) more *aggressive* tourism *publicity*; (vi) development of *packaged tours*; (vii) visits and tours have become viewed as *status symbols*. The demand for tourist services and products depend upon attraction of a destination and/or on the activities that might draw tourists to an area. Examples of activities sought by tourists are: (1) leisure (for example sun-seeking, sightseeing); (2) recreation and sports; (3) entertainment (for example, theatres, casinos, nightclubs); (4) culture (interests in history, pagentry, archaeology); (5) religion (pilgrimage, ceremonies); (6) conventions and exhibitions (for example, conferences, meetings, exhibitions, trade displays); (7) business travel; (8) medical or social visits.

The structure of the tourism industry is highly fragmented in terms of size, styles, geographical location and the ownership pattern of its operating units; however, it has four major common characteristics:

(i) Inflexibility of supply, for example, the hotel bedroom or the restaurant dining room cannot be adjusted to fluctuations in demand; these cannot be stored for periods of peak demand.
(ii) Tourism services are perishable, that is, any unoccupied bed in a hotel or seat in a plane represents a loss which affects industry's profitability and ability to compete.
(iii) Fixed location and, therefore, the importance of communication methods such as advertising and/or sales promotion in order to bring the customer to the tourist destinations where the service can be consumed.
(iv) Relatively large financial investments are required for every modern tourist establishment, and therefore both the level of risk and the return on investment are of critical importance to tourism management.

In recent years, because of growing interest in tourism marketing, a number of studies have been published in this area. The early publications focused on sales promotions and advertising [Taylor, 1964; Seaberg, 1971] and other studies were on the identity of customers [Bloomstrom, 1968] and the size of the market [Medlik, 1972; Beavis, 1971].

MARKET SEGMENTATION

The tourist market could be segmented by: *(i) age group; (ii) number of trips taken per annum/season; (iii) education; (iv) occupation; (v) income groups; (vi) purpose of trip(s)*. The last category is the most popular one; hotels, travel agencies/tour operators and airlines identify among the various sub-segments of business, vacation, convention, personal emergencies, visit to relatives and other 'types' of travellers. The various elements in the marketing mix and plans are designed in order to exploit the different elasticities of demand for travel and tourism of these various segments. The marketing policies and packages offered include various prices, promotions and products for identical tourist destinations. The three main tourist market segments identified by tourist main travel reasons, together with their major marketing characteristics, are presented in Table 1 (p. 170).

In addition to the six main segmentation methods above, the tourism industry has recently employed also psychographic, benefit and distance travelled bases for segmentation:

(vii) Psychographic segmentation utilises consumer life style and personality differences to determine variance in buyer demands. For example, the tourism companies market differently to 'swingers' (young, unmarried, active, fun-loving, party-going people, seeking up-to-date tourist destinations and fast-paced hedonistic living) than to ordinary families seeking a relatively cheap summer packaged tour holiday. Indeed tour operators and travel agencies price differently these tourism products and services.

The uses of psychographic segmentation in tourism, are suitable for:

(a) predicting behaviour: by identifying a tourist market segment and understanding why its members are interested in making a tourism related decision, we can estimate the probability that they will react in a certain way, or at least predict several possible reactions;
(b) client interaction: the process of psychographic segmentation allows more effective communication between a customer and the travel agent or the hotelier. A more meaningful dialogue, with more information, will flow either way;
(c) anticipation of future tourism market needs: with valuable information flowing in from customers, it will provide a better opportunity to analyse future customers' requirements. It will also help provide a basis for determining future tourism objectives;
(d) relevance of practice: by understanding the behavioural patterns of customers, tourism services and products can be tailored to meet the changing customers' needs and demands. The idea is to meet as many as possible of the needs of a target market.

(viii) Benefit segmentation: Tourists could be segmented according to the particular benefits they are obtaining through the purchase of the tourist product. In using benefit segmentation, the task is to determine the major benefits that tourists might be looking for in the tourist product class, the kind of tourist who might be looking for each benefit, and the existing tourist destinations which come close to delivering each benefit. The goal

TABLE 1

SOME MAJOR TOURIST SEGMENTS AND THEIR MAIN MARKETING CHARACTERISTICS

Marketing Characteristics	*Main Tourist Segments* Holiday Tourists	*Business Tourists*	*Visitors (Common interest tourists)*
1. Typical Destination	Resort-orientated	Big City	Visit friends, relatives education, pilgrimage
2. Seasonality	High; marketing mix can assist however in spreading demand levels	No seasonality	Partial seasonality
3. Length of Stay	Could be influenced by promotion/ communication	Normally short and cannot be prolonged by advertising	Prefer long stay. This will be prolonged if the costs of additional stay are 'reasonable'
4. Mode of Transport	Varied mode(s) of transport. Time spent on the way to destinations is part of the holiday or package tour	Airplane invariably. The objective is to reach the destination as soon as possible	The cheapest mode of transport
5. Hotel Accommodation User	Yes. Normally rather stops at un-expensive hotels/pensions	Yes, normally expensive hotels	Only at a very limited degree. Particularly interested in B&B establishments
6. Requires Entertainment	Yes. Very much so. Normally the entertainment is part of the tourist package	Yes, but to a limited degree	No.
7. Price Sensitivity	Very sensitive (high price elasticity of demand)	Rather insensitive (low price elasticity of demand)	Sensitive (middle price elasticity of demand)
8. Role of Advertising/ Marketing Communication	Very important (The potential tourist can be influenced)	Rather limited	Quite important particularly sales promotions are important
9. Tour Package(s) Importance	Of great interest and demand	Of no appeal at all	Limited appeal

of benefit segmentation is to find a group of people all seeking the same benefit from a tourist product [Moutinho, 1982: 103]. Once people have been classified into benefit segments, each segment is evaluated in terms of demographics, life style, personality, volume of consumption and other factors which are essential to developing a complete understanding of the people who make up each segment.

(ix) Distance travelled: This is an additional important criterion for segmenting tourist markets [Etzel, 1982: 11]. Distant travellers usually

comprise the larger and more profitable segment, while nearer travellers are more attracted although less profitable. Segmentation with distance criteria proves useful in this age of high costs when price is a major factor in destination choice.

The tourists' needs could be classified as follows: (i) common needs – common to all catering customers, for example, eat, drink, rest, be sheltered, etc.; (ii) general tourist's needs, for example entertainment, distractions, novel eating experiences, etc.; (iii) specific tourist needs, for example, understanding menus, be relieved of currency conversion problems.

In addition, tourists' needs include 'additive' needs, that is, products and services that are 'a must' for the average tourist. For example, tourists 'own' newspaper(s), cigarettes from countries of origin, alcohol, iced water, preparation of coffee/tea as the tourist is used to, etc. Segmentation is at the core of modern tourism marketing thought since it enables the tourist firm to: (i) achieve a better competitive position for existing destinations; (ii) more effectively position an existing destination by appealing to a limited market; (iii) identify gaps in the market which represent new tourist product opportunities; (iv) identify potential new tourists for the product.

The concept of market segmentation is the basic point of origin for all tourism marketing strategies. The ultimate purpose of market segmentation is an increased tourist satisfaction which is the result of tourist product benefits, which in turn results from tourist product use.

FACTORS AFFECTING THE TOURISM MARKET

The major problem in marketing the tourism product is to create a need/want that might lead to tourists choice of a destination. In the process of decision making, the potential tourist is influenced by three sets of variables as follows: (i) social and personal determinants of tourist behaviour; (ii) tourism stimuli factors; and (iii) destinations considerations (Figure 1).

Tourist marketing plays a critical role in determining and influencing many of the variables included in all the three sets. It is obvious that advertising, promotion and the travel agents (distribution) play a major role in shaping the tourism stimuli, and – to some extent the quality/quantity of tourism information as well as the image, cost/value, and expectations of a destination (set (iii)). Tour operators in particular – and to some extent, also travel agents – have an extremely important marketing role to play in influencing (potential) tourists' behaviour (set (i)), via market segmentation, and tourists' products – particularly package tours development. In the process of developing 'new' tourist packages to suit various tourists needs, pricing and location decisions also play important roles, as discussed in more detail later in this article. The four main marketing tools: product development, promotion, pricing and distribution/location, are indeed of major importance in shaping out

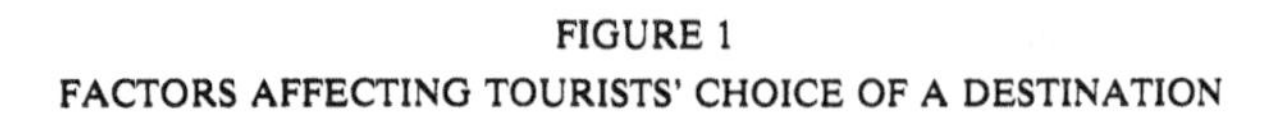

FIGURE 1
FACTORS AFFECTING TOURISTS' CHOICE OF A DESTINATION

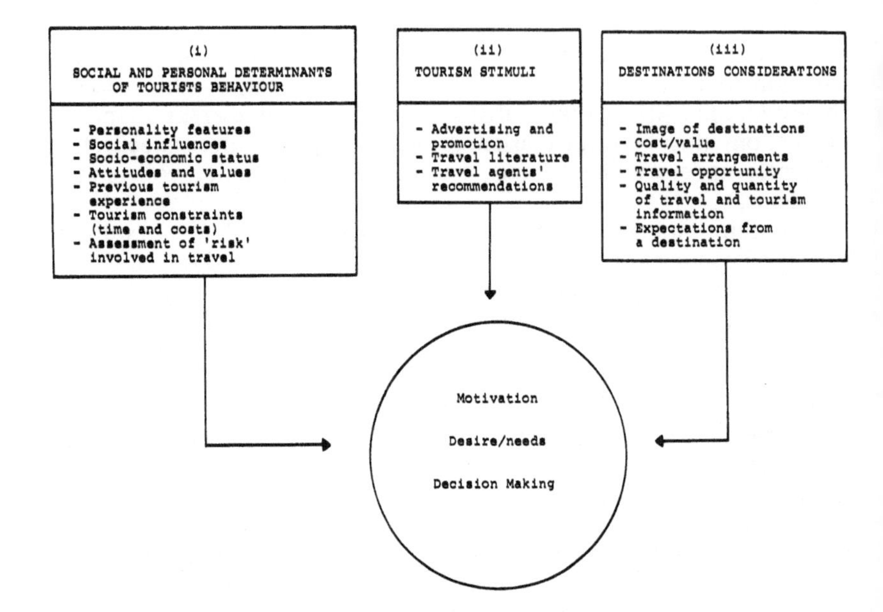

effective marketing strategy for the tourism organisation. However, in practice, the efficient deployment of marketing mix (or marketing controllable) variables, depend not just on possible tourists market segments, but also on: (i) other tourism marketing objectives; (ii) tourism non-controllable factors, and (iii) the structure of the tourism industry (see Figure 2).

From review and study of the published literature on tourism it emerges that there are five major objectives in this industry, as follows:

(1) Satisfying Tourists' Needs.

The ability to know and to meet customers' needs relative to the competition, endows the tourist firm with a set of differential advantages such as cost leadership, appropriate service quality, specialisation on a certain clientele or function (e.g. convention hotels), proper location; and may be likened to a capital asset. Indeed, satisfying customers' needs is the basis of marketing management and its importance has increased even more lately because of the increase in competition among hotels.

(2) Maximising Occupancy (of a bed in a hotel or a seat on a plane)

This has, of course, a major influence on the volume of business and on profitability. Consequently, an alternative measure of profitability can be, for example, the bedroom occupancy for a period, especially for the season. The scale or size of hotels has traditionally been expressed in

FIGURE 2
THE TOURIST MARKETING SYSTEM

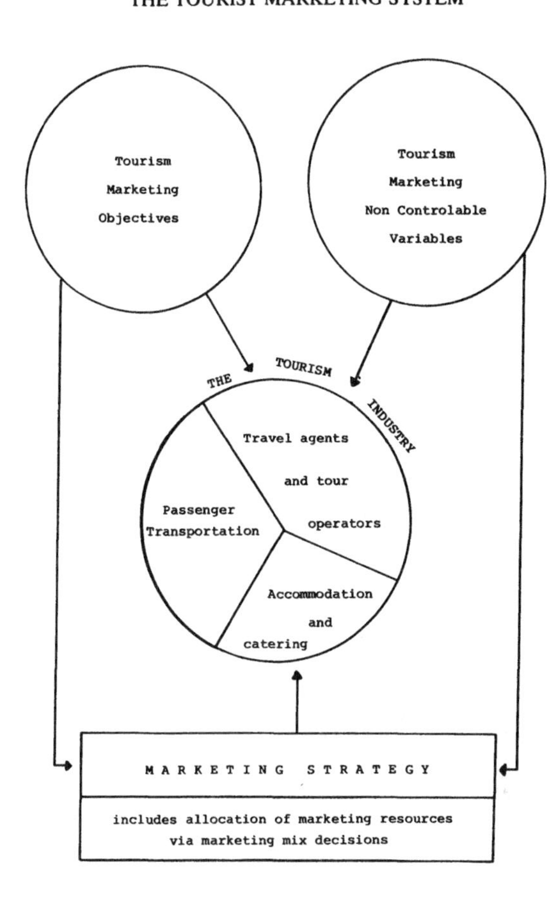

terms of bedroom capacity. But an alternative measure in terms of bed occupancy is better, because it takes into consideration the usage of single or double bedrooms.

(3) Maximising Return on Investment

This is an important factor especially for the large, publicly owned hotels, airlines or tour operators. Up to 90 per cent of the total capital investment in a hotel is invested in fixed assets of two kinds; first, in land and building, and second – investment in the interior assets. The rate of return on investment is usually measured and expressed by the pay-back method and a relatively low figure (that is, a long pay-back term of up to 12 years) is usually accepted.

(4) Maximising Tourist Establishment's Total Profit

This is often considered the most obvious measure of management performance. However, the question immediately arises – how profit should be defined, measured and indeed what is the 'desired' level of profit? Lately, profitability can no longer aspire to be the sole end of all business activity, although still very important as a vehicle to ensure survival and growth.

(5) Achieving a Stable Occupancy

Attaining a *stable*, high bed or seat occupancy in a hotel, restaurant or airline throughout the year is viewed as a measure of productivity, efficiency and viability of the tourist organisation. The reason for this objective being so popular is because sales are typically correlated with profitability, although it is clear that occupancy increase is sometimes bought at the expense of profitability.

Besides the above-mentioned five objectives there are other alternative objectives for being in the tourism business which were not explored in this article. The most well-known ones are: spreading the risk of investments; growth; market share; increasing tourists' loyalty, improving tourist destinations' image, etc. Tourism marketing objectives reflect the conditions existent in the industry and effect – together with the non-controllable variables – the selection of a marketing strategy, as indicated in Figure 3 later in this study.

The non-controllable variables affecting tourism are:

(i) *Economic factors* including: (a) *foreign exchange regulations*: the rates of exchange restrict the amount of foreign (or domestic) currency the tourist could legally obtain and affect also the total cost of his/her holiday or visit; (b) *government economic policy*, including taxation imposed on tourist services (for example, the airport tax recently imposed on tourists to Portugal has had a negative effect on the short-term demand for visits to that country). Government's economic policy effects Gross National Product (GNP) and the disposable income. Research on travel propensities indicates that tourism increases double the rate of increase in the GNP; (c) *inflation and recession* have a negative impact on the demand of tourism products. Inflation has affected the price of tourism and travel, particularly as the prices of petrol and wages to industry's employees have gone up. The increase of flight costs have effected flight prices and have led to a decrease in the occupied capacity in most airlines. The 'break-even' load factor for most airlines is 55 per cent of plane seats and, therefore, airlines have come under even more pressure to increase the number of seats taken in every flight.

(ii) *Competition variables*: the competition in the tourism industry has recently increased significantly. In addition, other retail services have recently become more interested in selling tourist packages/products. In the UK, W.H. Smith diversified in the

1970s from the newspaper and stationery business into travel agency business. This was influenced by the cash flows from stationery/books that peak before Christmas and fall sharply in the new year. The travel agency business generates profits in January–February (when summer holiday bookings are being made), as well as in the summer that are 'slack seasons' for W.H. Smith's main line (the stationery business).

Competition has increased not just in the travel agencies and tour-operator sectors, but also in the carrier industries, particularly airlines, charters and overland (bus) companies, as well as amongst hotel (chains and independents), caterers, restaurants, etc.

(iii) *Risk and uncertainty variables*: the impact of these could be seen mainly in the increase of insurance premiums and cancellation costs, to offset the security, political, weather/climate risks and/or unpredicted increases in the costs of transport, as a result of changes in the rates of exchange and/or the cost of petrol.

THE TOURISM MARKETING MIX

The marketing mix in tourism is – in practice – different from the traditional marketing mix for products, although basically selecting a tourist destination is like selecting a product in a shop. The difference arises from the fact that successful tourism marketing operations must combine the selection of a destination (which is a function of destinations images) with the accessibility and delivery of the destination chosen (which is largely a function of the method of transport or transit feasibility in terms of time and costs).

The planning of an efficient marketing mix is facilitated through marketing research. In tourism, the objectives of marketing are to understand customers at two levels [Lewis, 1983: 82].

(i) What are the determining factors in a consumer choice of one tourism establishment (hotel, travel agency, airline, tour-operator, destination, restaurant, casino, etc.), rather than another?

(ii) What are the consumer's perceptions of the various offerings (tourist destinations, hotels, restaurants, etc.) available?

If a tourist establishment will be able to answer these two questions, it will have at its disposal a set of efficient marketing mixes that will enable it to reach the organisational objectives despite the competition's efforts.

Tourism marketing mix includes the traditional four elements [McCarthy, 1983: 217]: Product, Promotion, Price and Place (distribution). In tourism, however, the first two elements are much more important. Indeed a recent study [Renagham, 1981] suggests that there are only three *major* elements in the tourism mix: (i) the product-service mix, (ii) the presentation mix and (iii) the communication mix. The presentation mix includes variables such as atmospherics or employees' appearance. A study carried out by the author [Meidan, 1976] on Public Houses Selection Criteria indicates that one of the most important attributes that pub customers look for in a public house is atmosphere! Employees' appearance is also very important (for example, airlines hostesses or fast food chain employees' uniforms).

The Product Mix

In practice, tourism product-mix has three major components: (i) attractions of destinations (site of location, images of destinations, events, natural beauty/characteristics); (ii) facilities (accommodation, catering, entertainment, and recreation, facilities); (iii) accessibility (good roads, airports, ports, etc.). The combination and final presentation of the tourist product mix rests mainly with tour operators and travel agents. These have played an increasing role in marketing of tourism in the last decade or so, by their offering of a greater variety of package tours products.

A package tour is designed to fit the requirements of a particular group of travellers. Packaged tours are of three types [Lundberg, 1980: 114–5]: (i) *escorted tours* – when an experienced tour operator travels with the group, handling all basic details, from hotel reservations to tour schedule; (ii) *unescorted package tours* – these are more flexible enabling the tourist to budget in advance his basic expenses, for example, transport, accommodation and certain meals; (iii) *group tours* – these are groups of 15 or more people travelling together who might be members of a club or organisation and who co-operate and finance together a 'special' trip to a chosen destination. The tourist product should change its 'image' over time according to developments in the tourist market-place. A good example of this image-changing of a tourist location is the island of Bermuda. Until 1945, Bermuda was thought of mainly for its market garden trade, although tourists – sailing in by boats – were a major source of income to the island's economy. After the Second World War, with the increasing use of aircraft for passengers' transport, Bermuda has acquired the image of a major *winter resort* destination particularly for North American tourists. With the further developments of modern aircraft and the increase in range and load of newer aeroplanes, Bermuda has changed its image as a tourist destination yet again, and has become a *summer resort*.

Intangible products like travel and tourism can seldom be tried out, inspected or tested in advance. Nevertheless, some major attempts are currently being made in this industry to 'tangibelise' promises of delivery [Levitt, 1981]. An example is with hotels that wrap their drinking glasses in fresh bags, or neatly shape the end piece of toilet tissue into a fresh-looking arrowhead to indicate with clarity that the 'product' has been prepared for *your* use and comfort.

The Promotion-Mix

Tourist promotion is persuasive communication about the various tourist destinations and their service offerings. Various possible advertising objectives can be sorted into whether their aim is to inform, persuade, or remind. The inform category includes objectives such as: telling the tourist market about the new products, new uses, price changes, description of services; reducing tourists' fears; and building a destination image. The persuasion category includes objectives such as building destination preferences, and encouraging switching from other destinations.

In the tourism advertising campaign, it is important to ensure that essential parts of the promotional message are remembered by a significant number or percentage of the tourist target groups. The messages must create or reinforce existing positive attitudes or images and correct negative attitudes or image elements.

The tourism communication programme should include the following [Moutinho, 1982: 106]: (i) the establishment of special objectives for each component of campaign to use; (ii) clearly defined audience segments and tourist target groups; (iii) the creation of useful, salient and creative messages and USPs (unique selling propositions) through market research; (iv) utilisation of creative media scheduling to reach the audiences with adequate frequency; (v) promotion of well-faced behavioural changes in messages; (vi) use of feedback to evaluate the campaign's progress over time. Sales promotion plays an integral role in the total promotional programme of tourist firms. Provision of brochures is often more important than advertisements in the newspapers and magazines. Promotional literature must give descriptive background before the destination decision-making. It can describe alternatives to influence the type of vacation to take and areas to visit.

The tourist market-place is completely dependent on the presentations and descriptions in printed and/or audiovisual form. A promotional aid is meant to show tourists the destination's merits, that is, product benefits that will ultimately help create demand for the destination product. Effective promotional tools depend heavily on creative design and copy, high quality paper and high standard full-colour printing. Creative aspects of printed material are essentially concept formulation, design, layout and copy writing. A recurring problem in tourism advertising [Hawkins, *et al.*, 1980: 149] is: at *whom* should the promotional effort be aimed and *what* should be said to the prospective tourist? Normally a basic starting point for tourism marketing effort is a marketing plan. The market plan should include careful selection of market segments. A systematic and logical selection of target segments will render more efficient efforts and/or reduce marketing costs while increasing tourist product demand.

The objective of tourism marketing is to satisfy consumers of tourism products. The generally accepted marketing approach is that there are four major marketing controllable variables that can be manipulated by the marketing organisation in order to reach organisational objectives: product, place, price and promotion. Within tourism marketing, however, only promotion could be controlled in the short term. (Promotion decisions involve decisions on media strategy and costs and these could be easily determined in the short term.) Product decisions involve planning and price alterations require risk assessment, both of which could not be decided or altered at short-time intervals. Therefore, in tourism marketing the promotional tools play an extremely important role in effecting the outcome of the overall marketing effort.

Pricing

Pricing is a vital marketing task that requires significant attention. This element of the marketing mix is very much affected by both the competition and the role of inflation. Overall there should be a tendency towards a more accurate price policy. Pricing in tourism is a complex matter, particularly where the individual suppliers, airlines, hotel groups and so on determine their prices independently of one another. The final price at which the tourist products will be sold covers the costs incurred in making the product available, the costs of marketing it, and a desired level of return or profit [Miller, 1980: 26]. Product demand is an important factor in pricing decisions. Since different market segments have differing needs and wants, the intensity of their demand for a given tourist product may differ. Pricing goals pursued by the tour operator or tourist establishment can include pricing to realise a target market share, pricing to meet or prevent competition or pricing subordinated to tourist product differentiation [Moutinho, 1982]. One of the basic characteristics of the tourism industry is the high level of *fixed costs* it operates at [Powers, 1979: 33]. This certainly applies in the hotel industry and/or the large airline carriers. Consequently, the industry should be very much market-orientated, that is, individual establishments should attempt to get a high market share in their respective markets in order to achieve profitability.

The supplier of tourist products should have two main objectives in view, in price setting: (1) to attract as many customers as possible to the selected segments; and (2) to do this under the most profitable conditions. This does not necessarily mean that he should price according to the cost of servicing the tourist. This cannot be done unless the tourist firm has reliable information on several factors: (a) the nature of demand facing the tour firm in each segment and the price which the potential tourist is 'willing to pay'; (b) the price levels charged by rival or competing services and tourist establishments; (c) full knowledge of the tourist firm's full costs of supplying the products. *In the long run*, the firm will not be able to survive if the price is lower than its full costs.

Price tactics in tourism should be used to exploit different price sensitivities. For example, compare the flight fares which are paid by tourists during summer vacations when children are not at school and flight ticket prices during the 'slack' tourist season, for example, October/November.

However, to successfully charge discriminatory prices in this way there must be no inter-segment leakage, otherwise customers will resell the service, as indeed very recently happened with the reselling of United Air Line travel coupons in the United States. Indeed inertia or ignorance of conditions in other segments are not very effective segment seals [Pizam and Reichel, 1979: 42]. Service differences also permit the charging of different prices which are not proportional to the 'production' costs of such differentiation: for example, in the travel business it may be possible to successfully sell to a businessman a trip through your agency simply because you might be able to offer (at a higher price) a 'fuller package' that is, car rental services, hotel booking of destination, etc. As specified above, tourism development might enable the use of price as a flexible, useful tool in increasing a firm's profitability. However, Promotion, Advertising and Distribution are also important tools which can effectively assist in increasing the profitability.

Promotion and advertising can appeal to preferences in such a way that discriminatory pricing becomes possible. A famous restaurant in Chicago was advertised as the most expensive local in the world. This appeal to exclusivity and implied quality made possible the selling of tables at disproportionately high prices (up to $1,000 per table per evening in the mid-1960s). American Express can successfully charge £20 p.a. vis-à-vis Access Card no-charge policy because of a certain image which American Express has created around its 'special' service and the type of customers using its service. ('You are welcome wherever you go with AMEX card'.) Such promotion must in fact be accompanied by an adequate degree of coverage (distribution/place) otherwise both the advertising campaign and the tourist firm price policy would not succeed.

There is no universally accepted pricing method in tourist establishments. Indeed the approach to pricing varies quite considerably, depending on the sector of the industry, as well as the price level of each individual establishment. In any one particular establishment (hotel, restaurant, airline, tour-operator), one may observe a different approach in the pricing of a product or service from that adopted in the pricing of a slightly different product/service. The different approaches to pricing result mainly from what link there is between direct cost and the selling price. Whatever the different approaches to pricing in the tourism business they are all variants of two well-established pricing methods, namely: cost-plus pricing and rate of return pricing [Kotas, 1975: 146–7].

Distribution

The most crucial question for tourism distribution analysis is what channels are the most productive and whether a new channel strategy is needed? [Goodrich, 1977: 10–13]. A distribution strategy should be the problem of determining the basic way in which the industry will try to sell its products to designated end markets. When deciding a tourism distribution policy, the leading factors should be the market coverage, the cost of distribution and the effectiveness in generating sales in terms of motivation and image of the channels. The tourism industry relies on airlines, tour operators and travel agents for most point-of-sale contacts, and selling these must be supported by information services, publicity material, training seminars, joint special promotions and trade advertising.

The major distribution channels in the tourism industry are: (i) Travel Agents; (ii) Tour Operators; (iii) Hotels and/or Hotel Representatives; (iv) Airlines; (v) Automated Reservation Services and, finally, (vi) Centralised Reservation Systems, mainly through group marketing arrangements.

Hotels sell directly to the tourists, as well as through all other five alternative intermediaries mentioned above. All the other intermediaries – with the exception of travel agencies – sell through each other. Travel agencies sell only directly to tourists:

(i) Travel agents: This is the most important channel of distribution in the tourism industry. There are about 4,500 ABTA (Association of British Travel Agents) offices in this country and, therefore, investigations on potential and actual travellers' attitudes toward the major criteria for selecting a travel agency, for a package tour holiday are of real importance. A research investigation undertaken recently by the author [Meidan, 1979: 27] indicates that travel agency selection depends on a large number of variables (see Table 2) and that their importance varies from one group of customers to another. Customers' age, social economic background, stage in family life cycle, level of education, occupation, etc., are some of the factors that affect customers' needs, wants and behaviour and therefore influence their travel agency selection. As criteria for selecting an agency are different for various age groups, the travel agency should define its area of competitive capability and concentrate on those segments of the holiday market which it can serve best. The package tour quality is recognised as the most important selling point in this industry and, therefore, the tour package quality has to be improved and differentiated. Differentiation will also lead to an increase in the variety offered which stands as a separate factor, rather important for younger customers.

(ii) Tour operators: Their main assets are professional knowledge and financial resources. The packaged tourist products that tour operators offer are sold mainly through retail travel agents. The tour operators are backed by large financial and travel organisations (for example, Midland Bank, Thomas Cook) and their success depends mainly on high load on aircraft and high occupancy rates at hotels. The major contribution of tour operators to tourism marketing has been in two aspects:

(a) They have significantly contributed to the *'standardisation' of the tourist product* by developing a variety of 'attractive tourist/holiday packages;

(b) Because of their financial backing, many tour operators have

TABLE 2

MAIN CRITERIA AFFECTING TOURISTS' SELECTION OF A TRAVEL AGENCY*

1. Package Price
2. Subsequent price surcharge
3. Terms of payment (e.g. credit, etc.)
4. Inflight entertainment
5. Inflight comfort
6. Inflight service
7. Hotel amenities
8. Hotel comfort
9. Hotel service
10. Insurance scheme available
11. Variety in choice of destinations
12. Variety in holiday travelling activities offered (e.g. golfing, safaris, cruise, etc.)
13. Variety in choice of hotels
14. Availability of agency representatives at resorts
15. Free time during tours
16. Advance booking requirement
17. Prompt booking confirmation
18. Assistance with visa handling
19. Travel agency reputation
20. Travel agency financial standing
21. Travel agency location
22. Number of offices (branches) of travel agency
23. Travel agency office layout
24. Travel agency interior decoration
25. Sufficient brochures provided
26. Agency advertisement on TV
27. Agency advertisement in magazines
28. Agency advertisement in newspapers
29. Agency advertisement in other media (posters, radio, etc.)

**Source*: Meidan, A., 1979, 'Travel Agency Selection Criteria', *Journal of Travel Research*, Vol. XVIII, No. 1. Summer, pp. 26–32.

acquired transport and lodging facilities (airlines, hotels, etc.) at various tourist destinations which required from them major marketing efforts to attract tourists. This has been done by large-scale advertising and promotional efforts and recently, we have witnessed competitive price wars amongst the major tour operators.

Most of the sales performed by tour operators are being done through retail travel agents who normally receive ten per cent commission.

(iii) Hotels and hotel representatives: Hotels sell either directly to private or business customers, or indirectly, mainly through travel agents. Most hotels emphasise the direct sales function and devote major efforts and resources – mainly through promotion – to this channel. Sales through hotel representatives are popular, particularly in the United States, and it is a form of indirect selling.

(iv) Airlines: These sell flight tickets and/or rooms mainly to overseas destinations. Airlines sell mainly indirectly – through travel agents; however, direct sales to customers are also common.

(v) Automated Reservation Services (ARS): These are indirect channels for certain tourism products and services, particularly in the hotel business. The ARS main function is to supply travel agents – around the world – with available hotel rooms at hotels anywhere. This computerised service is offered for a fee to hotels worldwide.

(vi) Centralised reservation systems: These sell, promote and accept room reservations. This is done through franchising arrangements and/or through group marketing which has recently gained wider acceptance, and is currently employed on a large scale by a substantial proportion of the lodging establishments in the hotel industry. The main characteristics of group marketing are:

(a) joint participation to the promotion activities by all the establishments in the group, sharing costs and benefits, in order to get more tourist bookings;
(b) negotiation with bulk purchases of hotel services on one hand, and suppliers of hotel equipment on the other;
(c) use of standardised equipment and furnishings and joint use of marketing (and management) advisory service;
(d) collective overseas marketing activities to spread costs; normally members of group marketing in the tourism business advertise common hotel tariff to boost occupancy.

The base of membership to these groups is uniform quality standards and prices by all the hotel members, the individual hotel/establishments being offered some kind of 'monopolistic' protection (that is, in a certain geographical region there should be a restricted number of establishments that are members of the marketing group and, therefore, customers are referred to these hotels).

MARKETING STRATEGIES

The basic objectives of tourism's strategy are: to match the tourism firm's strengths with market opportunities; to avoid threats posed by competition and environmental changes; and to remedy weaknesses in the firm's organisation and operations. It is not enough to generate tourist arrivals or achieve a certain market share, but, rather, it is necessary to produce profitable tourist product sales and profitable market penetration.

There are four major stages in the formulation of a marketing (Figure 3), as follows: (1) segmenting the market, that is identification of potential tourists' destinations and needs; (2) defining constraints, particularly environmental and competitive factors [Meidan and Lee, 1982: 170]; (3) formulation of tourism marketing objectives; and (4) allocation of marketing resources (chiefly through the tourism marketing mix, discussed earlier in this paper).

Tourism marketing strategies can be broadly categorised into two groups: (a) *growth strategies*, comprising marketing strategies whose overall predominant character is related to a certain pattern of objective of market growth; and (b) *competitive (or market share) strategies*, comprising strategies that focus on tourism's market share competitive position. Whichever strategy a tourism firm decides to apply, it is significantly determined by the marketing objectives and the target market.

FIGURE 3
TOURISM MARKETING STRATEGY – MAIN STAGES

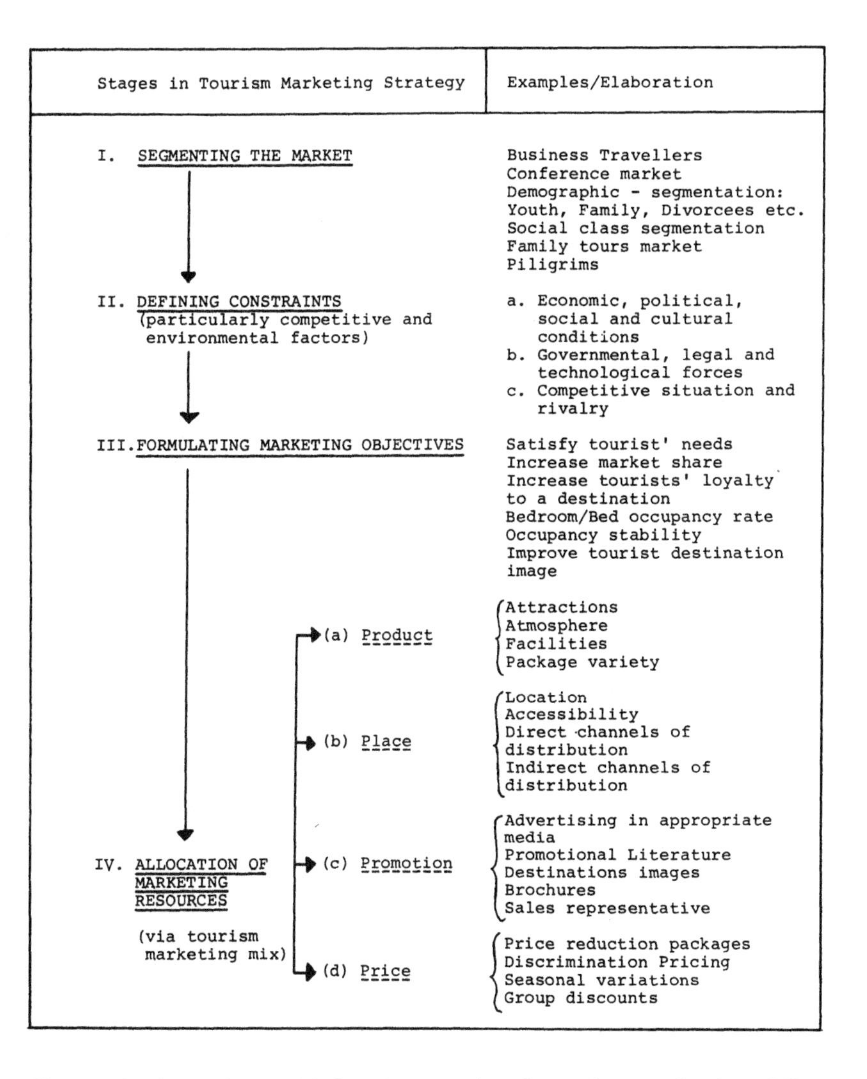

Stages in Tourism Marketing Strategy	Examples/Elaboration
I. SEGMENTING THE MARKET	Business Travellers Conference market Demographic - segmentation: Youth, Family, Divorcees etc. Social class segmentation Family tours market Piligrims
II. DEFINING CONSTRAINTS (particularly competitive and environmental factors)	a. Economic, political, social and cultural conditions b. Governmental, legal and technological forces c. Competitive situation and rivalry
III. FORMULATING MARKETING OBJECTIVES	Satisfy tourist' needs Increase market share Increase tourists' loyalty to a destination Bedroom/Bed occupancy rate Occupancy stability Improve tourist destination image
IV. ALLOCATION OF MARKETING RESOURCES (via tourism marketing mix) — (a) Product	Attractions Atmosphere Facilities Package variety
(b) Place	Location Accessibility Direct channels of distribution Indirect channels of distribution
(c) Promotion	Advertising in appropriate media Promotional Literature Destinations images Brochures Sales representative
(d) Price	Price reduction packages Discrimination Pricing Seasonal variations Group discounts

The marketing mix would then have to be planned accordingly, whilst external factors would presumably have been given due attention.

For example, it is important to attempt to reduce the problem of tourism seasonality and improve hotel capacity utilisation by promoting all-year tourism zone, creating new off-peak demand and by attracting other activities to hotel capacity. A 'pipe-line' strategy (a continuous charter flights programme) could be used in the low season, carrying specific 'interest target groups'. To maximise tourist satisfaction and to best utilise the facilities year-round, some action must be taken to minimise the level of variation of demand from the peak to the off-season. Two specific strategies for dealing with this situation are the multiple use (involving supplementing peak season attractions) and price differentials [Moutinho, 1982: 110]. Basically there are three major strategies for tourism as follows:

(i) Market Penetration Strategy

This usually focuses on gaining market share at the expense of competitors. This may be achieved through creating a differential advantage via any of the elements of the marketing mix. This is undoubtedly the most popular strategy prevalent amongst tourist firms. A well-planned penetration strategy would also win new tourists through its better understanding of their needs.

(ii) Market Extension Strategy

This is designed to reach new types of tourists by modifying the firm's present tourist products by planning in advance of the actual launching of a new tourist product, its life could be extended or stretched out through predetermined actions designed to sustain its growth and profitability.

(iii) Market Development Strategy

This means that the tourist firm will seek new classes of tourists for its products or will add salient product characteristics to the existing line. This strategy seeks to widen its appeal to attract tourists from segments of the market which the firm in the past has not concentrated on. Such a strategy may either attempt to receive the new types of tourists in addition to its traditional ones, or may resolve to replace its past market segment appeal. Of the marketing mix variables, the most important factors that should be considered when this strategy is adopted are quite obviously promotion and product development. The market development strategies are of three types: (a) tourist product differentiation strategy; (b) reformulation strategy; and (c) innovatory strategy.

The tourist product differentiation strategy: This is designed to differentiate each tourist sub-product in real or psychological terms. A differentiated marketing strategy should be applied with different marketing mixes designed to satisfy several market segments. Promotional expenditures may increase as unique promotional mixes are developed for each market segment.

The reformulation strategy: This includes specific tourist programmes which are designed to ameliorate some attributes of the tourist products, in order to satisfy the needs of the present tourist market. A product reformulation strategy means that the tourist firm sets out to build upon its present market through developing new products. The application of this strategy may help to define the particular range of tourist products which would match with the specific motivations of the target tourist market.

The innovatory strategy: This focuses on expanding the tourism target markets either by segmenting the broader market or converting non-tourists. An innovation strategy means that the tourist organisation will seek to satisfy new tourists with new tourist products and services. A real innovation strategy searches for significant tourism innovations, not just 'new and improved' products.

More recent studies on tourism marketing strategies [Meidan and Lee, 1983: 22] indicate that strategy selection in this industry should be based on four factors: (1) the size of the segment or submarket; (2) tourists' sensitivity to the differences between tourist hotels, airlines, travel agencies, etc.; (3) the distinctiveness of these tourist establishments and companies; and (4) competitors' marketing strategies.

CONCLUSIONS

Operating in an environment of competition, inflation and world-wide recession, the tourism industry must place greater emphasis on more efficient and objective-orientated marketing management. The world spending on tourism today exceeds $500 billion per annum, greater than the total world spending for health care or for military purposes. The employment of a marketing approach and relevant marketing methods will enhance the tourist firms with improved profitability and a larger market share. This could be achieved, in practice, via tourism marketing that is basically a three-stage process: (i) analysis of the tourist's needs; (ii) designing of a product/package to meet these needs; and (iii) communicating the availability of the tourist product via advertising, sales promotions and public relations. Unfortunately, too many tourist firms omit the first two stages and concentrate mainly on the third, leaving out marketing planning and policy. As every tourist organisation must consider how it can build and protect a strong competitive and growth position, the critical question is the selection of an appropriate marketing strategy. The present article suggests six different marketing strategies for tourism that might be suitable to different tourist market/product/ competition situations.

REFERENCES

Beavis, J., 1971, *Report on the Inter-Hotel Comparison Survey 1970*, University of Strathclyde.

Bloomstrom, R.L., 1968, *Profile of the Guest*, New York: American Hotel and Motel Association.

Bosman, J., 1976, 'Prospects for the British Hotel Industry', *Long Range Planning*, December.

Burkart, A.J. and S. Medlik, 1975, *Tourism – Past Present and Future*, London: Heinemann.

Butlin, R.F., 1977, 'The Holiday Market – Facts and Forecasts', *ADMAP* (UK) June.

Etzel, M.J. and A.G. Woodside, 1982, 'Segmentary Vacation Markets', *Journal of Travel Research* 20, Spring.

Goodrich, J.N., 1977, 'Differences in Perceived Similarity of Tourism Regions: A Spatial Analysis', *Journal of Travel Research*, Summer.
Hawkins, D.E., Shafer, E.L. and J.M. Rovelstod, (eds.) 1980: *Tourism Marketing and Management Issues*, Washington: George Washington University Press.
Lattin, G.W., 1977, *Modern Hotel and Motel Management*, New York: W.H. Freeman.
Levitt, T., 1981, 'Marketing Intangible Products and Product Tangibles' *The Cornell HRA Quarterly*, August.
Lewis, R.C., 1983, 'Getting the Most from Marketing Research', *The Cornell HRA Quarterly*, November.
Kotas, R. (ed.), 1975, *Market Orientation in the Hotel and Catering Industry*, Surrey University Press in association with Intertext Publishing Ltd.
Lundberg, D.E., 1980, *The Tourist Business*, 4th ed., New York: CBI Publishing.
McCarthy, E.J., 1983, *Basic Marketing: A Managerial Approach*, 7th ed., Homewood, IL: Richard D. Irwin.
Medlik, S., 1972, *Profile of the Hotel and Catering Industry*, Heinemann.
Meidan, A., 1976, 'Pub Selection Criteria – A Factor Analysis Approach', in M.J. Baker (ed.), *Buyer Behaviour*, (Proceedings of MEG National Conference, Strathclyde University, July).
Meidan, A., 1979, 'Travel Agency Selection Criteria', *Journal of Travel Research* Vol. XVIII, No. 1.
Meidan, A., 1980, 'Hotel Industry Marketing Management Profiles', in M.J. Baker and M.A. Saren (eds.), (Proceedings of European Academy for Advanced Research in Marketing, Strathclyde).
Meidan, A., and B. Lee, 1982, 'Marketing Strategies for Hotels', *International Journal of Hospitality Management*, Vol. 1, No. 3.
Meidan, A., and B. Lee, 1983, 'Marketing Strategies for Hotels: A Cluster Analysis Approach', *Journal of Travel Research*, Vol. XXI, No. 4, Spring.
Miller, J., 1980, *Menu Pricing and Strategy*, New York: CBI Publishing.
Moutinho, L., 1982, *An Investigation of Vacation Tourist Behaviour in Portugal*, Ph.D. dissertation, Sheffield University, UK.
Powers, T.E., 1979, 'Introduction to Management in the Hospitality Industry, New York: Wiley Service Management Series.
Pizam, A., and A. Reichal, 1979, 'Big Spenders and Little Spenders in US Tourism', *Journal of Travel Research*, Vol. XVIII, No. 1.
Renaghan, L.M., 1981, 'A New Marketing Mix for the Hospitality Industry', *The Cornell HRA Quarterly*, August.
Seaberg, A.G., 1971, *Menu Design Merchandising and Marketing*, IL: Institutions Magazine.
Taylor, D., 1964, *Hotel and Catering Sales Promotion*, Atlanta, GA: Iliffe.

Marketing Package Holidays

by

A.J. Burkart*

Package holidays form a significant part of tourism and are a comparatively recent one too. This article examines some of the marketing implications. It argues that the package tour operators have created a distinct special kind of tourism product which has been responsive to the marketing techniques available to manufacturers of consumer goods.

INTRODUCTION

The package holiday, technically known as an inclusive tour, has become a major contributor to the growth of tourism, particularly in the United Kingdom, Scandinavian and West German markets. It consists of a combination of transport and accommodation sold at a single price as a complete product which we shall discuss below. The mode of transport is overwhelmingly by air and, unless otherwise indicated, the term package holiday will be deemed to read package holiday by air.

The first tour operator offering package holidays by air was Horizon Holidays, controlled by V. Raitz. But the principle is claimed to be found much earlier [Williams, 1968: 373]. In the immediate aftermath of war the restrictions imposed on operators by the air transport licensing system kept growth low initially, but by the end of the 1960s, the package holiday industry had taken shape and the package holiday itself had become a major force in tourism, especially in outward tourism from the UK to the Mediterranean. With the Civil Aviation Act 1971 and the new licensing regime it brought, a degree of stability was attained and the orderly marketing of package holidays could be developed.

THE PRODUCT

It is not easy to define or identify the real product in the case of package holidays. In particular, the identification of the destination as the product [Medlik and Middleton, 1973: 28] seems inadequate in this case, however important it may be in general. Jenkins [1982: 93] offers a more promising formulation, pointing out that while every package holiday must of

* Since this article was written, the results of an empirical inquiry, 'Choosing a Country for a Holiday: Knowledge v. Fantasy', by Christine Gray and Marion Herbert, has been published in the proceedings of the ESOMAR seminar, June 1983.

course have a location, in the short-haul 'sun-lust' market there is a good deal of substitutability between a large number of resorts, with price being a major determinant of the substitution-effect. There is a good case for departing to some extent from the concept of the destination as the product. A study of the tour operators' brochures, that is, their catalogues, shows that a typical package holiday, the product, consists of about 14 days to be spent in a modern whitewashed hotel, preferably on the sea-shore, but nevertheless with a swimming pool surrounded by a green lawn, and with a bar close by, the whole scene being bathed in sunlight from a cloudless sky. This is the product in the package tour market.

The foregoing description is not frivolous. A carefully manufactured tourism product has resulted from the activities of the tour operators, by the contracting for hotel and aircraft space. Whereas traditionally the tourism product has been identified with the destination or the resort, in the package holiday we have a product which is destination-indifferent. The location of the hotel and the destination is no longer felt to be a prime factor in the choice of a holiday. The hotel and its amenities are seen as the resort: even the swimming pool is no accident, but forms a centre for the social life of the hotel. Although a particular holiday may be located in Spain, it is not Spain itself that is sought.

The physical characteristics of the product are largely given and unchangeable, and the scope for effective product differentiation is accordingly limited. In fact, the leading operators appear to emulate the brand leader, or even to imitate him, leaving the smaller tour operators to find their niche on locational factors rather than on product characteristics. One consequence of this is that there is a marked consistency of product which is rarely found in tourism. Even so, there is considerable variation even within a single operator's range; Thomsons' *Summer Sun* brochure for 1983 offered 336 resorts. Within that total, there are different dates of departure, different airports of departure and so on, each forming a different product or at least different variations on the product. The need for consistency of product is well-understood in the consumer goods field – it is accepted that the packet containing cornflakes in London must not contain sawdust in Aberdeen!

REGULATION OF PACKAGE HOLIDAYS

There is comparatively little economic regulation in tour operation. Internationally, the operations of the (largely) chartered aircraft will require the usual consents, but they have so far not attracted the complex system under which scheduled airlines labour. Within the UK jurisdiction, there are two licensing requirements to be met by air travel organisers (this is a slightly wider term than tour operator). First, the air travel organiser must obtain from the Civil Aviation Authority an air travel organiser's licence. The main purpose of this has been to enable the CAA to monitor the financial strength and well-being of the tour operator (for an account of this, see Burkart [1974]). Second, tour operators are required to be bonded. This requirement arose from instances of British package holidaymakers being stranded on some foreign beach unable to return home, after their tour operator had collapsed. The proceeds of the bond are to be used for the sole purpose of rescuing the stranded tourists, not for meeting the claims of other creditors. After the collapse in the mid-1970s of a major tour operator, the government of the day levied an Air Travel Reserve Fund to be used as a long-stop to the proceeds of bonding.

The original initiative for this elaborate manifestation of consumer protection came from the Association of British Travel Agents (ABTA) to which most travel agents and tour operators belong. In the early days ABTA ran its own common fund and in order to protect the fund, ABTA required that retail travel agents should only sell the tours of tour operator members of ABTA and, vice versa, tour operators should use only ABTA retailers to sell their tours. This exclusive dealing meant that the package holiday trade was entirely in the hands of ABTA. In due course, this agreement was referred to the Restrictive Trades Practices Court which, however, found that the exclusive dealing agreement was not 'not in the public interest'. It is hard to assess the net effect. ABTA has become an extremely strong trade association, since membership is essential to be able to trade in inclusive tours. On the other hand, there appears to be no evidence that ABTA has ever acted in admitting to membership, in any way in restraint of trade, or refused membership for unworthy reasons. The development of inclusive tours has undoubtedly brought a new and much demanded product to the market, and this in itself has ensured reasonable prosperity for the travel agent. It is against this background that the role of the retail travel agent will be examined.

THE RETAIL TRAVEL AGENT

Approximately 85 per cent of the traffic goes through retail travel agents. Although airlines and the larger tour operators often have a small network of retail outlets, the conventional travel agent is the main channel of distribution. Because of the nature of the tourism product as a service, the functions of the travel agent are rather limited. First, the travel agent provides a local point where the intending holidaymaker can get information. This information will for the most part be found in the tour operators' brochures, rather than from the knowledge and experience of the travel agent. This is not to reduce the importance of the travel agent; it merely underlines the nature of the package holiday, namely, that it is a standardised product which cannot be altered. This product is fully described in the brochure. The information function of the travel agent, in the context of package holidays is, above all, to stock and distribute the tour operators' brochures. Second, the retail travel agent provides a communication service between the intending holidaymaker and the operator. This is conducted by the travel agent by his having access to the operators' reservations systems. It is of course always open to the customer to deal directly with the tour operator, but there is no evidence of any major swing from the retail travel agent. Third, the travel agent provides a point locally through which payment can be made.

With the rapid growth of communications technology, the question arises – could all these functions be handled better by use of modern technology? Already the travel trade in Britain is one of the largest users of Prestel. Nevertheless, the physical shop seems to attract customers, and if one argues by analogy, the proliferation of retail outlets for building societies suggest that other services than tourism and travel need an outlet on the high streets too.

The tour operator's brochure acts at the retail level as a surrogate product. The effective distribution of the brochure becomes a major marketing aim, and the marketing of package holidays can be seen as a two stage operation: first, to get the brochure distributed, directly and through travel agents; and second, to take bookings for holidays described in the brochure. Here again, the consistency of the product is important – there is no way in which the retail travel agent can modify the product locally.

PRICING

It has been recognised from the earliest attempts to produce and market package holidays that demand would be highly price-elastic. At first, this was established by the use of second-line aircraft, which led to inclusive tours being priced below the level of the available scheduled fares. But the advent of modern jet aircraft led in turn to lower unit costs, and competition between operators turned almost entirely upon price. Recently, the larger operators have re-priced their tours between the date of the first publication of their brochure and the first operations of the season, sometimes adding specific price guarantees. The vigorous price competition involved has in the past led to a concentration of the market into the hands of the six or so largest operators. Keen prices lead to small margins and the largest tour operators tend to be closely associated with large groups with interests other than tourism.

An effect of the marked price elasticity has been that conventional market segmentation has not been pursued. The largest operators apparently see their market as including virtually the whole undifferentiated population. The smaller operators are in any event largely localised undertakings or serve some clear speciality, and rather over half the licensed air travel organisers are dealing with less than 10,000 seats per annum.

Parallel to the determination of the consumers' price is the question of the commission payable to the travel agent. Current orthodoxy suggests ten per cent of the price but, in practice, additional remuneration and incentive bonuses for staff are widespread. The pitfalls of a commission battle are clearly recognised but, nevertheless, especially vigorous retailers are suitably rewarded.

CONCLUSIONS

The first point to be made in conclusion is that the emergence of the package holiday in the hands of the tour operator has relieved the airline and the hotels from the necessity of undertaking their own marketing. Since they are only concerned with a part-product, the marketing is more efficiently conducted by the tour operator who may be seen quite properly as manufacturing a true tourism product. This benefit extends also to the national tourist office or similar body in the destination country. If, as we think, the public are largely indifferent to the country, the national tourist office will be better employed in persuading tour operators to package holidays, to see that their country has a place in the brochure, rather than trying to increase awareness among the public at large. In this context, it is important to see that the tour operator has created a consistent standardised product. It is of the essence of the classical marketing of consumer goods that each item shall be identical with its peers. Tourism products generally tend not to display that identity and, as a result, one is bound to say that they are not really marketed at all.

Second, the tour operator has produced the brochure, itself a tangible product, to stand in for the intangible product – the package holiday. It may be noted that one operator's brochure is very much like those of other operators. Little attempt is made to differentiate the product. In fact, we claim that tour operators make no attempt to do so. Rather, the main weapon in the competitive struggle is simply price. Demand for package holidays has proved to be highly price-elastic, and all operators both large and small have strenuously fought their competitors on price, even to the extent of permitting discounting at the retail level.

It seems plausible to assert that there will always be a place in the marketing of travel and tourism, even in an era of expanding electronic technology, for the retail travel agent. Certainly there is currently considerable pressure in the market for travel agency businesses. In the UK, the sale of holidays by mail has never achieved a success that would lead one to see a threat to the retail travel agent. About ten per cent of package holidays are sold direct to the public. Of course, the larger operators, in particular, may well wish to have more control at the retail level and acquire a retail chain for that purpose, or open branch offices of their own. But this is not true direct selling, merely the acquisition of directly owned retail outlets.

It is perhaps characteristic of a service that it should attract government regulation, codes of conduct, etc. There is felt to be a strong case for the protection of the consumer in circumstances where *caveat emptor* is hard to apply. In the case of package holidays, there are two areas where the consumer needs protection; he may be misled about the quality of the product – his holiday may disappoint him; quite different is the case where his tour operator collapses just before or during his actual holiday. The history of tour operating industry has shown that innovation in marketing is not inconsistent with a proper regard for the consumer.

REFERENCES

Burkart A.J., 1974, 'The Regulation of Non-Scheduled Air Services in the United Kingdom 1960 to 1972', *Journal of Industrial Economics*, Vol. xxiii, No. 1.

Jenkins, C.L., 1982, 'The Use of Investment Incentives for Tourism Projects in Developing Countries', *Journal of Tourism Management*, Vol. 3, No. 2.

Medlik, S. and V.T.C. Middleton, 1973, 'The Tourist Product and its Marketing Implications', *International Tourism Quarterly*, Vol. 13.

Williams, J.E.D., 1968, 'Holiday Traffic by Air', *Institute of Transport Journal*, May.

The Impact of New Technology on Services Marketing

by

Nigel Piercy

New information processing technology has already had a clear impact on the operational aspects of service organisations of all kinds, but what is only now becoming apparent is its fundamental impact on marketing systems. This last impact is of particular note in the service sector. Discussed in this paper are: the nature of new technology in marketing, the significance to information–communication systems, and the power created by the control of informational resources. This analysis is illustrated from the retailing sector and extended to other service organisations. The conclusion advanced is that the informational change currently faced is of a strategic nature and that organisations face an urgent need to formulate marketing/information technology strategies.

SERVICES MARKETING

The academic debate as to whether services are the same as products, and thus whether services marketing is a comparable activity to product marketing, continues [e.g. Middleton, 1983], with some distinction attempted between 'service products' and 'product service' [Christopher, *et al.*, 1980], and stances being taken at almost all possible points on the available spectrum.

In fact, this argument is set aside for present purposes on the grounds that its resolution does not seem to be apparent or, indeed, particularly useful. For instance, taking the criterion of differences in operational marketing, it might be argued that there is as much or more difference between the small engineering firm – competing on service by adapting its offerings to individual customer specifications – and the national producer of packaged consumer goods, as between that last firm and the retailer marketing its packaged goods to the end user.

In fact, the major thrust of this paper is to suggest that such debates are largely superseded by other concerns. The concern of the literature has been with the tardiness of the service sector in adopting marketing departmentation and the outward signs of formalised marketing: 'It is ironic that service businesses, which are necessarily in the most direct contact with consumers, seek to be the last kind of firm to adopt a consumer marketing oriented marketing concern' [Bessom, 1973]. Others have emphasised the need to develop a new theory of services marketing [Rothwell, 1974; Grönroos, 1982], though largely in line with the traditional model provided for marketing products.

The interest here is in an issue of rather deeper significance: the impact of new information processing technology on marketing and, in particular, its impact on marketing at the level of retailing goods and services to consumers or other users. The point is that new technology undermines so much of the received model of corporate marketing systems – in organisation, information, distribution and communications – that new, different marketing structures and concepts are emerging in product marketing [Piercy, forthcoming], thus arguably invalidating much of the prescriptive marketing approach to the services sector. This last point emerges again at the end of the paper. The illustrations used here apply to the retailing of goods through stores to consumers, but the conclusions reached may easily be adapted to the context of many of the other industries served by *The Service Industries Journal* – particularly, for example, hotels and catering, tourism, business and financial services and the leisure industry.

Given this initial definition of context, it is also perhaps necessary to clarify the view being taken here of 'marketing'. As before, this is no proper setting for a debate about formal definition which has been attempted by others [e.g. Crosier, 1975]. The view taken here – however arbitrary it may be considered – is that marketing may be taken to include activities of three kinds: (a) *marketing strategy* – the formulation of product–market direction and competitive stance; (b) *marketing programmes* – the planning and implementation of policies at the customer interface in 'product' policy, pricing, communications and services; and (c) *marketing information* – the processing of data on markets, marketing effectiveness, and the environment.

While this paradigm may seem idiosyncratic, it has some foundation in businessmen's perceptions of marketing [e.g. Hague, 1971], and has the advantage of allowing for most views on and definitions of marketing.

In particular, this framework clears the way for the central argument to be developed here: that the impact of new technology on marketing is being, and will increasingly be, felt through its effect on marketing information, which feeds back to both marketing programme management, marketing strategy formulation and, hence, to organisational and corporate marketing issues.

With the underlying assumptions about the nature of services marketing declared, the structure of the article is built around this last contention. First, we examine the nature of new information technology (NIT) and the scope of its impact at operational and strategic levels. Second, we examine the specific implications of NIT for marketing information systems. Third, taking the retailing of consumer goods as context, it is possible to illustrate the strategic and political nature of the

NIT and marketing information interaction. This leads finally to the identification of a need for an explicit marketing/information technology strategy in retailing firms, and by implication others in the service sector.

NEW INFORMATION TECHNOLOGY

The case for adopting a proactive managerial or strategic – rather than technical or operational – stance towards new technology has recently been formulated by one writer in the following terms: (a) NIT is a high expenditure activity and continues to grow; (b) information processing is increasingly the means of 'delivering the services' which are central to many business operations; (c) NIT is offering new business and management opportunities of a strategic nature; (d) NIT is affecting all functions and levels of management; (e) NIT is obviously central to developing and upgrading management information systems; (f) as well as management, other stakeholders – unions, consumers, suppliers, and governments – are concerned with, and seeking to influence, the use of NIT; and (g) lack of management involvement has been associated with information processing failures [Earl, 1984].

To this list must be added concern for the increased potential for social control – in terms of measuring employee performance, restricting the way people do their work, collating information about employees, and affecting career development [Land, 1984] – and for changing, particularly centralising, management and organisational control systems [Mansfield, 1984].

Clearly interest here lies primarily in the impact of NIT on 'delivering services' and strategic issues in the marketing area, but the point should first be underlined that the nature of the changes created – or, at least, initiated – by NIT, are more fundamental than simply improving the speed and efficiency of operations.

The Nature of NIT-induced Change

That NIT induces change cannot be denied, but what should be emphasised is the progression or trend of that change, and its degree, with what this implies for business and marketing strategy.

In considering the way in which organisations use computing generally, Hedberg [1980] suggested three phases of change: a first phase where designers of information systems attempt to increase the efficiency of data processing tasks; a second phase, where systems are designed to avoid organisational change; and a third phase, in which systems designers attempt to use the technology to shape the structure and tasks of the organisation itself. Land [1984] suggests that most UK computer users are still in the first and second phases of the Hedberg model, implying that what is currently faced is the somewhat more fundamental disruption in organisations involved by a third phase change.

Long [1984] illustrates the progression of change in the case of a firm where field sales personnel have frequently to telephone a sales office to obtain information for customers and to input orders. First phase automation involves adopting microcomputers for the telephone clerks to store information for retrieval and to input orders. The second phase involves providing the sales force with portable terminals to access a central data base, thus eliminating the clerks and some salesmen. The third phase would involve direct electronic communication between the customer and the centralised data base, developing 'telemarketing', and removing the need for much of the sales force.

Partly as a result of such a progression, it is argued that NIT-induced change is deep-seated rather than peripheral, and of strategic rather than operational impact.

One may point to the diverse impacts of NIT on such issues as: the degree and type of control exercised by management in organisations – and hence, through management style the organisational climate; the structure of organisations – since structure may be conceived as a framework of information flows – and thus on the roles and relationships within that structure; the pattern of jobs – and thereby at the individual level on motivation, satisfaction and performance, and at the macro-level on employment and educational requirements; and thus on the entire nature of the organisation. Most particularly, the concept of organisational boundaries is weakened in the sense that electronic communications and information processing heighten the already existing trend towards 'quasi-integration' [Blois, 1977] between apparently independent organisations – the key interaction here is that between the environmental dependency of an organisation and the effect of electronic networking, and this lies at the heart of the analysis pursued below.

Indeed, the central point is that in marketing as in other areas of business, many of our traditional, underlying assumptions about business and organisations are thrown into disarray [Handy, 1980].

Views about the direction of change faced vary from the pessimistic view of all-powerful multinational corporations and a 'technological elite' dominating business [Doll, 1981], to a scenario of 'democratic free enterprise' and the growth of 'organic networks and multi-dimensional matrices combining rigorous accountability with autonomous operations' [Halal, 1982]. This said, it is also notable that some see the consequences of NIT as unavoidable, while others take a more deterministic view of managerial choices:

> The research shows that popular predictions about the radical and automatic advantages of new technologies are exaggerated ... management has a choice of means and ends in the use of new technology; these choices can and should be identified and evaluated in advance of change [Buchanan, 1982].

Indeed, it is the existence of such choice which underpins this present view of NIT-induced change in services marketing.

In addition, considering the general nature of NIT, Earl [1984] makes the point that new information technologies are: (a) *multiple* – since there are now many generic and specific information–communication technologies, each likely to stimulate its own portfolio of applications and management problems; (b) *dispersing* – for instance, into distributed, local, end-user and personal information processing; (c) *dynamic* – in that the rate of change continues to accelerate, bringing the risk of 'management and organisational dyspepsia'; and (d) *pervasive* – in the organisations, functions, and people affected and involved.

Taking the progressive and pervasive nature of NIT-induced change in business, its fundamental nature, and the significance of managerial choices, as given, the immediate strategic importance to the service sector has been illustrated by Earl [1984] in the following examples: (a) American Airlines placed terminals with travel agents for seat reservation enquiries which would display data on any subscribing airline but were programmed to show American Airlines first; (b) Commercial Union used a similar method to break into the American insurance broking business and – through the necessary work on developing special hardware and software – are now in the 'computing business' as well; (c) Merrill Lynch used NIT to enter and develop a market segment left by other financial institutions through the Cash Management Account; (d) Reuters invested in communications technology to develop a specialised, global information service for the financial sector – developing a new product-market and increasing profitability – at a time of poor performance by traditional news agencies. The implication of such cases is that NIT is both a competitive weapon and a key to increased productivity, but also a means of delivering new services and entering new businesses.

With these points relating to services marketing and NIT established, attention now turns to their interaction in one particular area of the services sector – the channel of distribution for consumer products – to demonstrate certain of the strategic implications for managers and researchers.

MARKETING INFORMATION SYSTEMS

It was noted that one element of marketing has concentrated on marketing information, perhaps typified by the prescriptive comment that 'good information is a facilitator of successful marketing action and indeed, seen in this light marketing management becomes first and foremost an information processing activity' [Christopher, 1980]. Indeed, this concept of marketing has been developed in a more analytical vein by others to evaluate the organisation of marketing:

> The organisation of a firm is designed for the purpose of processing environmental information .... Accordingly, we propose to look at the environment as a generator of information and at the marketing department as a processor of environmental information [Nonaka and Nicosia, 1979].

The implications of an information processing model of marketing have led to an information–structure–power model of the marketing organisation [Piercy, forthcoming], one element of which is pursued below.

The focus here is on information and environmental dependency. The central propositions are outlined below, and the practical implications are evaluated in the next section of the article.

First, an organisation 'knows' its competitor and market environments through the information system it operates – however formal or informal that system may be. Intervening variables include the process of 'enactment' in the sense that 'the human *creates* the environment to which the system then adapts. The human does not *react* to an environment, he enacts it' [Weick, 1969]. In addition to the technical inefficiencies of marketing information systems in scanning to provide 'valid' information (Aguilar, 1967; Piercy and Evans, 1983], more fundamentally the information system represents a structure imposed by an organisation on its environment:

> Theoretically information systems are designed and created to provide the information the decision maker requires, but that is an impossible task because the decision maker does not know what he needs, only what is available. The available information provides clues to what is considered organizationally important, and provides the information which will tend to be used by decision makers [Pfeffer and Salancik, 1978].

Thus, regardless of the technology, the information system involves construction or structuring of the environment.

Second, by implication the control of that process of structuring and construction is a source of power. At one level information is a source of power simply because it is a resource upon which others rely for their own activities, but the phenomenon is more pervasive still. If one accepts the notion that in organisational terms information is a source of: unity or common ground among decision makers; collective memory and cohesiveness among individuals; stability in decisions; re-assurance; delaying decisions; or ritual and conciliation [Piercy and Evans, 1983], then information may be seen also as a more covert source of influence on organisational functioning. Indeed, information has been increasingly recognised as a political weapon, used in the pursuit of goals through organisationally non-sanctioned behaviour through such activities as: the use of secrecy [Pfeffer, 1977]; the control of decision premises, alternatives, and information about alternatives [Pfeffer, 1981]; and the shaping of the 'agenda' for decision making [Bachrach and Baratz, 1962].

Third, and again by implication, control of information is central to obtaining formal power and less formally sanctioned political strength in an organisation. In the sense and to the extent that information is: a construction of the perceived environment; a source of uncertainty coping in relation to contingencies which are – or are perceived as – critical to organisational performance; and a source of control over the environment, and that decision making is surrounded by contingencies of uncertainty and conflict, then the party controlling information is in a powerful position to determine the agenda for decision making, to bargain with others and hence, to influence significant outcomes. This argument applies both intra-organisationally to determining the power and politics of the marketing department and other sub-units within a firm [Piercy, forthcoming], but also to inter-organisational relationships.

This brings us to a focus on the relationship between manufacturers and the wholesalers and retailers of their products, in terms of NIT-induced change in the location of information processing capacity and control.

MACRO-MARKETING INFORMATION SYSTEMS IN DISTRIBUTION CHANNELS

If the channel of distribution is seen as a service-filled space existing between manufacturers and consumers, then the contention may be advanced:

> If space in the channel is conceived not simply in geographical or physical terms, but also in terms of psychological and sociological distance – including such aspects as familiarity, trust, images, frequency of interaction and face-to-face communication – then it can be suggested that retailers enjoy a considerable advantage over suppliers. In particular, they enjoy a considerable *informational* advantage. [Piercy, 1983].

Firstly, that advantage relates simply to *access* to market and competitive data in terms of closeness to the market-place, but also in the availability of facilities and resources for market and product testing, advertising effectiveness evaluation, and the like.

However, the practical value of that access is far greater with the application of NIT. At present the parallel trends of adoption of electronic point-of-sale equipment – in particular scanning facilities – and the bar coding of manufacturer products suggest the development of an extremely powerful marketing information resource.

At the time of writing, the diffusion of these technological innovations appears to be accelerating. For instance, in the grocery market, by 1983, 80 per cent of packaged goods were source-coded, and the number of scanning stores had reached 75 (more than twice the number in 1981) [POS News, 1984].

To these specific innovations – adopted primarily for their impact on in-store operational efficiency – must be added the *networking* effect associated with NIT. This term is taken, for present purposes, to mean the electronic communication links between individuals and organisations, manifested in 'electronic mail', interactive television sets in the consumer's home, cable television, and so on. The ability to communicate electronically to numerous remote locations – virtually instantaneously – provides the catalyst which may lead in the very near future to the operationalisation of a major potential – the distributed or macro-marketing information system.

While the marketing information system (MkIS) has normally been seen as a corporate function, as noted above, the concept of organisational boundaries is becoming increasingly less relevant, and we may see the emergence of the type of distributed information system illustrated in Figure 1.

FIGURE 1
A MACRO-MARKETING INFORMATION SYSTEM

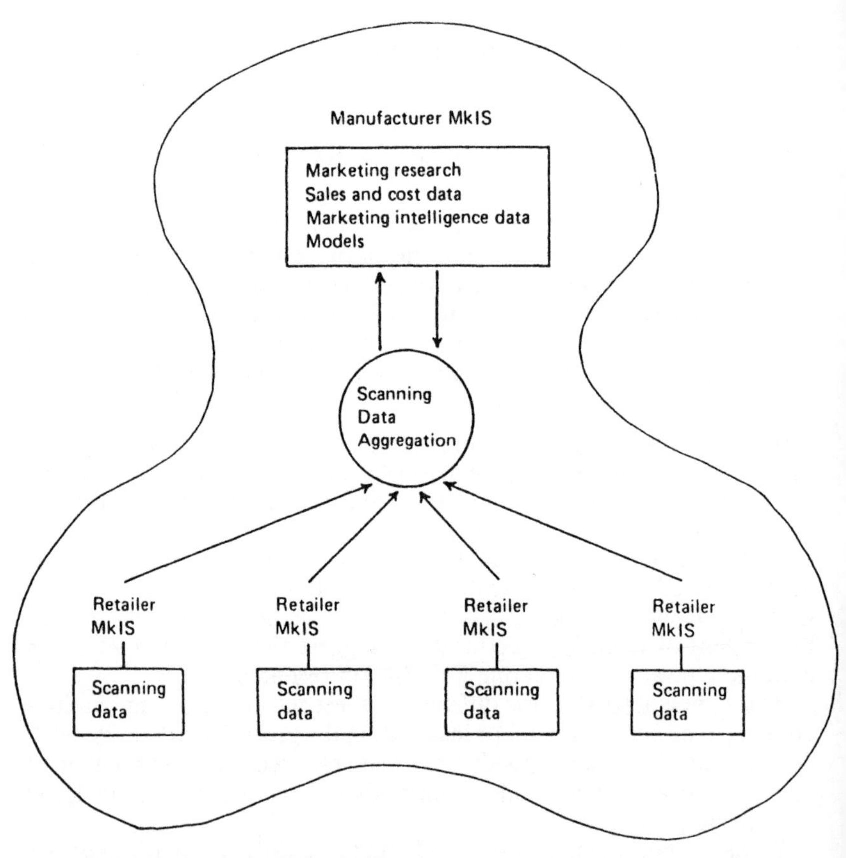

Source: Piercy and Evans [1983]

Conceptually, the channel may be seen as a network of information based on electronic links between manufacturers, distributors and consumers. However, as well as data access and networking, the retailer also enjoys the key advantage of information *control*. Bearing in mind the earlier commentary on the power and politics of information, one may identify retailer marketing information strategies of the type listed in Table 1.

TABLE 1

RETAILER MARKETING INFORMATION STRATEGIES

Strategies	*Advantages to the Retailer*
Conflict	Power in managing conflict for self-interest
Competition	Leverage in negotiation and bargaining
Commercial	Income from sales of marketing information
Co-operation	Reduction of total channel of distribution costs through integration and information sharing

Control by retailers of marketing information – or variations in the degree and type of information sharing – may be manifested in *conflict*: through building data monopolies, the retailer's informational advantages may be used simply as a competitive weapon in dealing with manufacturers – or less extremely in *competitive* behaviour, as part of the bargaining process. On the other hand, *commercial* information strategies are open – where information is sold to manufacturers – taking the service organisation into a new area of business as a marketing information processor and as a seller. Finally, the distributed information system may provide the basis for joint decision-making and *co-operative* marketing in the channel of distribution, with information-sharing in both directions and participation by manufacturers and retailers in participative strategic decisions. While empirical data remain limited, the American experience would seem to suggest the existence of all these strategies [Piercy, 1982].

Whichever situation prevails – and we return shortly to the importance of making an explicit choice of strategy – the underlying implication is that the NIT/marketing information interaction provides a further source of erosion of the position of the manufacturer and a corresponding elevation in that of the retailer. This has implications for the location of decision-making in the channel and for the organisational structures adopted for marketing.

First, informational advantages may be manifested in retailer marketing initiatives in product policy, pricing and communications typifying the channel of distribution for packaged goods. The well-known case of Marks and Spencer dominating R & D, product policy and pricing for goods, may well prove to be prototypical.

Second, this growing change in the locus of marketing decision-making power is likely to be manifested in organisational change – and indeed there are signs that the 'traditional' manufacturer marketing department is disintegrating: (a) some manufacturers are abandoning product and brand management – at one time the classic route to 'marketing orientation'; (b) marketing department responsibilities are being reduced – partly as a result of concentrated power in retailing – as the financial and strategic significance of decisions in such areas as advertising and promotion increases through greater top management intervention, cross-functional committees, and formal corporate planning; (c) in some areas the business sector or programme manager now comes between the chief executive and the marketing department, reducing the latter's role in strategy formulation and integration; (d) Trade Marketing departments are growing – separate from marketing – out of key account selling to deal directly with major retailer customers; (e) NIT is reducing the size of the marketing department and its co-ordinative and informational roles, and thus its power in the organisation, particularly in the key area of managing external interfaces and dependencies [Piercy, forthcoming].

The corollary is that the powerful, integrated marketing department may emerge in the channel of distribution – providing the source of formal management and control of product development – and branding, pricing, marketing communications and marketing information systems. The signs already evident are of increased unified departmentation of marketing, the greater use of product and brand management, more formally organised marketing research, and the appointment or designation of more chief marketing executives in retailing firms. The suggestion is therefore that the transfer of marketing power to the retailing firm is being accompanied by the relocation of the formal marketing organisation.

Finally, let us consider the implications of this type of change: first, for the retailer/manufacturer relationship, and second, more broadly for others in the service sector.

INFORMATION STRATEGY

If one accepts the premise that NIT-induced change affects: information systems, the structure of inter-organisational relationships, and intra-organisational structures, in the way argued above, then one is led to the conclusion that the change – in the phases now faced – is of a fundamental, strategic nature, rather than being peripheral or operational.

The implication in the retailer/manufacturer setting discussed above is that strategic choices are faced by management relating to: the conflictual or co-operative stance to be taken, the allocation of marketing decision-making initiative and power, and the reorganisation of marketing to reflect the new realities.

The suggestion here is that a proactive management approach to this area of change is likely to be more satisfactory than a reactive or passive attitude towards NIT. For this reason it is proposed that the issues above provide a management agenda, drawing on an analysis of the emerging NIT scenario and corporate needs and business opportunities, to make choices for the future [Piercy, 1984].

Secondly, and more broadly, a similar proposition may be advanced for other service organisations. The 'electronic market-place' suggests that the integration of marketing functions, the control of marketing decisions, and the formal organisation of marketing is emerging rapidly as a key strategic issue for the service organisation in many sectors. If this case is granted, then, as for retailers, the need is for a development of explicit strategies for marketing information and marketing organisation – the structure of which is detailed elsewhere [Piercy and Evans, 1983; Piercy, forthcoming].

Broadly, such a process involves a strategic analysis of (a) the technological scenario – the applications of NIT to operations and management in the long-term future [Benjamin, 1982]; (b) organisational impacts – in structural and management terms; (c) market impacts – on both customers and suppliers; (d) company needs and resources [Piercy, 1984]. While such a prescription is generally valid in all organisations, for the reasons noted above, it would be both particularly apt and urgent in the services sector marketing area.

REFERENCES

Aguilar, F.J., 1967, *Scanning the Business Environment*, New York: Macmillan.

Bachrach, P. and M.S. Baratz, 1962, 'Two Faces of Power', *American Political Science Review*, Vol.56.

Benjamin, R., 1982, 'Information Technology in the 1990s: A Long-Range Planning Scenario', *Management Information Systems Quarterly*, June.

Bessom, R.M., 1973, 'Unique Aspects of Marketing Services', *Arizona Business Bulletin*, November.

Blois, K.J., 1977, 'Problems in Applying Organizational Theory to Industrial Marketing', *Industrial Marketing Management*, Vol.6.

Buchanan, D.A., 1982, 'Using the New Technology: Management Objectives and Organizational Choices', *European Journal of Management*, Vol.1, No.2.

Christopher, M., Kennedy, S.H., McDonald M., and G. Wills, 1980, *Effective Marketing Management*, Farnborough: Gower.

Christopher, M., MacDonald, M., and G. Wills, 1980, *Introducing Marketing*, London: Pan.

Crosier, K., 1975, 'What Exactly Is Marketing?', *Quarterly Review of Marketing*, Vol.1, No.2.

Doll, R., 1981, 'Information Technology and its Socioeconomic and Academic Impact', *Online Review*, Vol.5, No.1.

Earl, M., 1984, 'Emerging Trends in Managing New Information Technologies', in Piercy, N. (ed.), *The Management Implications of New Information Technology*, Beckenham: Croom Helm.

Grönroos, C., 1982, 'An Applied Service Marketing Theory', *European Journal of Marketing*, Vol.16, No.7.

Hague, D.C., 1971, *Pricing in Business*, London: Allen & Unwin.

Halal, W.K., 1982, 'Information Technology and the Flowering of Enterprise', *European Journal of Management*, Vol.1, No.2.

Handy, C., 1980, 'Through the Organizational Looking Glass', *Harvard Business Review*, January/February.

Hedberg, B., 1980, 'The Design and Impact of Real-Time Computer Systems', in Bjorn-Anderson, N., Hedberg, B., Mercer, D., Mumford, E., and A. Sole, (eds.), *The Impact of Systems Change in Organizations*, Alphen: Sijtoff and Noordhoff.

Land, F., 1984, 'The Impact of Information Technology on the Work Place', in N. Piercy (ed.), *The Management Implications of New Information Technology*, Beckenham: Croom Helm.

Long, R., 1984, 'The Application of Microelectronics to the Office: Organisational and Human Implications', in N. Piercy (ed.), *The Management Implications of New Information Technology*, Beckenham: Croom Helm.

Mansfield, R., 1984, 'Changes in Information Technology, Organisational Design and Managerial Control', in N. Piercy (ed.), *The Management Implications of New Information Technology*, Beckenham: Croom Helm.

Middleton, V.T.C., 1983, 'Product Marketing – Goods and Services Compared', *Quarterly Review of Marketing*, Vol. 8, No. 4.

Nonaka, I., and F.M. Nicosia, 1979, 'Marketing Management, Its Environment and Information Processing: A Problem of Organizational Design', *Journal of Business Research*, Vol. 7, No. 4.

Pfeffer, J., 1977, 'Power and Resource Allocation in Organizations', in Staw, B.M., and G.R. Salancik (eds.), *New Directions in Organizational Behavior*, Chicago: St Clair.

Pfeffer, J., 1981, *Power in Organizations*, Marshfield, MA: Pitman.

Pfeffer, J., and G.R. Salancik, 1978, *The External Control of Organizations: A Resource Dependence Perspective*, New York: Harper & Row.

Piercy, N., 1982, 'How Retailers Use Marketing Information in the USA', *Retail and Distribution Management*, Vol. 10, No. 5.

Piercy, N., 1984, 'Retailer Marketing – Informational Strategies', *European Journal of Marketing*, Vol. 17, No. 6.

Piercy, N., forthcoming, *Marketing Organisation: An Analysis of Information Processing, Power and Politics*, London: Allen & Unwin.

Piercy, N., and M. Evans, 1983, *Managing Marketing Information*, Beckenham: Croom Helm.

POS News, 1984, 'The Progress in Bar-Coding and Scanning During 1983', *POS News*, No. 1.

Rothwell, J.M., 1974, *Marketing in the Service Sector*, Cambridge, MA: Winthrop.

Weick, K.R., 1969, *The Social Psychology of Organizing*, Reading, MA: Addison-Wesley.

The Strategy of Customer Service

by

Martin Christopher

This article explores the role of Customer Service in an organisation's marketing effort and suggests an approach to the development of appropriate strategies. Customer service here is defined in its broadest sense of providing 'time and place utility' which might more simply be expressed as the provision of 'availability'.

INTRODUCTION

One of the best selling management books of recent years, *In Search of Excellence* [Peters and Waterman, 1982], has alerted managers and others to the simple truth that customers create sales and the most successful companies are those that create the most customers *and keep them*. It may seem strange that such obvious axioms should provide the basis for a book that appears on executives' desks around the world. Nevertheless, it has taken a major recession to focus many organisations' attention upon the customer more sharply than was often the case in the past. The lessons of *In Search of Excellence* extend beyond a concern for customer relations, but it is perhaps in this field that the greatest scope for improvement lies in the 'non-excellent' company. It is upon the development of effective strategies for customer service that this article is centred and in particular the means by which an organisation can achieve a sustainable competitive advantage based upon such a strategy.

Two factors have perhaps contributed more than anything else to the growing importance of customer service as a competitive weapon. One is the continual development of customer expectations; in almost every market the customer is now more demanding, more 'sophisticated' than he or she was, say, 30 years ago. Likewise in industrial purchasing situations we find that buyers expect higher levels of service from vendors, particularly as more manufacturers convert to 'just-in-time' manufacturing systems. The second factor is the slow but inexorable transition towards 'commodity' type markets. By this I mean that increasingly the power of the 'brand' is diminishing as technologies of competing products converge thus making product differences difficult to perceive – at least to the average buyer. Take, for example, the current state of the personal computer market. There are so many competing models which in reality are substitutable as far as most would-be purchasers are concerned. Unless one is particularly expert it is difficult to use product features as the basis for choice.

Faced with a situation such as this the customer may be influenced by price or by 'image' perceptions but overriding these aspects may well be 'availability' – in other words – is the product in stock, can I have it now? Since availability is clearly one aspect of customer service we are in effect saying that the power of customer service is paramount in a situation such as this. Nor is it only in consumer markets that we are encountering the force of customer service as a determinant of purchase; as we shall note shortly, there is much evidence from industrial markets of the same phenomenon. On top of all this we have seen the growth of the 'service' sector in many Western economies. Over 50 per cent of the GNP of the United Kingdom is derived from the non-manufacturing sector and every year the percentage increases. The marketing of services should not call for any different philosophy from that underlying the marketing of physical products. Rather it calls for possibly an even greater emphasis upon availability, particularly given the 'perishability' of the service product. Nevertheless, both service products and tangible products are increasingly dependent for their success upon the supplier's ability to enhance their appeal through the 'added value' of customer service.

WHAT IS CUSTOMER SERVICE?

It is sometimes suggested that the role of customer service is to provide 'time and place utility' in the transfer of goods and services between buyer and seller. Put another way, there is no value in a product or service until it is in the hands of the customer or consumer. It follows that making the product or service 'available' is what, in essence, the distribution function of the business is all about. 'Availability' is in itself a complex concept, impacted upon by a galaxy of factors which together constitute customer service. These factors might include, for example, delivery frequency and reliability, stock levels and order cycle time, as they impact upon availability. Indeed, it could be said that ultimately customer service is determined by the interaction of all those factors that affect the process of making products and services available to the buyer.

In practice, many companies have varying views of customer service. LaLonde and Zinszer [1976] in a major study of customer service practices found that in the industries they surveyed a range of views existed as to what constituted 'customer service'. Some of the definitions of service they encountered are shown in Table 1. What all these definitions have in common is that they are concerned with relationships at the buyer/seller interface. This same study suggested that customer service could be examined under three headings: (1) pre-transaction elements; (2) transaction elements; and (3) post-transaction elements.

The *pre-transaction* elements of customer service relate to corporate policies or programmes, for example, written statements of service policy, adequacy of organisational structure and system flexibility. The

TABLE 1
TYPICAL DEFINITIONS OF CUSTOMER SERVICE

'All activities required to accept, process, deliver and bill customer orders and to follow up on any activity that erred'

'Timeliness and reliability of getting materials to customers in accordance with the customer's expectation'

'A complex of activities involving all areas of the business which combine to deliver and invoice the company's products in a fashion that is perceived as satisfactory by the customer and which advance our company's objectives'

'Total order entry, all communications with customers, all shipping, all freight, all invoicing and total control of repair of products'

'Timely and accurate delivery of products ordered by customers with accurate follow-up and inquiry response, including timely delivery of invoice'

Source: LaLonde and Zinszer [1976].

transaction elements are those customer service variables directly involved in performing the physical distribution function, for example, product availability, order cycle time, order status information and delivery reliability. The *post-transaction* elements of customer service are generally supportive of the product while in use, for instance, product warranty, parts and repair service, procedures for customer complaints and product replacement.

Many commentators have defined various elements of customer service, but the most commonly occurring seem to be:

Order Cycle Time
Consistency and Reliability of Delivery
Inventory Availability
Order-size Constraints
Ordering Convenience
Delivery Times and Flexibility
Invoicing Procedures and Accuracy
Claims Procedure
Condition of Goods
Salesman's Visits
Order Status Information

In any particular product/market situation, some of these elements will be more important than others and there may be factors other than those listed above which have a significance in a specific market. Indeed, the argument that will be developed in this article is that it is essential to understand customer service in terms of differing requirements of different market segments and that no universally appropriate list of elements exists; each market that the company services will attach different importance to different service elements.

It is because of the multivariate nature of customer service and because of the widely differing requirements of specific markets that it is essential for any business to have a clearly identified policy towards customer service. It is surprising perhaps that so few companies have defined policies on customer service, let alone an organisation flexible enough to manage and control that service, when it is considered that service can be the most important element in the company's marketing mix. A considerable body of evidence exists which supports the view that if the product or service is not available at the time the customer requires it, and a close substitute is available, then the sale will be lost to the competition. Even in markets where brand loyalty is strong a stock-out might be sufficient to trigger off brand switching. In industrial markets, too, the same pressures on purchasing source loyalty seem to be at work. Perreault and Russ [1976] surveyed industrial purchasing officers using examples of standardised products and found that distribution service was considered second in importance only to product quality as a deciding criterion for vendor selection. Moreover, more than one-third of these purchasing officers indicated that they would cancel the order if it were not available for shipment when ordered. These findings were further reinforced in a study by Cunningham and Roberts [1974]. This investigation of the valve and pump manufacturing industry evaluated the service provided by suppliers of steel castings and forgings. Delivery reliability emerged as the primary element influencing the choice of supplier.

In the light of this and other evidence it is suggested that there are three basic requirements for the management of customer service [Herron, 1982]:

(1) Define an overall company philosophy of customer service in terms of attitude, organisation and responsibilities;
(2) Develop internal standards for customer service, based on careful studies that have explored the quantitative trade-offs between various levels of customer service and the costs of achieving such levels, so as to identify the most profitable policy for each customer segment; and
(3) Inform customers what they might expect by way of customer service (perhaps in more general terms than the company defines its policies internally).

To achieve the most effective deployment of corporate resources in developing a customer service policy along the lines broadly defined above, a number of prerequisites exist:

The differing perceptions of the various parties to the purchasing decision in terms of customer service must be recognised;
The trade-off potential between the various components of the customer service mix must be evaluated; and
The unique customer service requirement of each product/channel/market segment must be identified.

If cost-effective customer service policies are to be successfully developed and implemented within the firm, it is imperative that a formalised logic is adopted and closely followed. Customer service is too important and too costly to be left to chance.

THE COMPONENTS OF CUSTOMER SERVICE

It is a common fault in marketing to fail to realise that customers do not always attach the same importance to product attributes as the vendor. Thus, it sometimes happens that products are promoted on attributes or features that are less important to the customer in reality than other aspects. A floor cleaner that is sold on its ease of application, for example, will not succeed unless 'ease of application' is a salient benefit sought by the customer. If 'shine' or the need for less frequent cleaning are important to the customer, then we might be better advised to feature those aspects on our promotion. The same principle applies in customer service: which aspects of service are rated most highly by the customer? If a company places its emphasis upon stock availability but the customer regards delivery reliability more highly, it may not be allocating its resources in a way likely to maximise sales. Alternatively, a company that realises that its customers place a higher value on completeness of orders than they do on, say, regular scheduled deliveries could develop this to its advantage.

There is, thus, a great premium to be placed on gaining an insight into the factors that influence buyer behaviour and, in the context of customer service, which particular elements are seen by the customer to be the most important. The use of market research techniques in customer service has lagged behind their application in such areas as product testing and advertising research, yet the importance of researching the service needs of customers is just as great as, say, the need to understand the market reaction to price. In fact, it is possible to apply standard, proven market research methods to gain considerable insight into the ways that customers will react to customer service.

The first step in research of this type is to identify the relative source of influence on the purchase decision. If we are selling components to a manufacturer, for example, who will make the decision on the source of supply? This is not always an easy question to answer as, in many cases, there will be several people involved. The purchasing manager of the company to whom we are selling may only be acting as an agent for others within the firm. In other cases, his influence will be much greater. Alternatively, if we are manufacturing products for sale through retail outlets, is the decision to stock made centrally by a retail chain or by individual store managers? The answers to these questions can often be supplied by the sales force. The sales representative should know from experience who the decision-makers are.

Given that a clear indication of the source of decision-making power can be gained, the customer service researcher at least knows *who* to research. The question still remains however – which elements of the vendor's total marketing offering have what effect on the purchase decision? Ideally, once the decision-making unit in a specific market has been identified, an initial, small-scale research programme should be initiated which would be based on personal interviews with a representative sample of buyers. The purpose of these interviews is to elicit, *in the language of the customers*, first, the importance they attach to customer service *vis-à-vis* the other marketing mix elements such as price, product quality, promotion and so on and second, the specific importance they attach to the individual components of customer service.

DESIGNING THE CUSTOMER SERVICE PACKAGE

To compete effectively in any market requires the ability to develop some differential advantage over competing companies and their product or service offerings. Sometimes, this differential advantage may be in terms of distinctive product attributes or related benefits as perceived by the customer. On other occasions, it may be price or, alternatively, the product may be promoted in such a way that it acquires a distinctive image in the eyes of the market. In just the same way, customer service can be used to develop a differential advantage and, indeed, there can be a major benefit to the company in using customer service in this way. For example, in competitive markets where real product differentiation may be difficult to establish and where to compete on price would only lead to profit erosion, it makes sense to switch the marketing emphasis to customer service.

The current battle in the office copier market provides a case in point: Xerox, the early leader in this field, have found that competition has become increasingly severe from products which, to the potential customer at least, seem to offer the same product benefits. Pressure on margins is considerable and price cutting would not provide a lasting solution for Xerox. Instead, they have switched the emphasis to service. Their advertisements underline this point. A recent advertisement in the business press for Xerox copies stated:

> Because the best way to get new customers is to keep your current ones happy, Xerox offers the largest service force in the business. Over 30,000 men and women worldwide.
>
> Parts inventories and parts distribution systems are all part of our job. That's why we have distribution centres around the globe.
>
> So, chances are, our technical representatives will always have what you need where you need it. Whenever possible, we standardise parts so that they're interchangeable from country to country. That way we can take better care of our copiers and our customers.

Similar approaches have been made by companies such as Digital Equipment and Caterpillar who have built up commanding positions in their markets and maintained them through the effective use of customer service. Earlier it was stressed that it is important to establish those components of the total customer service mix which have the greatest impact on the buyer's perception of us as a supplier. This thinking needs to be carried right through into the design of the customer service offering. This offering can best be described as the customer service 'package', for it will most likely contain more than one component.

The design of the package will need to take account of the differing needs of different market segments so that the resources allocated to customer service can be used in the most cost-effective way. Too often, a uniform, blanket approach to service is adopted by companies which does not distinguish between the real requirements of different customer types. This can lead to customers being offered too little service or too much. Several authors have suggested ways in which competitive service packages might be designed. In a recent presentation Shycon and Ritz [1982] described one approach to the development of such a package which contained the following steps:

> Determining competitive customer service practices and policies within each product and market channel;
> Identifying and measuring key elements which led to becoming a preferred, or 'Most Favoured Supplier';
> Measuring the impact of each aspect of service on market share and profitability;
> Assessing the performance of the company on each of these service components; and
> Redesigning the corporate service package to emphasise effective service expenditures and de-emphasise ineffective ones.

They identified in a study of one firm's customers that sensitivity to different service elements varied considerably by market channel, geographic area and product category. More importantly, they isolated two distinct effects of different service levels: first, a short-term effect on sales; and second, a long-term effect on achieving a more favoured position with the buyer. For this particular company selling to a specific market segment they were able to suggest an improved service package designed to influence the purchasing decision-maker in order to achieve a more favoured long-term position. Recommendations for the redesigned service package included:

(1) In designing the distribution system, consider the added buyer influence and the impact on sales of a 'market presence', that is, proximity of stock to key markets;
(2) Provide quantity price brackets, encouraging the buyer to 'stretch' for a lower price through purchasing greater quantities – especially at the lowest quantity levels;
(3) Offer promotion incentives, especially to lower volume customers;
(4) Support promotions with superior distribution service;
(5) Provide incentives to reduce 'customer responsible' emergency shipment needs;

(6) Concentrate on improved on-time delivery consistency; and
(7) Recognise the influence of sales and service personnel on sales levels achieved.

The precise composition of the customer service package for any market segment will depend on the results of the analysis described earlier. It will also be determined by budgetary and cost constraints. If alternative packages can be identified which seem to be equally acceptable to the buyer, it makes sense to choose the least cost alternative. For example, it may be possible to identify a customer service package with high acceptability which enables the emphasis to be switched away from a high level of inventory availability towards, say, improved customer communication. Once a cost-effective package has been identified in this way, it should become a major part of the company's marketing mix – 'using service to sell' is the message here. If the market segments we serve are sensitive to service, then the service package must be actively promoted. One way in which this can be achieved with great effect is by stressing the impact on the *customer's* costs of the improved service package, for example, what improved reliability will do for his own stock planning; what shorter lead-times will do for his inventory levels; how improved ordering and invoicing systems will lead to fewer errors; and so on. All too often, the customer will not appreciate the impact that improved service offered by the supplier can have on his, the customer's, bottom line.

CONCLUDING COMMENTS

Beyond the simple presentation of a marketing message based around an improved customer service package lies the opportunity to develop tailor-made service offerings, particularly to key accounts, based on 'negotiated' service levels. The idea here is that no two customers are alike, either in terms of their requirements or, specifically, in terms of their profitability to the supplier. One UK-based company in the consumer electronics field identified that whilst three of its major customers were roughly equivalent in terms of their annual sales value, there were considerable differences in the costs generated by each. For example, one customer required delivery to each of its 300-plus retail outlets, whilst the others took delivery at one central warehouse. Similarly, one company paid within 30 days of receiving the invoice, the others took nearer to 40 days to pay. Again, one of the three was found to place twice as many 'emergency' orders as the others. Careful analysis of the true costs showed that the profitability of the three customers differed by over 20 per cent. Yet, each customer received the same value-related discounts and the same level of customer service!

Conducting such a 'customer account profitability' analysis can provide the supplier with not only the basis on which to negotiate price but also a basis for 'negotiating' service. Whilst companies in the United States tend to be familiar with the importance of relating price discounts to customer related costs, because of Robinson-Patman legislation, it is rarely used elsewhere in a positive way. Thus, whilst the concept of paying more for an airmail letter than a surface letter is well established, say, it is less common to find a supplier offering different 'qualities' of service at different prices. Interestingly enough, the business manager who accepts the difference between First Class, Business Class and Tourist Class on the plane he takes to see his customer might never think of how that same principle could be applied to his own business!

REFERENCES

Cunningham, M.T., and D.A. Roberts, 1974, 'The Role of Customer Service in Industrial Marketing', *European Journal of Marketing*, Vol. 8, No. 1.

Herron, D.P., 1982, 'Making Dollars and Sense out of Customer Service', Working Paper, *SRI International.*

LaLonde, B.J., and P.H. Zinszer, 1976, *Customer Service: Meaning and Measurement*, Chicago: NCPDM.

Perreault, W.D., and F.A. Russ, 1976, 'Physical Distribution Service in Industrial Purchase Decisions', *Journal of Marketing*, Vol. 40, April.

Peters, T.J., and R.H. Waterman, 1982, *In Search of Excellence*, New York: Harper and Row.

Shycon, H.N., and C.J. Ritz, 1982, *Analytical Techniques to Evaluate Service Levels Required for Sales Growth and Profitability*, Waltham, MA: Shycon Associates.

Notes on Contributors

Gordon Foxall is a senior lecturer in marketing at Cranfield School of Management. He has lectured widely and acted as a consultant to several business and nonbusiness organisations. His main research interests are in consumer behaviour and industrial innovation and his books include *Consumer Choice* and *Corporate Innovation: Marketing and Strategy*.

John Lidstone is Deputy Managing Director of Marketing Improvements Ltd. He is an internationally recognised consultant and has wide industrial experience. He is the author of four books including the best-selling *Training Salesmen on the Job*. John Lidstone is a Council Member of the UK Management Consultants Association. In 1981, he was elected a member of the British Academy of Film and Television Arts for his services to management training films.

Christopher H. Lovelock is an associate professor at the Graduate School of Business Administration, Harvard University. He has written several seminal papers on the marketing of services and recently produced the well-received book, *Services Marketing*.

Donald Cowell is Dean of the Business School at Plymouth Polytechnic. A graduate of the Universities of Leeds and Bradford, he worked in the electrical engineering industry before taking up posts at the University of Bradford (Management Centre) and the University of Loughborough. His current interests include the marketing of services and he is the author of a book and a number of articles on this topic.

Keith J. Blois is Reader in Marketing at Loughborough University of Technology. He has contributed to European and American journals on a variety of topics including economic theory, marketing to organisations, industrial economics and social responsibility.

Barbara R. Lewis is a senior lecturer in management sciences at the University of Manchester Institute for Science and Technology. She is also the editor of the *International Journal of Bank Marketing*.

Simon Majaro is Director of Strategic Management Learning and a visiting professor at Cranfield School of Management. He has extensive business experience which includes the managing directorship of an EEC Unilever Company. He has headed the Marketing Department of the IMI, Geneva, and was a senior consultant with Urwick, Orr and Partners. His books include *International Marketing – A Strategic Approach to World Markets*, and *Marketing in Perspective*.

John Driver is a lecturer in the Department of Industrial Economics and Business Studies at the University of Birmingham. He has teaching and research interests in investment, pricing, consumer choice, marketing education and market research. He has published in economics and marketing journals and is the co-author (with Gordon Foxall) of *Advertising Policy and Practice*. He is also a consultant to various companies and other organisations.

Stanley Siebert is a lecturer in the Department of Industrial Economics and Business Studies at the University of Birmingham. He has written (with J.G. Addison) *The Market for Labour* and other papers for journals such as the *Economic Journal* and *Economica*. He has been a visiting professor at the University of North Carolina at Chapel Hill and is currently visiting the University of Wisconsin – Milwaukee.

Norman E. Marr is the managing director of a Northamptonshire consultancy firm concentrating on materials management and physical distribution. He has many years' operational experience in logistics and his Ph.D. is in marketing logistics.

Peter R. White is a senior lecturer in public transport systems at the Polytechnic of Central London. His research interests include rural transport, and he is the author of *Planning for Public Transport*. He has lectured widely and acted as a consultant to a number of organisations in the transport field.

David Yorke is a lecturer in management sciences at the University of Manchester Institute of Science and Technology. He has experience in industry and commerce in the field of market research. His research interests include the provision by local authorities of leisure services and he has made a special study of the marketing of public libraries. He has lectured widely to both profit and non-profit organisations on marketing planning.

Arthur Meidan is a senior lecturer in marketing and Director of the MBA Programme at Sheffield University, specialising in the marketing of services. His books, *Insurance Marketing* and *Bank Marketing Management*, have recently been published.

A.J. Burkart is reader in tourism at the University of Surrey. He is co-author with S. Medlik of a leading text, *Tourism Past Present and Future* and is consulting editor of *Tourism Management*.

Nigel Piercy is a senior lecturer in the Department of Business Administration and Accountancy, at the University of Wales Institute of Science and Technology, Cardiff. His publications include the books *Export, Strategy, Managing Marketing Information*, and *Marketing Organisation*. His research interests include retailer marketing and marketing information systems.

Martin Christopher is Professor of Marketing and Logistics Systems at Cranfield School of Management. He has lectured widely in Europe, North America and Australia and is editor of the *International Journal of Physical Distribution and Materials Management*. He acts as an advisor on marketing and logistics to a number of companies and is a Director of an international logistics consultancy.